Fortify and Shield: Security and Protection in Operating Systems

Table of Content

Chapter 1: The Foundations of OS Security

- Definition and importance of operating system security.
- The role of OS security in protecting sensitive data and ensuring system integrity.
- Overview of security models such as discretionary access control (DAC) and mandatory access control (MAC).
- Understanding how security models dictate access rights and permissions.
- Examination of key security components, including firewalls, antivirus software, and intrusion detection systems.
- The collaborative function of these components in maintaining a secure OS environment.
- Best practices for creating and managing user accounts.
- Password policies, user roles, and the principle of least privilege.
- The importance of auditing and monitoring for detecting and responding to security incidents.
- Strategies for implementing effective auditing and monitoring practices in an operating system.

Chapter 2: Threat Landscape Analysis

- Categorization of common threats, including malware, phishing, and social engineering.
- The impact of various threats on operating system security.
- Techniques for identifying vulnerabilities in operating systems.
- The role of vulnerability assessments in preemptive security measures.
- The process of risk analysis in determining potential security risks.
- Strategies for managing and mitigating identified risks.
- The importance of incident response plans in addressing security breaches.
- Steps to develop and implement effective incident response strategies.
- Exploration of current and emerging threats in the ever-evolving threat landscape.
- The significance of staying abreast of emerging trends for proactive security measures.

Chapter 3: Securing Network Communication

- Introduction to network security concepts within the operating system.
- The relationship between OS security and secure network communication.
- The role of firewalls in filtering network traffic and preventing unauthorized access.
- How intrusion detection systems monitor and respond to potential security threats.
- Utilizing VPNs for secure and encrypted communication over networks.
- Implementation and configuration of VPNs for enhanced OS security.
- Understanding the role of SSL and TLS in securing data transmission.
- Best practices for implementing and maintaining secure communication channels.
- Security considerations for wireless networks in an operating system environment.
- Strategies for securing Wi-Fi networks and protecting against unauthorized access.

Chapter 4: User Authentication and Authorization

- Overview of authentication methods, including passwords, biometrics, and multi-factor authentication.
- The strengths and vulnerabilities associated with each authentication mechanism.
- Understanding the concept of RBAC for user authorization.
- Implementing RBAC to control user access based on roles and responsibilities.
- The benefits and challenges of implementing single sign-on solutions.
- Integration of SSO to streamline user authentication across multiple systems.
- Utilizing access control lists to specify user permissions on resources.
- Fine-tuning access control through ACL configurations.
- The role of biometrics in enhancing user authentication.
- Implementing biometric authentication systems for heightened security.

Chapter 5: Data Encryption and Integrity

- Overview of encryption algorithms used to secure data.
- Evaluating the strengths and suitability of different encryption methods.
- Implementing file-level and disk-level encryption for data protection.
- The impact of encryption on data integrity and access.
- Understanding digital signatures as a means of ensuring data integrity.
- The process of generating, verifying, and managing digital signatures.
- The role of hash functions in maintaining data integrity.
- Selecting and implementing secure hash algorithms for various use cases.
- Strategies for secure data backup and recovery.
- Ensuring data integrity during backup processes and expedient recovery in case of data loss.

Chapter 6: Endpoint Security

- The importance of securing endpoints such as computers and mobile devices.
- Implementing endpoint protection solutions for comprehensive security.
- Evaluating the effectiveness of antivirus and anti-malware tools.
- Best practices for selecting, configuring, and maintaining these tools.
- Strategies for controlling and managing connected devices.
- Preventing unauthorized devices from compromising endpoint security.
- Implementing application whitelisting to control approved software.
- The role of blacklisting in preventing the execution of malicious applications.
- Guidelines for users and administrators to enhance endpoint security.
- Periodic assessments and updates to fortify endpoint protection.

Chapter 7: Patch Management and Updates

- Understanding the significance of timely updates and patches.
- The role of patch management in addressing vulnerabilities and enhancing system security.
- Strategies for deploying patches without disrupting system operations.
- The importance of testing patches before widespread deployment.
- Overview of automated patching tools for streamlined management.
- Implementing and configuring tools to automate the patching process.
- Responding to critical vulnerabilities with emergency updates.
- Balancing the need for rapid patch deployment with thorough testing.
- The importance of user awareness in the update process.
- Educating users on the significance of timely updates and their role in security.

Chapter 8: Security Best Practices and Future Trends

- Defining and implementing security policies to guide user behavior.
- The role of security policies in shaping a secure operating environment.
- Implementing continuous monitoring tools for real-time threat detection.
- Regular assessments to identify and address evolving security challenges.
- Developing comprehensive incident response plans for effective crisis management.
- Conducting drills and simulations to ensure preparedness.
- The importance of ongoing security training for users and IT staff.
- Fostering a culture of security awareness throughout the organization.
- Exploring emerging trends such as zero-trust architecture and AI-driven security.
- The potential impact of quantum computing on encryption and security practices.

Introduction

"In the fast-evolving digital landscape, the paramount importance of robust security and protection mechanisms in operating systems cannot be overstated. The eBook titled 'Fortify and Shield: Security and Protection in Operating Systems' serves as a comprehensive guide, delving into the intricacies of safeguarding operating systems from a myriad of potential risks. As technology advances, so do the threats that compromise the integrity and confidentiality of sensitive information. This groundbreaking eBook addresses this dynamic landscape by not only presenting an in-depth analysis of the current security challenges but also providing practical insights and strategies to fortify operating systems against evolving threats.

The eBook unfolds across eight chapters, each contributing to a holistic understanding of operating system security. The first chapter sets the stage by exploring the foundational concepts of operating system security, laying the groundwork for subsequent discussions. Moving forward, the second chapter delves into the evolution of cyber threats, offering a historical perspective that underscores the urgency of adapting security measures to the ever-changing threat landscape.

Chapter three provides a detailed examination of the vulnerabilities inherent in operating systems, identifying potential weak points that malicious actors may exploit. It then transitions seamlessly into the fourth chapter, where the eBook introduces various encryption techniques and access control mechanisms crucial for maintaining data integrity and confidentiality.

The fifth chapter takes a deep dive into the world of intrusion detection and prevention systems, elucidating how these tools serve as vigilant guardians, constantly monitoring and thwarting potential security breaches. Building upon this, the sixth chapter explores the nuances of secure software development practices, emphasizing the proactive role developers play in fortifying operating systems.

A pivotal aspect of operating system security lies in effective incident response and recovery strategies, which the seventh chapter thoroughly examines. Real-world case studies and scenarios are dissected, providing valuable lessons for mitigating the aftermath of security incidents. Finally, the eighth chapter peers into the future, discussing emerging trends and technologies shaping the next frontier of operating system security.

In essence, 'Fortify and Shield' is more than just a guide; it is an indispensable resource for anyone seeking to navigate the complex realm of operating system security. By combining theoretical insights with practical strategies, this eBook equips readers with the knowledge and tools needed to safeguard operating systems in an era where cyber threats continue to evolve and proliferate."

Chapter 1: The Foundations of OS Security

Definition and importance of operating system security. Operating system security refers to the set of measures and mechanisms implemented to safeguard the integrity, confidentiality, and availability of a computer's operating system. It is a critical aspect of overall information security, as the operating system serves as the foundation for all software applications and user interactions on a computing device. The importance of operating system security cannot be overstated, given that the OS is the primary interface between the hardware and software components, managing resources and facilitating communication. A secure operating system is vital for protecting sensitive data, preventing unauthorized access, and ensuring the reliable and consistent functioning of the entire computing environment.

One fundamental aspect of operating system security is confidentiality, which involves protecting sensitive information from unauthorized access or disclosure. This is achieved through access control mechanisms, encryption, and other security measures that restrict user privileges and ensure that only authorized individuals or processes can access confidential data. Without a robust operating system security framework, malicious actors could exploit vulnerabilities to gain unauthorized access to sensitive information, leading to data breaches, identity theft, or other forms of cybercrime.

Integrity is another crucial dimension of operating system security, focusing on the accuracy and reliability of data and system resources. A secure operating system must prevent unauthorized modifications to critical files, settings, or configurations, as tampering with these elements can compromise the overall stability and functionality of the system. By employing techniques such as file integrity checking and digital signatures, the operating system can detect and mitigate attempts to alter system components, preserving the integrity of the computing environment.

Availability is the third pillar of operating system security, emphasizing the need for continuous and reliable access to system resources. Security measures such as redundancy, failover mechanisms, and denial-of-service protection are implemented to ensure that the operating system remains accessible and functional, even in the face of malicious attacks or unexpected failures. Uninterrupted availability is crucial for maintaining business operations, preventing service disruptions, and minimizing the impact of security incidents on users and organizations.

Furthermore, operating system security plays a pivotal role in protecting against various types of cyber threats, including malware, viruses, and other malicious software. Security features such as antivirus programs, firewalls, and intrusion detection systems are integrated into the operating system to identify and neutralize potential threats. These measures are essential for preventing the spread of malware, safeguarding system resources, and maintaining the overall health of the computing environment.

User authentication and access control are foundational elements of operating system security, ensuring that only authorized individuals or processes can interact with the system. Strong password policies, multi-factor authentication, and role-based access controls contribute to effective user authentication, reducing the risk of unauthorized access and privilege escalation. By implementing these measures, operating systems can enforce the principle of least privilege, limiting user access to only the resources necessary for their specific tasks.

Security patching and updates are critical components of operating system security, as they address vulnerabilities and weaknesses that could be exploited by attackers. Regularly updating the operating system ensures that known security flaws are patched, reducing the risk of exploitation and enhancing overall system resilience. Timely and consistent patch management is crucial for mitigating emerging threats and maintaining a secure computing environment.

In the context of network security, the operating system plays a central role in controlling communication between devices and managing network configurations. Secure network protocols, encryption, and firewall capabilities integrated into the operating system contribute to the protection of data during transmission and prevent unauthorized access to network resources. This is particularly important in the interconnected and often vulnerable landscape of the internet, where cyber threats can originate from various sources.

In conclusion, operating system security is a multifaceted and indispensable aspect of overall information security. Its significance lies in the protection of sensitive data, the preservation of system integrity, and the assurance of continuous availability. A secure operating system serves as the bedrock for a resilient and trustworthy computing environment, safeguarding against a myriad of cyber threats. As technology evolves, the importance of operating system security continues to grow, and its implementation remains a critical consideration for individuals, organizations, and society as a whole.

The role of OS security in protecting sensitive data and ensuring system integrity.

Operating system (OS) security plays a pivotal role in safeguarding sensitive data and ensuring the integrity of computer systems. Sensitive data encompasses a wide range of information, including personal identifiers, financial records, and proprietary business data, all of which are at constant risk of unauthorized access and exploitation. The OS serves as the primary layer of defense against such threats, providing mechanisms to control and monitor access to sensitive information. Access control mechanisms, such as user authentication and authorization, are fundamental components of OS security. By implementing robust authentication processes, including strong password policies and multi-factor authentication, the OS ensures that only authorized users can access sensitive data, reducing the risk of data breaches and unauthorized disclosures.

Furthermore, OS security is crucial for protecting the integrity of the system itself. System integrity refers to the accuracy and reliability of data, configurations, and overall system resources. Any compromise to system integrity can have severe consequences, leading to data corruption, system malfunctions, or unauthorized modifications. Security measures like file integrity checking and digital signatures are integrated into the OS to detect and prevent unauthorized changes to critical system files. These mechanisms play a vital role in maintaining the stability and reliability of the entire computing environment, ensuring that the OS functions as intended and providing a secure foundation for applications and user interactions.

Encryption is another essential aspect of OS security that contributes significantly to both data protection and system integrity. By encrypting sensitive data at rest and in transit, the OS ensures that even if unauthorized access occurs, the data remains indecipherable and unusable to malicious actors. This not only protects the confidentiality of sensitive information but also adds an additional layer of defense against tampering or modification attempts. Encryption technologies, such as full-disk encryption and secure communication protocols, are integral components of OS security strategies aimed at fortifying the overall integrity of the computing environment.

In the context of user privilege management, OS security is instrumental in enforcing the principle of least privilege. This principle advocates for granting users the minimum level of access required to perform their specific tasks. By carefully managing user privileges, the OS minimizes the potential impact of security incidents, limiting the scope of unauthorized access and reducing the risk of privilege escalation. Role-based access control (RBAC) systems, implemented at the OS level, contribute to effective privilege management by assigning specific roles and permissions to users based on their responsibilities within the organization. This not only enhances the security posture but also ensures that sensitive data is only accessible to those with a legitimate need.

Operating system security is particularly crucial in preventing data breaches, a prevalent and potentially devastating threat to sensitive information. OS-level security measures, such as firewalls and intrusion detection systems, play a critical role in identifying and mitigating unauthorized access attempts. Firewalls, whether implemented as hardware or software solutions, monitor and control incoming and outgoing network traffic, acting as a barrier between the internal system and external networks. This helps prevent unauthorized access and the exfiltration of sensitive data. Intrusion detection systems complement these efforts by actively monitoring system and network activities for signs of malicious behavior, allowing for timely responses to potential threats and vulnerabilities.

Regular security updates and patch management are integral components of OS security practices aimed at maintaining the integrity of the system. Software vulnerabilities are discovered regularly, and without prompt updates, these vulnerabilities can be exploited by attackers to compromise system integrity. Operating system vendors release security patches and updates to address known vulnerabilities and enhance system resilience. Timely application of these updates is critical to ensuring that the OS remains secure and capable of withstanding emerging threats. Effective patch management is a proactive strategy that strengthens the OS's ability to defend against potential exploits and vulnerabilities, contributing to the overall protection of sensitive data.

Moreover, OS security extends its protective measures to the realm of network security, where the integrity of data during transmission is a significant concern. The OS manages network configurations, protocols, and encryption mechanisms to secure the communication between devices and protect data as it traverses networks. Secure network protocols, such as HTTPS, SSH, and VPNs, are implemented at the OS level to encrypt data in transit, preventing eavesdropping and unauthorized interception. Additionally, firewalls configured at the OS level control the flow of network traffic, blocking unauthorized access and enhancing the overall security posture of the system.

In conclusion, the role of operating system security in protecting sensitive data and ensuring system integrity is paramount in the landscape of modern computing. The OS serves as the linchpin of a secure computing environment, implementing a diverse array of security measures to thwart unauthorized access, prevent data breaches, and maintain the accuracy and reliability of system resources. Through access control mechanisms, encryption technologies, privilege management, and proactive security measures like patch management, the OS establishes a robust defense against the myriad threats posed by malicious actors. As technology continues to advance, the importance of OS security will only intensify, underscoring its critical role in safeguarding sensitive information and upholding the integrity of computer systems.

Overview of security models such as discretionary access control (DAC) and mandatory access control (MAC).

Security models, such as Discretionary Access Control (DAC) and Mandatory Access Control (MAC), are foundational frameworks designed to govern and regulate access to resources within computing systems. Discretionary Access Control is a widely used security model that empowers users with the ability to control access to their own resources. In DAC, individuals have discretion over granting or revoking access permissions to their files, directories, and other system objects. This model operates on the principle of ownership, where each resource is associated with an owner who determines the access rights for others. While DAC offers flexibility and simplicity, it poses challenges in terms of ensuring consistent and uniform security policies across an entire system, as it relies heavily on individual users to make access control decisions.

In contrast, Mandatory Access Control takes a more centralized and restrictive approach to access management. In a MAC system, access decisions are not at the discretion of individual users but are determined by a higher authority, typically a security policy defined by the system administrator or security administrator. This model is particularly prevalent in environments where data confidentiality is of utmost importance, such as military or government settings. MAC ensures a more stringent control over access permissions, as users cannot modify or override access decisions set by the security policy. This rigid control helps mitigate the risk of unauthorized access, but it may limit flexibility and user autonomy, making it less suitable for environments where users require greater control over their resources.

One notable example of a Mandatory Access Control model is the Bell-LaPadula model, which is designed to address the confidentiality requirements of secure systems. The Bell-LaPadula model enforces the "no read up, no write down" principle, meaning that a user with a certain security clearance cannot read information classified at a higher level but can write information to lower-level classifications. This prevents unauthorized users from accessing sensitive information, maintaining the confidentiality of data. While effective in high-security environments, the Bell-LaPadula model may not be suitable for all scenarios, as it may be overly restrictive for systems with different security requirements.

Another well-known security model is the Biba Integrity Model, which focuses on maintaining data integrity within a system. The Biba model enforces the principle of "no write up, no read down," meaning that users with lower integrity levels cannot write to objects with higher integrity levels and cannot read objects with lower integrity levels. This prevents the introduction of malicious or erroneous data into the system, preserving the integrity of information. However, like other MAC models, the Biba model may be perceived as inflexible in certain situations, as it strictly controls access based on predefined integrity levels.

Hybrid security models, such as Role-Based Access Control (RBAC), combine elements of both DAC and MAC to provide a more flexible yet controlled approach to access management. In an RBAC system, access decisions are based on predefined roles, each associated with specific responsibilities and permissions. Users are assigned to roles, and their access rights are determined by the permissions associated with those roles. This model simplifies administration by reducing the need for fine-grained access control while offering a level of centralized control over access decisions. RBAC strikes a balance between the autonomy granted by DAC and the strict control imposed by MAC, making it suitable for a wide range of organizational structures and security requirements.

The implementation of these security models is often complemented by access control mechanisms, such as Access Control Lists (ACLs) and Capability-based security. ACLs are commonly associated with DAC and provide a way to specify which users or system processes are granted access to objects, as well as what operations they can perform on those objects. ACLs offer a fine-grained approach to access control, enabling users to tailor permissions at the individual or group level. Capability-based security, on the other hand, is a concept that assigns tokens or "capabilities" to users, granting access based on possession of these capabilities. This approach is more closely aligned with the DAC model, emphasizing the user's discretion in controlling access to their resources.

The choice between DAC and MAC, or a combination of both in a hybrid model, depends on the specific security requirements and organizational needs. DAC is often favored in environments where user autonomy and flexibility are prioritized, such as in many business and personal computing settings. On the other hand, MAC is preferred in situations where centralized control and the highest levels of security are paramount, as seen in government or military contexts. Hybrid models like RBAC provide a compromise, allowing organizations to define and enforce access policies while still accommodating the diverse needs of users within the system.

In conclusion, security models, including Discretionary Access Control, Mandatory Access Control, and hybrid approaches like Role-Based Access Control, play a critical role in shaping access management within computing systems. These models provide frameworks for defining and enforcing access policies, each with its own advantages and limitations. The choice of a particular security model depends on factors such as the sensitivity of data, organizational structure, and the desired balance between user autonomy and centralized control. As the landscape of computing continues to evolve, the effective implementation of these security models remains essential in addressing the ever-growing challenges of information security and access management.

Understanding how security models dictate access rights and permissions.

Security models play a pivotal role in dictating access rights and permissions within computing systems, governing how users interact with resources and ensuring the confidentiality, integrity, and availability of sensitive information. One of the fundamental security models is Discretionary Access Control (DAC), where access decisions are at the discretion of individual users. In the DAC model, each resource, such as files, directories, or devices, is associated with an owner who has the authority to set access permissions. Owners can grant or revoke access rights for other users, providing a flexible and decentralized approach to access management. This model enables users to exercise control over their own resources, allowing them to tailor access permissions based on their specific needs. However, the flexibility of DAC comes with challenges, as it relies on the responsible and consistent decision-making of individual users, which may lead to inconsistencies and potential security vulnerabilities.

Mandatory Access Control (MAC) represents another paradigm in access management, offering a more centralized and rigid approach. In a MAC system, access decisions are predetermined by a higher authority, typically defined by a security policy enforced by the system administrator. Users do not have the discretion to modify or override access controls, as permissions are dictated by the security policy. This model is particularly prevalent in environments where strict control over data confidentiality is paramount, such as military or government settings. MAC ensures a more stringent and uniform application of access controls, reducing the risk of unauthorized access. However, the centralized nature of MAC may limit user autonomy and flexibility, making it less suitable for environments where users require more control over their resources.

The Bell-LaPadula model, a prominent example of a Mandatory Access Control model, focuses on preserving data confidentiality. It adheres to the principle of "no read up, no write down," meaning that users with a certain security clearance cannot read information classified at a higher level but can write to lower-level classifications. This approach prevents unauthorized access to sensitive information, maintaining the confidentiality of data. While effective in high-security environments, the Bell-LaPadula model may be overly restrictive for systems with different security requirements, as it strictly enforces access based on security clearances.

Complementing the focus on confidentiality, the Biba Integrity Model is another MAC model designed to preserve data integrity. The Biba model adheres to the principle of "no write up, no read down," preventing users with lower integrity levels from writing to higher integrity objects and from reading lower integrity objects. This model aims to prevent the introduction of malicious or erroneous data into the system, ensuring the integrity of information. Like other MAC models, the Biba model may be perceived as inflexible in certain situations, as it strictly controls access based on predefined integrity levels.

Hybrid models, such as Role-Based Access Control (RBAC), combine elements of both DAC and MAC to strike a balance between flexibility and control. In an RBAC system, access decisions are based on predefined roles, each associated with specific responsibilities and permissions. Users are assigned to roles, and their access rights are determined by the permissions associated with those roles. This model simplifies administration by reducing the need for fine-grained access control while offering a level of centralized control over access decisions. RBAC is suitable for a wide range of organizational structures and security requirements, providing a compromise that allows organizations to define and enforce access policies while accommodating the diverse needs of users within the system.

Access control mechanisms, such as Access Control Lists (ACLs) and Capability-based security, are often implemented within the context of these security models to further dictate access rights. ACLs, commonly associated with DAC, provide a way to specify which users or system processes are granted access to objects and what operations they can perform on those objects. ACLs offer a fine-grained approach to access control, enabling users to tailor permissions at the individual or group level. Capability-based security, on the other hand, is a concept that assigns tokens or "capabilities" to users, granting access based on possession of these capabilities. This approach is more closely aligned with the DAC model, emphasizing the user's discretion in controlling access to their resources.

Understanding how security models dictate access rights is essential for effective access management, as it directly impacts the security posture of computing systems. These models influence the design and implementation of access control policies, shaping the overall security architecture of an organization. The choice between DAC, MAC, or hybrid models like RBAC depends on factors such as the sensitivity of data, organizational structure, and the desired balance between user autonomy and centralized control. As organizations grapple with evolving security challenges, the intricate interplay between security models and access control mechanisms remains a critical consideration in establishing robust and resilient information security frameworks.

Examination of key security components, including firewalls, antivirus software, and intrusion detection systems.

A comprehensive examination of key security components, such as firewalls, antivirus software, and intrusion detection systems, is crucial for understanding their pivotal roles in fortifying the defenses of information systems against a myriad of cyber threats. Firewalls stand as one of the foremost elements in network security, serving as a barrier between internal networks and external, potentially malicious entities. These hardware or software-based systems scrutinize incoming and outgoing network traffic based on predetermined security rules, deciding whether to allow or block specific communication. Firewalls play a critical role in preventing unauthorized access, mitigating the risk of cyber attacks, and safeguarding sensitive data. By establishing a perimeter defense, firewalls contribute significantly to the overall security posture of an organization, acting as the first line of defense against various cyber threats, including malware and unauthorized access attempts.

Antivirus software represents another indispensable component in the realm of information security, specifically targeting the detection and mitigation of malicious software, commonly known as malware. This category encompasses viruses, worms, trojan horses, ransomware, and other types of malicious code designed to compromise the integrity and functionality of computer systems. Antivirus programs employ a range of techniques, such as signature-based detection, behavioral analysis, and heuristics, to identify and neutralize known and emerging threats. Regular updates to antivirus databases are critical to ensuring the software's effectiveness in recognizing new strains of malware. By scanning files, emails, and web traffic, antivirus software plays a crucial role in preventing the spread of malware, protecting both individual devices and entire networks from the potentially devastating consequences of cyber infections.

Intrusion Detection Systems (IDS) form a vital component of proactive security measures, focusing on the identification and response to unauthorized or suspicious activities within a network or system. These systems monitor and analyze network and system events, looking for patterns indicative of potential security incidents. IDS can be categorized into two types: Network-based Intrusion Detection Systems (NIDS) and Host-based Intrusion Detection Systems (HIDS). NIDS analyze network traffic, identifying anomalies or known attack signatures, while HIDS focus on the activities and behaviors of individual hosts or devices. The timely detection of security incidents allows organizations to respond promptly, preventing or minimizing the impact of cyber attacks. Intrusion Detection Systems play a crucial role in enhancing the overall situational awareness of an organization's security posture, enabling proactive responses to emerging threats.

Firewalls, antivirus software, and intrusion detection systems often work in tandem to create a layered defense strategy, commonly referred to as defense-in-depth. This multifaceted approach acknowledges the diversity and sophistication of modern cyber threats, recognizing that no single security component can provide foolproof protection. The synergy between these components allows organizations to address different aspects of security, creating a more resilient and adaptive defense mechanism. Firewalls establish a barrier at the network perimeter, preventing unauthorized access and controlling communication, while antivirus software focuses on identifying and eliminating malicious code. Intrusion Detection Systems complement these efforts by actively monitoring for patterns of malicious activity, enhancing the organization's ability to detect and respond to security incidents.

The effectiveness of firewalls, antivirus software, and intrusion detection systems is contingent on timely updates, regular monitoring, and proactive management. Firewalls need to be configured with up-to-date security policies, considering the evolving nature of cyber threats. Antivirus software requires frequent updates to its signature databases to recognize newly emerging malware variants. Intrusion Detection Systems must be tuned to the specific needs and characteristics of the organization's network, ensuring that they can effectively identify anomalous activities without generating an overwhelming number of false positives. Additionally, organizations should implement a continuous monitoring and response mechanism to address security incidents promptly and adapt their defense strategies based on emerging threats.

While these security components contribute significantly to the overall resilience of information systems, it is crucial to recognize that they are not silver bullets and should be complemented by other security measures. User education and awareness training, regular system patching and updates, and the implementation of strong access controls are essential elements of a holistic security strategy. Moreover, the evolving landscape of cybersecurity demands a proactive stance, with organizations staying abreast of emerging threats and continuously refining their security measures to address new challenges. Firewalls, antivirus software, and intrusion detection systems serve as key pillars in this dynamic and ever-changing security ecosystem, helping organizations navigate the intricate landscape of cyber threats and protect their valuable assets from compromise.

The collaborative function of these components in maintaining a secure OS environment.

The collaborative function of key security components, namely firewalls, antivirus software, and intrusion detection systems, is paramount in establishing and maintaining a secure operating system (OS) environment. These components operate synergistically to create a robust defense mechanism that addresses diverse cyber threats, safeguarding the integrity, confidentiality, and availability of the OS and its associated resources. Firewalls, acting as a frontline defense, play a pivotal role in controlling the flow of network traffic to and from the OS. By establishing a barrier between internal networks and external entities, firewalls prevent unauthorized access and filter communication based on predefined security rules. This collaborative effort significantly reduces the attack surface and minimizes the risk of malicious actors infiltrating the OS environment, fortifying the overall security posture.

Antivirus software contributes indispensably to the collaborative security framework by focusing on the identification and mitigation of malicious software. Operating within the OS environment, antivirus programs scan files, emails, and web traffic for known malware signatures or behavioral anomalies. Regular updates to antivirus databases are critical to ensuring the software's efficacy against emerging threats. The collaborative relationship between firewalls and antivirus software lies in their collective ability to address different aspects of security. While firewalls control network traffic and prevent unauthorized access, antivirus software proactively detects and eliminates malicious code, forming a comprehensive defense strategy that mitigates the risk of malware compromising the OS.

Intrusion Detection Systems (IDS) further enhance the collaborative security efforts by actively monitoring and analyzing network and system events within the OS environment. IDS, whether network-based (NIDS) or host-based (HIDS), play a crucial role in detecting and responding to unauthorized or suspicious activities. NIDS analyze network traffic for known attack signatures or anomalies, while HIDS focus on individual hosts or devices, monitoring their activities and behaviors. The collaborative function of intrusion detection systems with firewalls and antivirus software lies in their complementary roles. While firewalls create a perimeter defense, preventing unauthorized access, and antivirus software addresses known malware threats, IDS actively identifies and alerts on anomalous activities, offering a proactive layer of defense that enhances the overall situational awareness of the OS environment.

This collaborative approach, often referred to as defense-in-depth, recognizes the multifaceted nature of cyber threats and acknowledges that a single security component may not provide comprehensive protection. The interplay between firewalls, antivirus software, and intrusion detection systems creates a layered defense strategy that strengthens the OS environment's resilience. Firewalls establish a protective perimeter, controlling network communication; antivirus software proactively detects and eliminates malware; and IDS actively monitors for signs of unauthorized activities. Together, these components create a dynamic defense mechanism that adapts to the evolving threat landscape, providing a more robust and comprehensive shield against cyber threats.

The effectiveness of this collaborative security framework is contingent on continuous updates, vigilant monitoring, and proactive management. Firewalls require regular configuration updates to adapt to emerging threats and changes in network requirements. Antivirus software needs frequent updates to its signature databases to recognize new malware variants. IDS must be tuned to the specific characteristics of the OS environment to effectively identify and respond to anomalous activities. This ongoing maintenance ensures that the collaborative security components remain aligned with the evolving threat landscape, maintaining the integrity and effectiveness of the defense-in-depth strategy.

While firewalls, antivirus software, and intrusion detection systems form the core of this collaborative defense, it is essential to recognize that user education, access controls, and system patching are integral components of a holistic security strategy. User awareness and education contribute to a security-conscious culture, reducing the likelihood of social engineering attacks. Access controls restrict user permissions, minimizing the impact of security incidents. System patching addresses vulnerabilities and strengthens the OS environment's resilience. The collaborative function of these security components, coupled with a holistic security strategy, ensures a well-rounded defense that comprehensively addresses the diverse challenges posed by cyber threats to the OS environment.

In conclusion, the collaborative function of firewalls, antivirus software, and intrusion detection systems is instrumental in maintaining a secure operating system environment. This synergistic approach creates a defense-in-depth strategy that addresses various dimensions of cybersecurity, from controlling network traffic to proactively detecting malware and actively monitoring for unauthorized activities. The continuous updates, vigilant monitoring, and proactive management of these components contribute to a resilient and adaptive defense mechanism that protects the OS environment from evolving cyber threats. By recognizing the collaborative nature of these security components and integrating them into a comprehensive security strategy, organizations can establish a secure operating system environment that effectively mitigates the risks posed by an ever-evolving threat landscape.

Best practices for creating and managing user accounts.

Best practices for creating and managing user accounts are essential in establishing a robust and secure information technology environment. The process begins with a thorough understanding of user account lifecycle management, encompassing account creation, provisioning, maintenance, and deprovisioning. When creating user accounts, it is crucial to adhere to the principle of least privilege, granting users the minimum access necessary for their roles and responsibilities. This minimizes the risk of unauthorized access and potential security breaches. Additionally, a strong authentication mechanism, such as password policies that enforce complexity, length, and regular updates, should be implemented to enhance the security of user accounts. Multi-factor authentication (MFA) is another recommended practice, adding an extra layer of protection by requiring users to provide multiple forms of identification before gaining access.

The process of managing user accounts involves continuous monitoring and periodic reviews to ensure that access privileges align with the evolving needs of the organization. Regularly auditing user accounts helps identify and address any discrepancies, dormant accounts, or unauthorized access. Automating account management processes, when feasible, enhances efficiency and reduces the likelihood of human error. Implementing a role-based access control (RBAC) system streamlines user account management by associating permissions with specific roles, simplifying the assignment and revocation of access rights based on job responsibilities.

Secure account provisioning is a critical aspect of user account management. Automating the account creation process helps eliminate manual errors and ensures consistency in the application of security policies. Additionally, implementing an approval workflow for account creation requests adds an extra layer of control, preventing unauthorized accounts from being provisioned. Regularly reviewing and updating provisioning processes based on changes in organizational structure or user roles is essential to maintain an accurate and secure user account environment.

User account maintenance involves ongoing activities to keep account information accurate and up-to-date. This includes regularly reviewing and updating user account attributes, such as contact information and job roles. It is advisable to periodically remind users to update their passwords and review their account settings for any anomalies. Organizations should establish clear policies regarding the reuse of passwords and set expiration periods for passwords to mitigate the risk of compromised credentials. Leveraging automated tools for user account maintenance tasks, such as password resets and account updates, contributes to efficiency and accuracy.

Deprovisioning, or the process of disabling or deleting user accounts, is equally crucial to prevent former employees or external actors from exploiting dormant accounts. Implementing a timely and systematic deprovisioning process ensures that access is promptly revoked when users leave the organization or change roles. Automated deprovisioning tools can play a vital role in enforcing consistent and immediate account terminations, reducing the window of vulnerability associated with inactive accounts. Additionally, maintaining an audit trail of account deprovisioning activities helps organizations track and verify that appropriate steps were taken to secure the system.

To enhance overall security, organizations should conduct regular security awareness training for users, educating them on the importance of secure password practices, recognizing phishing attempts, and understanding the significance of adhering to security policies. Implementing strong access controls, such as segregation of duties, helps prevent conflicts of interest and ensures that no single user has excessive privileges that could lead to security vulnerabilities. Organizations should also have incident response plans in place, detailing procedures to follow in case of a security incident related to user accounts.

Furthermore, organizations should stay informed about emerging threats and vulnerabilities, updating security measures accordingly. Regularly conducting security assessments, penetration testing, and vulnerability scans on user account management systems can help identify and address potential weaknesses. Periodic reviews of security policies and practices ensure that they remain aligned with industry standards and regulatory requirements.

In conclusion, best practices for creating and managing user accounts are essential for maintaining a secure information technology environment. Adhering to the principle of least privilege, implementing strong authentication mechanisms, and utilizing multi-factor authentication are foundational steps. Continuous monitoring, automated processes, and periodic reviews contribute to effective user account lifecycle management. Secure provisioning, regular maintenance, and systematic deprovisioning help minimize security risks associated with user accounts. Additionally, user awareness training, strong access controls, and proactive security measures further enhance the overall security posture. As organizations navigate the ever-evolving landscape of cybersecurity threats, robust user account management practices remain a fundamental element in ensuring the confidentiality, integrity, and availability of sensitive information.

Password policies, user roles, and the principle of least privilege.

Password policies, user roles, and the principle of least privilege constitute critical elements in the realm of information security, working together to establish a robust defense against unauthorized access and potential security breaches. Password policies play a foundational role in securing user accounts by defining the requirements and constraints for passwords. A well-crafted password policy typically includes guidelines on password length, complexity, and expiration. It is essential to encourage users to create strong passwords that combine a mix of alphanumeric characters, symbols, and are not easily guessable. Regular password updates and the prohibition of password reuse enhance security by minimizing the risk associated with compromised credentials. Additionally, the implementation of multi-factor authentication (MFA) adds an extra layer of protection, requiring users to provide multiple forms of identification before gaining access.

User roles serve as an organizational framework for delineating responsibilities and access privileges based on job functions. Role-Based Access Control (RBAC) is a widely adopted approach that aligns user permissions with specific roles, streamlining access management. Assigning roles to users simplifies the process of granting and revoking access rights, ensuring that individuals have the minimum access necessary to perform their tasks. This not only enhances security but also streamlines administrative tasks, making it easier to manage user access in large and complex environments. Establishing clear and well-defined user roles is crucial for implementing the principle of least privilege.

The principle of least privilege is a fundamental concept in information security that advocates for granting users the minimum level of access required to perform their specific tasks and responsibilities. By restricting unnecessary privileges, the principle of least privilege aims to minimize the potential impact of security incidents and reduce the attack surface. In practice, this means that users should only be granted access to the resources and data necessary for their job functions, preventing unauthorized access or unintended modifications to critical systems. Implementing the principle of least privilege requires a comprehensive understanding of user roles, their associated responsibilities, and the specific access requirements of each role within the organization.

Effective password policies, user roles, and the principle of least privilege are interconnected components that form a cohesive security strategy. A well-designed password policy complements the principle of least privilege by ensuring that even if credentials are compromised, the potential damage is mitigated by frequent password updates, complexity requirements, and the use of multi-factor authentication. User roles, when aligned with the principle of least privilege, contribute to a fine-grained access control system, where access rights are precisely tailored to meet the needs of individual roles, minimizing the risk of privilege escalation and unauthorized access.

Implementing these security measures necessitates a collaborative and comprehensive approach. Password policies should be communicated clearly to users, accompanied by training programs to promote awareness of the importance of strong and secure passwords. Automated tools and systems play a crucial role in enforcing password policies, ensuring compliance and reducing the burden on administrators. Regular audits and reviews of user roles and permissions are essential to ensure that access privileges align with current job responsibilities and organizational needs. Periodic assessments of the overall security posture, including user accounts and access controls, contribute to the continuous improvement of the security framework.

In addition to safeguarding against external threats, these security measures are equally important in addressing insider threats. The principle of least privilege helps mitigate the risk of insider abuse by limiting employees' access to only what is necessary for their job functions. User roles and permissions should be regularly reviewed to prevent unauthorized access and ensure that terminated employees no longer have active accounts. Password policies, enforced through education and technology, add an additional layer of defense against potential insider threats.

Furthermore, these security measures align with regulatory requirements and industry standards, demonstrating a commitment to compliance and data protection. Password policies, when designed to meet specific regulatory requirements, contribute to the organization's adherence to data protection laws and confidentiality standards. User roles and the principle of least privilege are instrumental in ensuring that access controls align with the data protection principles of least access necessary, reducing the risk of non-compliance and associated legal repercussions.

In conclusion, password policies, user roles, and the principle of least privilege are integral components of a comprehensive information security strategy. Together, they form a cohesive framework that addresses access control, authentication, and authorization, reducing the risk of unauthorized access and potential security breaches. A well-implemented password policy, supported by user roles aligned with the principle of least privilege, creates a resilient security posture that balances usability and protection. As organizations navigate the evolving landscape of cybersecurity threats, these measures remain crucial in upholding the confidentiality, integrity, and availability of sensitive information.

The importance of auditing and monitoring for detecting and responding to security incidents.

The importance of auditing and monitoring in the context of information security cannot be overstated, as these processes play a pivotal role in detecting and responding to security incidents, thereby bolstering the overall resilience of an organization's cybersecurity defenses. Auditing involves the systematic examination and assessment of various aspects of an information system, including user activities, system configurations, and access controls, to ensure compliance with security policies and regulatory requirements. Through regular audits, organizations can establish a baseline understanding of the normal behavior and functioning of their systems, allowing for the identification of anomalies or deviations that may indicate potential security threats.

Monitoring, on the other hand, is an ongoing process that involves the continuous observation of system activities, network traffic, and user behavior in real-time. It serves as a proactive surveillance mechanism, enabling organizations to promptly detect and respond to security incidents as they unfold. The synergy between auditing and monitoring creates a comprehensive approach to cybersecurity, encompassing both periodic reviews of system configurations and real-time surveillance to identify and address emerging threats.

One of the primary benefits of auditing is its role in promoting accountability and transparency within an organization. By conducting regular audits, organizations can ensure that individuals and processes adhere to established security policies and procedures. Audits provide a mechanism for tracking changes to system configurations, user account permissions, and access logs, aiding in the identification of potential vulnerabilities or unauthorized activities. Moreover, audits contribute to regulatory compliance, as many industry standards and data protection laws require organizations to maintain a thorough record of security-related activities and demonstrate due diligence in safeguarding sensitive information.

Auditing is particularly crucial in maintaining the integrity and confidentiality of data. By reviewing access logs and system changes, organizations can identify and rectify any discrepancies or unauthorized alterations to critical data. This process not only helps in preventing data breaches but also enables organizations to trace the origin of security incidents, facilitating effective incident response strategies. Additionally, auditing assists in establishing a culture of continuous improvement, as organizations can learn from audit findings to enhance their security measures and address vulnerabilities proactively.

Monitoring complements auditing by providing real-time visibility into the dynamic landscape of an organization's information systems. Continuous monitoring enables the detection of anomalous activities or patterns that may signify a security incident. This proactive approach allows organizations to respond swiftly, minimizing the potential impact of a security breach. Monitoring encompasses various aspects, including network traffic analysis, intrusion detection, and endpoint security, offering a comprehensive view of the organization's overall security posture.

Detection is a crucial aspect of incident response, and monitoring serves as the frontline defense in this regard. By analyzing network traffic patterns and user behavior, organizations can identify indicators of compromise or malicious activities that may go unnoticed through traditional auditing alone. Real-time monitoring tools, such as Security Information and Event Management (SIEM) systems, play a pivotal role in aggregating and correlating security events across the organization, providing security teams with actionable insights into potential threats.

The importance of monitoring is further underscored by its contribution to incident response and mitigation strategies. In the event of a security incident, the ability to promptly detect and respond is paramount. Continuous monitoring enables security teams to identify and isolate compromised systems, investigate the root cause of incidents, and take decisive actions to prevent further damage. Timely response to security incidents is essential in reducing the dwell time of attackers within a network, limiting the potential for data exfiltration, and restoring the normal functioning of affected systems.

Furthermore, monitoring plays a vital role in compliance management by providing evidence of security controls and incident response activities. Many regulatory frameworks and standards, such as the Payment Card Industry Data Security Standard (PCI DSS) and the Health Insurance Portability and Accountability Act (HIPAA), require organizations to demonstrate due diligence in monitoring and responding to security incidents. A well-established monitoring infrastructure not only helps organizations meet these compliance requirements but also enhances their overall cybersecurity posture.

In conclusion, the importance of auditing and monitoring in detecting and responding to security incidents cannot be overstated. Auditing provides a structured and systematic approach to assessing and ensuring the compliance of information systems with security policies and regulations. It establishes a foundation for accountability, transparency, and continuous improvement within an organization. Monitoring, on the other hand, offers real-time visibility into the dynamic nature of security threats, enabling proactive detection and response to potential incidents. The synergy between auditing and monitoring creates a comprehensive and adaptive security framework that empowers organizations to safeguard their information assets, mitigate risks, and respond effectively to the ever-evolving landscape of cybersecurity threats. As organizations embrace these practices, they reinforce their ability to protect sensitive data, maintain the integrity of their systems, and uphold the trust of their stakeholders in an increasingly interconnected and digital world.

Strategies for implementing effective auditing and monitoring practices in an operating system.

Implementing effective auditing and monitoring practices in an operating system (OS) is critical for maintaining a robust security posture, detecting anomalies, and responding promptly to security incidents. A strategic approach begins with the establishment of a well-defined auditing framework, encompassing the identification of key audit trails, selection of relevant events, and the determination of audit policies. Auditing should be tailored to the specific security requirements and risks of the organization, considering factors such as regulatory compliance, the sensitivity of data, and the organization's overall threat landscape.

A fundamental strategy involves defining clear audit trails for critical system components, applications, and user activities. These trails serve as a record of events that can be reviewed during audits to identify security-related incidents. Audit trails may include logs of login attempts, file accesses, system configuration changes, and other relevant activities. By identifying and prioritizing the most critical audit trails, organizations can focus their monitoring efforts on areas with the highest impact on security.

Selecting the appropriate events to monitor is another crucial aspect of effective auditing. Organizations must identify the events that are most indicative of potential security threats or violations. For instance, monitoring failed login attempts, changes to privileged accounts, or access to sensitive files can help detect and respond to unauthorized activities. Collaboration with key stakeholders, including security professionals, system administrators, and compliance officers, is essential to ensure that the chosen events align with organizational objectives and compliance requirements.

To ensure the success of auditing strategies, organizations should implement comprehensive audit policies. These policies define the rules and conditions under which auditing is performed, specifying what events are logged, the level of detail recorded, and where the audit logs are stored. Careful consideration should be given to balancing the need for detailed logging with the potential impact on system performance and storage capacity. Additionally, organizations should establish procedures for regular reviews and updates of audit policies to adapt to evolving security requirements and address emerging threats.

The implementation of real-time monitoring tools, such as Security Information and Event Management (SIEM) systems, is instrumental in achieving effective auditing practices. SIEM solutions aggregate and correlate data from various sources, allowing organizations to monitor and analyze security events in real-time. These tools provide a centralized view of the OS environment, enabling security teams to detect anomalies, patterns of behavior indicative of threats, and potential security incidents. Integrating SIEM with other security technologies, such as intrusion detection systems and firewalls, enhances the overall visibility and responsiveness of the monitoring infrastructure.

Establishing baselines for normal system behavior is a proactive strategy that supports effective monitoring. By understanding what constitutes typical system activity, organizations can more readily identify deviations or abnormal patterns that may indicate a security incident. Baseline creation involves analyzing historical data and establishing benchmarks for metrics such as network traffic, user behavior, and system performance. Deviations from these baselines trigger alerts, enabling security teams to investigate and respond to potential security threats.

An essential element of effective auditing and monitoring is user activity tracking. Monitoring user actions, including logins, file accesses, and system changes, is critical for detecting insider threats and unauthorized activities. User activity logs contribute to accountability, allowing organizations to trace the actions of individuals in the event of a security incident. However, striking a balance between monitoring user activity for security purposes and respecting privacy concerns is crucial. Organizations should transparently communicate their monitoring practices to users and establish policies that align with legal and ethical considerations.

Regular auditing and monitoring reviews are integral components of a successful strategy. Periodic assessments of audit logs and monitoring reports help organizations identify trends, patterns, or recurring issues that may require further investigation or adjustments to security controls. Regular reviews also support the refinement of audit policies, ensuring that they remain aligned with evolving security requirements and compliance standards. Furthermore, audits can serve as valuable learning opportunities, enabling organizations to enhance their security posture based on insights gained from past incidents or vulnerabilities.

Automation plays a significant role in streamlining auditing and monitoring processes. Implementing automated tools for log collection, analysis, and reporting reduces the burden on security teams, enhances accuracy, and enables timely responses to security incidents. Automation can also facilitate the correlation of diverse data sources, helping organizations make sense of complex and interconnected events. Automated alerts and notifications ensure that security teams are promptly informed of potential security threats, enabling them to take immediate action.

Incorporating threat intelligence into auditing and monitoring practices enhances the organization's ability to identify and respond to emerging threats. By integrating information about current cyber threats, attack vectors, and vulnerabilities, organizations can tailor their auditing and monitoring strategies to focus on areas most likely to be targeted. Threat intelligence feeds can be utilized to create correlation rules in monitoring tools, enabling organizations to detect and respond to specific indicators of compromise or malicious activities.

Collaboration and communication are foundational to the success of auditing and monitoring strategies. Establishing clear lines of communication between security teams, IT administrators, and other stakeholders ensures that everyone is aligned on the goals of auditing and monitoring efforts. Regular training sessions and knowledge-sharing initiatives enhance the capabilities of personnel involved in auditing and monitoring, fostering a collaborative and informed security culture within the organization.

In conclusion, effective auditing and monitoring practices in an operating system are indispensable for maintaining a resilient cybersecurity posture. A strategic approach involves defining clear audit trails, selecting relevant events, establishing comprehensive audit policies, and implementing real-time monitoring tools such as SIEM systems. Baseline creation, user activity tracking, regular reviews, and the incorporation of automation and threat intelligence contribute to a proactive and adaptive auditing and monitoring strategy. Collaboration and communication among stakeholders play a pivotal role in ensuring the success of these efforts. As organizations navigate the complex landscape of cybersecurity threats, robust auditing and monitoring strategies remain essential for early detection, rapid response, and continual improvement of security measures.

Chapter 2: Threat Landscape Analysis

Categorization of common threats, including malware, phishing, and social engineering.

The categorization of common threats, including malware, phishing, and social engineering, is essential for understanding the diverse landscape of cybersecurity risks and implementing effective defense mechanisms. Malware, a portmanteau of malicious software, represents a broad category encompassing various types of harmful software designed to compromise the integrity, confidentiality, and availability of computer systems. This includes viruses, which attach themselves to legitimate programs and replicate when the infected program runs; worms, which spread independently by exploiting vulnerabilities; trojan horses, which disguise themselves as benign software to deceive users into installing them; and ransomware, which encrypts files and demands payment for their release. Each subtype of malware poses unique challenges, requiring tailored security measures to detect, prevent, and mitigate their impact on systems.

Phishing is a pervasive threat that involves deceptive attempts to trick individuals into divulging sensitive information, such as usernames, passwords, or financial details, by posing as a trustworthy entity. Phishing attacks commonly employ email, social engineering, or fraudulent websites to create a façade that mimics legitimate organizations or individuals. Spear phishing, a targeted form of phishing, customizes attacks to specific individuals or organizations, making them more difficult to detect. Vishing (voice phishing) and smishing

(SMS phishing) leverage phone calls and text messages, respectively, to deceive individuals. The success of phishing attacks often relies on exploiting human psychology, prompting users to act impulsively without verifying the authenticity of the communication.

Social engineering constitutes a broader category of threats that exploit human psychology and behavior to manipulate individuals into divulging confidential information, performing unauthorized actions, or unwittingly aiding an attacker. Beyond phishing, social engineering techniques include pretexting, where attackers create a fabricated scenario to elicit information, and baiting, which involves offering something enticing to lure individuals into compromising security. Impersonation, quid pro quo, and tailgating are additional social engineering methods that exploit trust, reciprocity, and physical access to gain unauthorized advantages. The effectiveness of social engineering lies in its ability to bypass traditional technological defenses, emphasizing the importance of user education, awareness training, and stringent access controls to mitigate these risks.

Ransomware, a subset of malware, has emerged as a particularly disruptive and financially motivated threat. This type of malware encrypts a user's files or entire system and demands a ransom for their release. Ransomware attacks often target individuals, businesses, and even critical infrastructure, seeking to exploit the value of data and the urgency of its recovery. The success of ransomware campaigns is often attributed to their ability to evolve rapidly, adopting new tactics and evasion techniques. As a response, organizations must implement a multi-faceted defense strategy that includes regular data backups, robust endpoint security, and user education to recognize potential ransomware vectors.

Zero-day exploits represent a unique and challenging category of threats that leverage vulnerabilities in software or hardware before the vendor releases a patch. Cybercriminals exploit these vulnerabilities to launch targeted attacks, often evading traditional security measures. The term "zero-day" refers to the fact that developers have had zero days to address and patch the vulnerability. Detection and prevention of zero-day exploits require advanced threat intelligence, behavior-based analysis, and the rapid deployment of security patches as soon as they become available. Organizations must maintain vigilance and stay informed about emerging threats to reduce the risk posed by zero-day exploits.

Distributed Denial of Service (DDoS) attacks pose a significant threat to the availability of online services by overwhelming a target system or network with a flood of traffic. DDoS attacks can be executed using various techniques, including volumetric attacks that flood the network with excessive traffic, protocol attacks that exploit vulnerabilities in network protocols, and application layer attacks that target specific applications or services. The motive behind DDoS attacks can range from financial extortion to ideological motivations. Mitigating the impact of DDoS attacks requires a combination of network infrastructure resilience, traffic filtering, and DDoS-specific mitigation services to maintain service availability.

Advanced Persistent Threats (APTs) represent a sophisticated and prolonged form of cyber-espionage where attackers, often nation-state actors or well-funded criminal groups, compromise targeted systems and maintain unauthorized access over an extended period. APTs involve meticulous planning, custom malware, and the use of various attack vectors, including spear phishing and supply chain attacks. The primary goals of APTs are data exfiltration, persistent monitoring, and the compromise of critical infrastructure. Detecting and responding to APTs require advanced threat intelligence, continuous monitoring, and robust incident response capabilities to identify and neutralize persistent threats.

Supply chain attacks exploit vulnerabilities in the interconnected networks of suppliers and service providers to compromise the security of a target organization. Adversaries may compromise the hardware, software, or firmware components supplied to a target, infiltrating their systems through seemingly trusted channels. These attacks can have far-reaching consequences, impacting multiple organizations within a supply chain. Mitigating the risks associated with supply chain attacks requires stringent vendor risk management, secure coding practices, and a comprehensive understanding of the organization's digital supply chain.

In conclusion, the categorization of common threats, including malware, phishing, social engineering, ransomware, zero-day exploits, DDoS attacks, APTs, and supply chain attacks, provides a comprehensive framework for understanding the dynamic and multifaceted nature of cybersecurity risks. Each threat category demands a tailored defense strategy, emphasizing the importance of a holistic approach that combines technological defenses, user education, and robust incident response capabilities. As organizations navigate the evolving landscape of cyber threats, the awareness and understanding of these threat categories become paramount in establishing effective cybersecurity postures that safeguard against a diverse range of risks.

The impact of various threats on operating system security.

The impact of various threats on operating system (OS) security is profound and multifaceted, encompassing a range of consequences that can compromise the integrity, confidentiality, and availability of computer systems. Malware, a pervasive threat in the digital landscape, poses significant risks to OS security. Viruses can corrupt or destroy files, disrupting normal system operation, while worms exploit vulnerabilities to replicate and propagate, potentially overwhelming the OS with malicious activity. Trojan horses, disguised as legitimate software, can create backdoors for unauthorized access. Ransomware, a specific form of malware, encrypts files and demands payment for decryption, causing data loss and financial harm. The impact of malware on OS security extends beyond immediate disruptions, as infected systems can become part of botnets, contributing to larger-scale cyber threats.

Phishing attacks, targeting human vulnerabilities rather than technical weaknesses, can have severe repercussions on OS security. By deceiving users into divulging sensitive information such as passwords or financial details, phishing compromises user accounts and potentially provides unauthorized access to the OS. The impact of phishing extends to the compromise of organizational data, the potential for identity theft, and the erosion of user trust. As phishing techniques evolve and become more sophisticated, OS security is challenged to adapt and implement effective countermeasures.

Social engineering, a broader category of threats, manipulates human psychology to exploit trust and obtain sensitive information or unauthorized access. Pretexting involves creating fabricated scenarios to elicit information, while baiting lures individuals into compromising security for promised rewards. Impersonation, quid pro quo, and tailgating leverage trust to gain unauthorized advantages. The impact of social engineering on OS security is significant, as it often bypasses traditional technological defenses, highlighting the need for user education and stringent access controls.

Ransomware, as a subtype of malware, inflicts severe consequences on OS security by encrypting files and demanding ransom for their release. The impact extends beyond financial losses, as organizations may face operational disruptions, reputational damage, and legal consequences. Critical systems and sensitive data may be rendered inaccessible, affecting business continuity and causing potential harm to the organization's relationships with clients and partners. The evolution of ransomware tactics, including targeted attacks on high-profile entities and the exfiltration of sensitive data, further underscores the gravity of this threat to OS security.

Zero-day exploits, targeting vulnerabilities before vendors release patches, have a profound impact on OS security. Exploiting unknown vulnerabilities allows attackers to compromise systems without immediate countermeasures. The impact includes unauthorized access, data breaches, and potential compromise of critical infrastructure. Organizations must navigate the challenges of detecting and mitigating zero-day exploits, emphasizing the importance of threat intelligence, rapid patch deployment, and advanced security measures to safeguard OS security effectively.

Distributed Denial of Service (DDoS) attacks, aimed at overwhelming a target system or network with excessive traffic, can severely impact the availability of OS resources. The impact includes service disruptions, degraded performance, and potential financial losses. DDoS attacks often exploit vulnerabilities in network infrastructure, causing widespread collateral damage. Mitigating the impact of DDoS attacks on OS security requires resilient network architecture, traffic filtering mechanisms, and specialized DDoS mitigation services to maintain service availability.

Advanced Persistent Threats (APTs), characterized by prolonged and sophisticated cyber-espionage campaigns, have a profound and persistent impact on OS security. APTs often remain undetected for extended periods, allowing attackers to compromise systems, exfiltrate sensitive data, and maintain persistent access. The impact extends to intellectual property theft, the compromise of critical infrastructure, and the erosion of organizational trust. Mitigating the impact of APTs requires advanced threat intelligence, continuous monitoring, and robust incident response capabilities to detect and neutralize persistent threats.

Supply chain attacks, exploiting vulnerabilities in interconnected networks of suppliers and service providers, have wide-ranging consequences for OS security. Compromised hardware, software, or firmware components can lead to unauthorized access, data breaches, and the compromise of critical systems. The impact extends beyond individual organizations, affecting multiple entities within a supply chain. Mitigating the impact of supply chain attacks requires stringent vendor risk management, secure coding practices, and a comprehensive understanding of the digital supply chain's interconnected nature.

In conclusion, the impact of various threats on operating system security is substantial and diverse. Malware, phishing, social engineering, ransomware, zero-day exploits, DDoS attacks, APTs, and supply chain attacks each present unique challenges that can compromise the fundamental pillars of OS security. From immediate disruptions to long-term consequences such as data breaches, financial losses, and reputational damage, the impact of these threats underscores the need for a comprehensive and adaptive security posture. Organizations must prioritize proactive measures, including user education, advanced threat intelligence, and continuous monitoring, to effectively safeguard against the evolving landscape of cyber threats and protect the integrity, confidentiality, and availability of operating systems.

Techniques for identifying vulnerabilities in operating systems.

Identifying vulnerabilities in operating systems (OS) is a critical aspect of cybersecurity, requiring a comprehensive approach that combines automated tools, manual assessments, and ongoing monitoring. One prominent technique for vulnerability identification involves the use of vulnerability scanners. These automated tools systematically scan OS components, applications, and network services to detect known vulnerabilities, misconfigurations, and potential security weaknesses. Vulnerability scanners leverage extensive databases containing information about known vulnerabilities and their associated patches, enabling organizations to assess and remediate potential risks efficiently. Regular scanning schedules, complemented by real-time monitoring, provide a proactive strategy to identify and address vulnerabilities promptly, reducing the window of exposure for potential exploits.

Penetration testing, often referred to as ethical hacking, is another technique for identifying vulnerabilities in operating systems. Penetration testers simulate real-world cyber-attacks to uncover weaknesses that may be exploited by malicious actors. These assessments involve a combination of automated tools and manual techniques to identify vulnerabilities that may not be detected by standard scanners. By mimicking the tactics, techniques, and procedures of actual attackers, penetration testing provides valuable insights into the organization's security posture. The results guide the development of effective remediation strategies and help prioritize actions based on the severity and potential impact of identified vulnerabilities.

Continuous monitoring of OS security is essential for promptly identifying emerging vulnerabilities and potential threats. Security Information and Event Management (SIEM) systems play a crucial role in this technique, aggregating and analyzing log data from various sources across the OS environment. By correlating events, SIEM systems can detect patterns indicative of potential security incidents or vulnerabilities. Continuous monitoring allows organizations to identify deviations from baseline behaviors, respond to incidents in real-time, and proactively address emerging threats. SIEM systems contribute to a holistic approach to vulnerability identification, integrating with other security measures to fortify the OS against evolving risks.

Threat intelligence feeds provide organizations with valuable information about emerging vulnerabilities, exploits, and cyber threats. Leveraging threat intelligence as a technique for vulnerability identification involves monitoring external sources, such as security advisories, industry reports, and information sharing platforms. By staying informed about the latest vulnerabilities affecting operating systems, organizations can prioritize patch management efforts and implement timely mitigations. Collaborating with external cybersecurity communities and sharing threat intelligence enhances the collective ability to identify and address vulnerabilities effectively, contributing to a more resilient security posture.

Manual code review and analysis represent an indispensable technique for identifying vulnerabilities in OS components and applications. Skilled security professionals meticulously examine source code and configurations to uncover potential weaknesses that automated tools might miss. Manual code review is especially crucial for identifying logic flaws, design vulnerabilities, and security issues specific to the organization's custom-developed applications. Integrating code review into the software development lifecycle promotes the early identification and remediation of vulnerabilities, reducing the likelihood of security incidents related to programming errors.

Fuzz testing, or fuzzing, is a dynamic technique for identifying vulnerabilities by bombarding an OS or application with unexpected and malformed inputs. Fuzzing tools systematically generate and inject a variety of input data, aiming to trigger software crashes, errors, or unexpected behaviors. By observing how the OS responds to these inputs, security professionals can identify potential vulnerabilities, buffer overflows, or memory leaks that may be exploited by attackers. Fuzz testing complements traditional vulnerability scanning methods by providing a more dynamic and unpredictable approach to identifying weaknesses in OS components.

Threat modeling is a proactive technique that involves assessing the potential security threats and vulnerabilities in an OS environment based on its architecture, design, and functionality. Security professionals, system architects, and developers collaborate to identify potential attack vectors, prioritize assets, and evaluate potential weaknesses in the OS design. Threat modeling helps organizations anticipate and address vulnerabilities before they manifest in the operational environment. By integrating threat modeling into the development and deployment processes, organizations can create a more secure foundation for their operating systems and reduce the likelihood of security incidents.

Network scanning is a technique focused on identifying vulnerabilities in OS-related network services. Tools such as port scanners and network mappers examine the OS's exposed network services, identifying open ports, active services, and potential entry points for attackers. Network scanning complements vulnerability scanning by providing insights into the accessibility and exposure of OS components to external networks. Regular network scanning helps organizations identify and secure potential ingress points, reducing the attack surface and fortifying the overall security posture of the operating system.

Container security scanning is a technique specifically tailored to environments leveraging containerization technologies. Containers encapsulate applications and their dependencies, creating a portable and efficient deployment unit. Container security scanning tools analyze container images for known vulnerabilities, misconfigurations, and security weaknesses. This technique ensures that OS components within containers are free from vulnerabilities that could be exploited by attackers. As organizations increasingly adopt containerized environments, integrating container security scanning into the development and deployment lifecycle becomes crucial for maintaining a secure operating system infrastructure.

Collaboration with the cybersecurity community, participation in bug bounty programs, and responsible disclosure initiatives represent a technique for identifying vulnerabilities by harnessing the collective knowledge and expertise of the wider security community. Engaging with ethical hackers, security researchers, and independent experts allows organizations to receive feedback on potential vulnerabilities in their operating systems. Bug bounty programs incentivize security researchers to responsibly report vulnerabilities, providing organizations with an additional layer of defense against potential exploits. The collaborative approach fosters a culture of transparency, accountability, and continuous improvement in OS security.

In conclusion, identifying vulnerabilities in operating systems requires a multifaceted and proactive approach that leverages automated tools, manual assessments, continuous monitoring, threat intelligence, code review, fuzz testing, threat modeling, network scanning, container security scanning, and collaboration with the cybersecurity community. By combining these techniques, organizations can create a robust and adaptive strategy for identifying and mitigating vulnerabilities in their operating systems. A comprehensive approach ensures that potential weaknesses are addressed across the entire OS environment, reducing the risk of exploitation and fortifying the security posture against the evolving landscape of cyber threats.

The role of vulnerability assessments in preemptive security measures.

Vulnerability assessments play a pivotal role in preemptive security measures, serving as a cornerstone for organizations aiming to proactively identify and address potential weaknesses in their systems, networks, and applications. At its core, a vulnerability assessment is a systematic and organized process of identifying, quantifying, and prioritizing vulnerabilities within an information system. This proactive approach enables organizations to stay ahead of potential threats, enhance their security posture, and mitigate risks before they can be exploited by malicious actors.

One fundamental aspect of vulnerability assessments is their ability to provide organizations with a comprehensive understanding of their attack surface. By systematically scanning and analyzing the infrastructure, networks, and applications, vulnerability assessments help identify potential entry points that could be exploited by cyber adversaries. This holistic view enables organizations to gain insights into the overall security landscape, allowing them to prioritize and allocate resources effectively to address the most critical vulnerabilities that could pose a significant threat to the integrity, confidentiality, and availability of their systems.

Preemptive security measures, driven by vulnerability assessments, empower organizations to take a proactive stance in addressing potential risks before they can be leveraged by attackers. Through regular and systematic assessments, organizations can identify vulnerabilities that may arise from misconfigurations, outdated software, or inadequate security controls. This proactive identification of vulnerabilities allows organizations to implement remediation measures promptly, reducing the likelihood of exploitation and fortifying the resilience of their systems against potential threats.

Vulnerability assessments contribute significantly to risk management by providing organizations with a quantifiable understanding of the potential impact associated with identified vulnerabilities. By assigning severity levels or risk scores to vulnerabilities, organizations can prioritize remediation efforts based on the level of risk each vulnerability poses. This risk-based approach ensures that resources are allocated efficiently, focusing on vulnerabilities with the highest potential for exploitation and impact on the organization's overall security posture.

Moreover, vulnerability assessments support compliance efforts by helping organizations adhere to industry regulations and standards. Many regulatory frameworks require organizations to conduct regular vulnerability assessments as part of their security and compliance measures. By proactively identifying and addressing vulnerabilities, organizations can demonstrate due diligence and compliance with regulatory requirements, mitigating the risk of non-compliance-related legal and financial repercussions.

The continuous nature of vulnerability assessments is crucial for maintaining an adaptive security posture. Threat landscapes evolve, new vulnerabilities emerge, and the IT infrastructure undergoes changes over time. Regular assessments ensure that organizations remain vigilant in the face of evolving cybersecurity threats. By integrating vulnerability assessments into their routine security practices, organizations can establish a proactive and continuous improvement cycle, fostering a security culture that adapts to emerging risks.

The role of vulnerability assessments extends beyond mere identification to include the crucial aspect of prioritization. Not all vulnerabilities are created equal; some may pose a higher risk to the organization than others. Vulnerability assessments aid in prioritizing remediation efforts by considering factors such as the potential impact on business operations, the ease of exploitation, and the criticality of the affected systems. This prioritization allows organizations to focus on addressing the most pressing vulnerabilities first, maximizing the efficiency of their security efforts.

Furthermore, vulnerability assessments contribute to incident prevention by identifying weaknesses before they can be exploited. This proactive approach is particularly valuable in preventing security incidents related to known vulnerabilities. By addressing vulnerabilities in advance, organizations reduce the likelihood of successful cyber-attacks, protecting their systems, data, and users from potential harm. Prevention, as facilitated by vulnerability assessments, is a key element in maintaining the confidentiality, integrity, and availability of information assets.

The data-driven insights provided by vulnerability assessments contribute to informed decision-making within organizations. Security professionals and decision-makers can use the results of vulnerability assessments to understand the organization's risk profile, allocate resources strategically, and make informed decisions about security investments. The actionable intelligence derived from vulnerability assessments empowers organizations to prioritize remediation efforts based on risk severity, business impact, and overall security strategy.

Collaboration and communication are integral components of preemptive security measures facilitated by vulnerability assessments. By fostering collaboration between security teams, IT administrators, and other stakeholders, organizations can create a shared understanding of the security landscape and collectively work towards mitigating identified vulnerabilities. Effective communication ensures that all relevant parties are informed about the risks and remediation efforts, creating a unified front against potential threats.

In conclusion, the role of vulnerability assessments in preemptive security measures is paramount in building a resilient and proactive defense against evolving cyber threats. By systematically identifying, quantifying, and prioritizing vulnerabilities, organizations can take proactive steps to address potential weaknesses before they can be exploited by malicious actors. Vulnerability assessments contribute to risk management, compliance efforts, incident prevention, and informed decision-making. Their continuous and data-driven nature empowers organizations to adapt to changing threat landscapes, fostering a security culture that prioritizes proactive measures to safeguard the confidentiality, integrity, and availability of their information assets. As organizations navigate the complex and dynamic field of cybersecurity, vulnerability assessments remain a foundational element in building and maintaining robust preemptive security measures.

The process of risk analysis in determining potential security risks.

Risk analysis is a multifaceted and iterative process integral to determining potential security risks within an organization's information system. It serves as a foundational component of a comprehensive risk management framework, allowing organizations to systematically identify, assess, and prioritize risks to their assets, operations, and objectives. The process begins with the identification of assets, including information, technology, personnel, and physical infrastructure, that are critical to the organization's functioning. By understanding the landscape of assets, organizations gain insights into the potential threats and vulnerabilities that may pose security risks.

Threat identification is a key step in risk analysis, involving the recognition of potential sources of harm that could exploit vulnerabilities and negatively impact assets. Threats can manifest in various forms, including cyber threats such as malware, phishing, and denial-of-service attacks, as well as physical threats like natural disasters, theft, or sabotage. The diverse nature of threats requires organizations to maintain a dynamic and up-to-date understanding of the threat landscape to effectively analyze potential security risks.

Simultaneously, the identification of vulnerabilities, or weaknesses within the organization's systems, processes, or controls, is a critical aspect of risk analysis. Vulnerabilities can arise from outdated software, misconfigurations, lack of user awareness, or gaps in physical security measures. The process involves scrutinizing the organization's infrastructure, applications, and operational procedures to pinpoint areas where exploitation could occur. Thorough vulnerability identification sets the stage for a more accurate and comprehensive risk analysis.

Once threats and vulnerabilities are identified, risk assessment comes into play. This involves evaluating the likelihood of a threat exploiting a vulnerability and the potential impact on the organization if such an event were to occur. Probability and impact assessments aid in assigning risk levels to different scenarios, allowing organizations to prioritize their mitigation efforts. Probability assessments consider factors such as historical data, threat intelligence, and the organization's security posture, while impact assessments analyze the potential consequences of a security incident on the organization's assets, operations, and reputation.

Quantitative risk analysis involves assigning numerical values to the probability and impact of identified risks, facilitating a more precise and measurable approach to risk assessment. Organizations may use statistical models, historical data, or industry benchmarks to quantify the likelihood and impact of various risks. By assigning numerical values, organizations can calculate a risk score for each identified risk, aiding in the prioritization of mitigation efforts based on the severity and potential impact on the organization.

Qualitative risk analysis, on the other hand, focuses on subjective assessments of the probability and impact of identified risks. This approach involves the use of risk matrices, risk heat maps, or expert judgment to categorize risks into high, medium, or low priority. Qualitative risk analysis is often more accessible and quicker to implement, making it a valuable tool for organizations seeking a rapid assessment of potential security risks. However, it may lack the precision and granularity offered by quantitative analysis.

Risk prioritization is a crucial step in the risk analysis process, guiding organizations to allocate resources effectively to address the most critical and impactful risks first. Prioritization is typically based on a combination of quantitative and qualitative assessments, taking into account the risk scores, business impact, and organizational priorities. By establishing a hierarchy of risks, organizations can develop targeted mitigation strategies that address the most significant threats and vulnerabilities, thereby enhancing the overall security posture.

Risk mitigation involves the development and implementation of strategies to reduce the probability and impact of identified risks. Mitigation measures may include implementing security controls, applying patches, conducting employee training, enhancing physical security measures, or implementing redundancy and backup systems. The goal is to either eliminate or reduce the likelihood of a risk event occurring or minimize its impact if it does occur. Organizations must carefully consider the cost-effectiveness, feasibility, and impact of mitigation measures, aiming for a balance that aligns with their risk tolerance and overall business objectives.

Risk monitoring and review are continuous processes that ensure the organization's risk analysis remains current and aligned with its evolving risk landscape. The dynamic nature of the threat landscape, technological advancements, and changes in the organizational environment necessitate ongoing monitoring to identify new threats, vulnerabilities, or changes in the risk landscape. Regular reviews of the risk analysis process allow organizations to refine their risk assessments, update mitigation strategies, and adapt to emerging security challenges.

Communication and documentation are integral components of the risk analysis process, facilitating transparency and understanding across the organization. Effective communication ensures that key stakeholders, including executives, management, and frontline employees, are aware of the identified risks, mitigation strategies, and the organization's overall risk posture. Comprehensive documentation provides a record of the risk analysis process, enabling organizations to demonstrate due diligence, comply with regulatory requirements, and support informed decision-making.

In conclusion, the process of risk analysis in determining potential security risks is a systematic and continuous undertaking that enables organizations to proactively identify, assess, and mitigate threats and vulnerabilities. By comprehensively identifying assets, threats, and vulnerabilities, organizations lay the groundwork for a nuanced risk assessment. Quantitative and qualitative risk analysis methods aid in evaluating the likelihood and impact of risks, guiding organizations in prioritizing their mitigation efforts. Risk prioritization, mitigation, and ongoing monitoring form a dynamic cycle that aligns with the evolving threat landscape and organizational changes. Effective communication and documentation foster transparency and informed decision-making, ensuring that organizations can navigate the complexities of the modern risk environment and fortify their security postures against potential threats.

Strategies for managing and mitigating identified risks.

Strategies for managing and mitigating identified risks encompass a holistic and adaptive approach, crucial for organizations seeking to safeguard their assets, operations, and objectives in an ever-evolving threat landscape. Risk management is an ongoing process that involves not only identifying and assessing risks but also developing and implementing effective mitigation strategies to reduce the likelihood and impact of potential adverse events.

One fundamental strategy for managing identified risks is the implementation of robust security controls. These controls, ranging from access management and encryption to intrusion detection systems and firewalls, serve as proactive measures to prevent or detect security incidents. By establishing a comprehensive set of security controls tailored to the organization's risk profile, industry regulations, and best practices, organizations can create layers of defense that collectively contribute to a resilient security posture.

Regular and timely software patching is a critical strategy to mitigate risks associated with software vulnerabilities. Keeping operating systems, applications, and firmware up-to-date with the latest security patches is essential for closing potential entry points for attackers. A proactive patch management strategy ensures that identified vulnerabilities are addressed promptly, reducing the window of opportunity for exploitation and enhancing the overall security resilience of the organization.

Employee training and awareness programs constitute a crucial strategy for managing risks associated with human factors. Employees, as both users and potential targets of social engineering attacks, play a pivotal role in the organization's security posture. By educating personnel on security best practices, recognizing phishing attempts, and promoting a security-conscious culture, organizations can significantly reduce the risk of human-related security incidents. Regular training sessions and awareness campaigns contribute to building a vigilant and security-aware workforce.

Creating and regularly testing an incident response plan is an essential strategy for managing risks associated with security incidents. Incidents such as data breaches, system compromises, or denial-of-service attacks are inevitable, and a well-prepared and tested incident response plan enables organizations to respond effectively when such events occur. This strategy involves defining roles and responsibilities, establishing communication protocols, and conducting simulated exercises to ensure a coordinated and efficient response to security incidents.

Organizations should consider the strategy of implementing a robust and proactive risk monitoring system. Continuous monitoring of the IT environment allows for the timely detection of emerging threats and vulnerabilities. Automated tools, security information and event management (SIEM) systems, and threat intelligence feeds contribute to real-time monitoring, helping organizations identify deviations from the baseline and potential indicators of compromise. Proactive risk monitoring enables organizations to detect and respond to security incidents promptly, minimizing the impact on the organization.

Data encryption is a vital strategy for managing risks associated with the confidentiality of sensitive information. Encrypting data both at rest and in transit ensures that even if unauthorized access occurs, the data remains unreadable and protected. Encryption technologies, such as full-disk encryption, secure communication protocols, and encryption of stored data, contribute to safeguarding sensitive information from potential breaches or unauthorized disclosures.

Redundancy and resilience in infrastructure design represent an effective strategy for managing risks associated with system availability. Implementing backup systems, redundant components, and failover mechanisms ensures that critical services and operations can continue even in the face of hardware failures, natural disasters, or malicious attacks. This strategy minimizes the impact of potential disruptions, contributing to business continuity and reducing the overall risk to the organization.

Risk transfer through insurance is a strategy organizations may employ to manage financial risks associated with security incidents. Cybersecurity insurance policies provide financial protection against the costs of data breaches, legal liabilities, and other expenses associated with security incidents. While insurance does not eliminate security risks, it can serve as a valuable risk management tool by transferring some of the financial burden associated with security incidents to the insurance provider.

Collaboration and information sharing with industry peers and cybersecurity communities represent a collective strategy for managing risks on a broader scale. By participating in information-sharing platforms, organizations can gain insights into emerging threats, vulnerabilities, and attack techniques. Collaborative efforts contribute to a shared understanding of the threat landscape, enabling organizations to adopt proactive measures collectively and strengthen their collective defenses against common adversaries.

Supply chain risk management is a strategy focused on managing risks associated with third-party vendors, suppliers, and service providers. Organizations often rely on external entities for various services and components, and vulnerabilities in the supply chain can pose significant risks. Implementing stringent vendor risk management practices, conducting due diligence on third-party security postures, and establishing contractual obligations for security standards contribute to mitigating risks associated with the supply chain.

Regular security audits and assessments serve as a strategic approach to continuously evaluate and validate the effectiveness of security controls and risk mitigation measures. Conducting internal and external security audits, penetration testing, and vulnerability assessments helps organizations identify gaps in their security defenses, ensuring that mitigation strategies remain robust and aligned with the evolving threat landscape.

Flexibility and adaptability are overarching strategies for managing risks in an environment characterized by rapid technological advancements and evolving threat landscapes. Organizations should embrace a dynamic risk management approach that allows for continuous assessment, adaptation, and improvement of security measures. Regularly reassessing risks, updating mitigation strategies, and incorporating lessons learned from security incidents contribute to building a resilient risk management framework.

In conclusion, effective strategies for managing and mitigating identified risks involve a combination of proactive measures, including the implementation of security controls, regular patching, employee training, incident response planning, risk monitoring, data encryption, redundancy, risk transfer through insurance, collaboration with the cybersecurity community, supply chain risk management, security audits, and a flexible and adaptive risk management approach. These strategies collectively contribute to creating a comprehensive and resilient risk management framework that enables organizations to navigate the complex and dynamic landscape of cybersecurity risks while safeguarding their assets, operations, and objectives.

The importance of incident response plans in addressing security breaches.

The importance of incident response plans in addressing security breaches cannot be overstated in the contemporary landscape of cybersecurity threats. An incident response plan serves as a strategic blueprint, providing organizations with a systematic and well-defined approach to detect, respond to, mitigate, and recover from security incidents effectively. As the digital landscape becomes increasingly complex and sophisticated threats evolve, having a well-prepared incident response plan is paramount for organizations to minimize the impact of security breaches on their operations, reputation, and overall resilience.

One key aspect of incident response plans is their role in fostering a proactive security posture. By outlining specific procedures and predefined roles, incident response plans empower organizations to anticipate potential security incidents and prepare for a swift and coordinated response. This proactive stance enables organizations to reduce the time it takes to detect and contain a security breach, limiting the potential damage and disruption to critical systems and services. Additionally, a well-documented incident response plan ensures that all relevant stakeholders understand their responsibilities and are prepared to execute their roles effectively in the event of a security incident.

Incident response plans play a crucial role in reducing the dwell time of security breaches, which refers to the duration between the occurrence of a security incident and its detection and containment. Rapid detection and containment are essential in mitigating the impact of security breaches, preventing further compromise of systems, data, and sensitive information. The structured and predefined processes outlined in incident response plans enable organizations to swiftly identify and isolate compromised systems, limiting the potential for lateral movement and escalation by attackers.

Moreover, incident response plans contribute significantly to the preservation of digital forensic evidence. In the aftermath of a security breach, understanding the scope, nature, and tactics of the attack is crucial for conducting a thorough post-incident analysis. Incident response plans guide organizations in preserving digital evidence, ensuring that critical information is collected, documented, and analyzed to understand the root cause of the incident. This forensic analysis not only aids in the immediate response to the breach but also informs future security improvements and helps organizations refine their incident response capabilities.

Another essential aspect of incident response plans is their role in facilitating effective communication during a security incident. Clear and timely communication is critical for coordinating the response efforts, informing stakeholders, and managing the public relations aspect of a security breach. Incident response plans typically include communication protocols, defining how internal and external stakeholders will be notified, what information will be shared, and who will be responsible for liaising with law enforcement, regulatory bodies, and the media. This communication strategy is essential for maintaining transparency, building trust, and mitigating reputational damage during and after a security incident.

Furthermore, incident response plans contribute to compliance with regulatory requirements and legal obligations. Many industries and jurisdictions mandate that organizations implement incident response capabilities to protect sensitive information and respond to security incidents promptly. Having a well-documented incident response plan not only helps organizations comply with these regulatory requirements but also demonstrates due diligence in safeguarding sensitive data and maintaining a commitment to security best practices. Compliance with these standards not only protects organizations from potential legal consequences but also enhances their overall reputation and trustworthiness.

Incident response plans serve as a valuable tool for organizational learning and continuous improvement in the realm of cybersecurity. Post-incident reviews and debriefings, as outlined in the incident response plan, provide an opportunity for organizations to assess the effectiveness of their response efforts, identify areas for improvement, and update their incident response procedures accordingly. This feedback loop is crucial for building a resilient security posture, as it allows organizations to adapt to emerging threats, refine their incident response capabilities, and enhance their overall cybersecurity maturity over time.

The importance of incident response plans extends beyond technological considerations to encompass the human element of cybersecurity. A well-prepared incident response plan accounts for the psychological and emotional impact of a security breach on employees and stakeholders. It outlines procedures for providing support, guidance, and communication to employees during and after a security incident, helping to manage stress, anxiety, and potential confusion. By addressing the human factor in incident response, organizations can foster a culture of resilience, ensuring that employees are equipped to navigate the challenges posed by security breaches effectively.

Incident response plans also contribute to the containment of reputational damage arising from security breaches. A swift and well-coordinated response, guided by the incident response plan, helps organizations control the narrative surrounding the incident. Proactive communication, transparency, and a demonstrated commitment to resolving the issue can mitigate the negative impact on public perception. Incident response plans provide a structured framework for managing public relations during and after a security breach, allowing organizations to rebuild trust and credibility.

Moreover, incident response plans play a vital role in facilitating cross-functional collaboration within organizations. Security incidents often require collaboration between IT, legal, human resources, public relations, and executive leadership. Incident response plans define the roles and responsibilities of each stakeholder group, promoting a coordinated and unified response. This collaborative approach not only enhances the effectiveness of incident response efforts but also fosters a culture of shared responsibility for cybersecurity across the organization.

In conclusion, the importance of incident response plans in addressing security breaches is multifaceted and indispensable in the dynamic landscape of cybersecurity threats. These plans provide organizations with a proactive and systematic approach to detect, respond to, mitigate, and recover from security incidents effectively. From reducing dwell time and preserving digital evidence to facilitating effective communication, compliance with regulations, organizational learning, and managing reputational damage, incident response plans are a cornerstone of a resilient cybersecurity strategy. By embracing the principles outlined in these plans, organizations can navigate the complexities of security breaches with agility, minimize the impact on their operations and reputation, and ultimately enhance their overall cybersecurity posture.

Steps to develop and implement effective incident response strategies.

Developing and implementing effective incident response strategies is a comprehensive and systematic process critical to an organization's cybersecurity resilience. The foundation of this endeavor lies in a well-structured plan that delineates the steps, roles, and responsibilities needed to detect, respond to, mitigate, and recover from security incidents. The initial step involves conducting a comprehensive risk assessment to identify potential threats, vulnerabilities, and critical assets within the organization. By understanding the risk landscape, organizations can tailor their incident response strategies to address the specific challenges they may face.

Once the risk assessment is complete, the next step is to define the objectives and scope of the incident response plan. Organizations need to articulate the goals of their incident response strategies, such as minimizing the impact of incidents, preserving digital evidence, and ensuring compliance with regulatory requirements. The scope should encompass the entire organization, including different departments, systems, and network components that may be affected by security incidents. Clearly defining the plan's objectives and scope lays the groundwork for developing targeted and effective incident response strategies.

The development of an incident response team is a pivotal step in implementing effective strategies. This team comprises individuals with diverse skills, including IT professionals, legal experts, communication specialists, and representatives from relevant departments. Assigning specific roles and responsibilities to team members ensures a coordinated and efficient response to security incidents. Regular training, simulations, and drills help the incident response team build and maintain the skills necessary for effective collaboration and response during actual incidents.

Creating an incident response plan involves establishing a set of documented procedures and guidelines for responding to security incidents. The plan should include predefined steps for incident detection, analysis, containment, eradication, recovery, and lessons learned. Detailed procedures should cover technical aspects, such as system isolation and forensic analysis, as well as non-technical aspects, including communication protocols, coordination with law enforcement, and post-incident reviews. A well-structured incident response plan serves as a crucial reference document during high-stress situations, providing guidance and direction for the response team.

Incident detection mechanisms are vital components of effective incident response strategies. Implementing robust monitoring tools, intrusion detection systems, and security information and event management (SIEM) systems enables organizations to identify unusual or suspicious activities that may indicate a security incident. Continuous monitoring, real-time alerts, and anomaly detection mechanisms contribute to early incident detection, reducing the dwell time between the occurrence of an incident and its identification.

Furthermore, organizations need to establish communication protocols both within the incident response team and with external stakeholders. Clear lines of communication are crucial during security incidents to ensure that relevant information is disseminated promptly and accurately. Internal communication channels facilitate collaboration among team members, while external communication protocols outline how the organization will interact with law enforcement, regulatory bodies, customers, and the media. Transparency and timely communication are key elements in maintaining trust and managing the public perception of the incident.

Implementing effective incident response strategies requires organizations to integrate threat intelligence into their processes. Staying informed about the latest threat actors, tactics, techniques, and procedures enhances the organization's ability to detect and respond to emerging threats. Continuous monitoring of threat intelligence feeds, industry reports, and information sharing platforms enables organizations to adapt their incident response strategies based on the evolving threat landscape. Integrating threat intelligence provides context to incidents, allowing organizations to tailor their response efforts to the specific characteristics of the threat actors.

Once an incident occurs, the response team must swiftly analyze the situation to understand the nature and scope of the incident. This involves conducting a detailed forensic analysis to identify the attack vector, determine the extent of the compromise, and gather digital evidence. Forensic tools and techniques help the response team reconstruct the timeline of events, assess the impact on systems and data, and identify indicators of compromise. The forensic analysis forms the basis for containment and eradication efforts, guiding the response team in mitigating the incident's impact.

Containment is a critical step in incident response strategies, aimed at preventing the further spread of the incident within the organization's network. This involves isolating compromised systems, restricting unauthorized access, and implementing temporary measures to halt the incident's progression. The goal is to limit the impact of the incident on critical assets and data, buying time for eradication and recovery efforts. Effective containment strategies require a thorough understanding of the incident's dynamics and potential vectors for lateral movement.

Eradication involves permanently removing the root cause of the incident from the organization's systems. This step may include patching vulnerabilities, removing malware, and addressing misconfigurations that allowed the incident to occur. Eradication efforts aim to eliminate the possibility of a recurring incident by addressing the fundamental weaknesses in the organization's infrastructure. The response team collaborates with IT and security teams to implement long-term solutions that fortify the organization against similar incidents in the future.

Recovery is a multifaceted process involving the restoration of affected systems, data, and services to normal operation. This step requires a careful balance between speed and thoroughness, ensuring that systems are brought back online efficiently without reintroducing vulnerabilities or compromises. Backups play a crucial role in the recovery process, enabling organizations to restore critical data and configurations to a pre-incident state. Post-incident reviews and evaluations inform the recovery process, providing insights into areas that require improvement for future incidents.

Lessons learned are a fundamental component of effective incident response strategies. Following the resolution of an incident, organizations conduct a thorough review to analyze the response efforts, identify strengths and weaknesses, and extract valuable insights for continuous improvement. This reflective process involves evaluating the effectiveness of the incident response plan, the performance of the response team, and the organization's overall resilience to security incidents. Lessons learned contribute to refining incident response strategies, updating documentation, and enhancing the organization's ability to adapt to evolving threats.

Continuous improvement is an ongoing aspect of effective incident response strategies. Organizations need to regularly review and update their incident response plans, ensuring that they remain aligned with the organization's evolving risk landscape, technological environment, and regulatory requirements. Regular training sessions, simulations, and drills help the incident response team stay sharp and prepared for various scenarios. The feedback loop established through continuous improvement fosters a culture of adaptability, ensuring that incident response strategies remain effective and relevant in the face of emerging threats.

In conclusion, developing and implementing effective incident response strategies involves a comprehensive and continuous process that encompasses risk assessment, team development, plan creation, incident detection, communication protocols, threat intelligence integration, forensic analysis, containment, eradication, recovery, lessons learned, and continuous improvement. By following these steps and embracing a proactive and adaptive approach, organizations can enhance their ability to detect, respond to, and recover from security incidents effectively, minimizing the impact on their operations, reputation, and overall cybersecurity resilience.

Exploration of current and emerging threats in the ever-evolving threat landscape.

The ever-evolving threat landscape in the realm of cybersecurity is a dynamic and complex ecosystem where adversaries continually innovate to exploit vulnerabilities and achieve their malicious objectives. Current and emerging threats pose significant challenges to individuals, organizations, and nations, requiring continuous vigilance and adaptation to stay ahead of the curve. One prevalent and persistent threat is malware, a term encompassing a variety of malicious software designed to infiltrate systems, steal sensitive information, or disrupt normal operations. With the constant evolution of malware variants, including ransomware, spyware, and trojans, cybercriminals can deploy sophisticated attacks, demanding ransoms, exfiltrating data, or creating covert channels for unauthorized access.

Ransomware, in particular, has surged to the forefront of cybersecurity concerns, with attacks targeting individuals, businesses, and critical infrastructure. These attacks involve encrypting a victim's data and demanding payment, often in cryptocurrency, for its release. The ransomware landscape has evolved to include increasingly sophisticated tactics, techniques, and procedures (TTPs), such as double extortion, where attackers not only encrypt data but also threaten to leak sensitive information if the ransom is not paid. This dual-threat strategy intensifies the impact on victims and underscores the need for robust defense mechanisms.

Phishing remains a prevalent and adaptable threat, relying on social engineering to deceive individuals into divulging sensitive information or clicking on malicious links. Spear phishing, a targeted form of phishing, tailors deceptive messages to specific individuals or organizations, leveraging personal information to increase credibility. Vishing, or voice phishing, involves manipulating individuals through phone calls to extract confidential information. As phishing techniques evolve, incorporating more convincing tactics and leveraging current events, individuals and organizations must enhance their awareness and employ advanced detection mechanisms to thwart these deceptive campaigns.

Social engineering extends beyond phishing to encompass a broader range of manipulative tactics aimed at exploiting human psychology. Cybercriminals exploit trust, authority, or urgency to manipulate individuals into divulging information, clicking on malicious links, or performing actions that compromise security. The rise of deepfake technology further amplifies the threat, allowing malicious actors to create convincing, yet fabricated, audio and video content. These deepfake techniques can be leveraged for impersonation or disinformation campaigns, posing challenges for authentication and trust in the digital realm.

The Internet of Things (IoT) introduces new dimensions to the threat landscape, as the proliferation of connected devices presents opportunities for cybercriminals to exploit vulnerabilities. Insecure IoT devices can be co-opted into botnets for large-scale attacks, such as distributed denial-of-service (DDoS) assaults. The lack of standardized security measures in many IoT devices poses challenges for consumers and organizations alike, creating potential entry points for cyber adversaries seeking to compromise network integrity or launch attacks on a broader scale.

Nation-state actors and advanced persistent threats (APTs) continue to be major contributors to the evolving threat landscape. State-sponsored cyber espionage, sabotage, and influence operations pose substantial risks to geopolitical stability and global cybersecurity. APT groups, characterized by sophisticated techniques, stealthy persistence, and strategic targeting, often focus on long-term objectives, such as stealing sensitive intellectual property or undermining critical infrastructure. As nation-states increasingly engage in offensive cyber operations, the boundaries between traditional warfare and cyber conflict blur, necessitating international cooperation and robust cybersecurity strategies.

Supply chain attacks have emerged as a potent threat vector, leveraging the interconnected nature of global supply chains to compromise targeted entities. Adversaries infiltrate the supply chain to introduce malicious code, compromise hardware components, or exploit vulnerabilities in software dependencies. The SolarWinds incident exemplifies the magnitude of supply chain attacks, where a compromised software update led to widespread breaches affecting numerous organizations. These attacks underscore the need for rigorous supply chain security measures, including code integrity checks, vendor assessments, and secure update mechanisms.

The expanding attack surface presented by cloud computing introduces new challenges and opportunities for cyber adversaries. Cloud services offer efficiency and scalability, but misconfigurations, weak access controls, and inadequate data encryption can expose organizations to data breaches and unauthorized access. Additionally, cloud-native threats, such as insecure application programming interfaces (APIs) and container vulnerabilities, demand specialized security measures to protect cloud environments effectively. As organizations transition to cloud-based infrastructures, securing cloud assets becomes paramount in mitigating evolving cyber threats.

The rise of cryptocurrency introduces novel challenges in terms of facilitating illicit activities and enabling ransomware payments. Cryptocurrencies provide a degree of anonymity and decentralization that appeals to cybercriminals seeking to evade traditional financial controls. Privacy-focused cryptocurrencies and privacy coins further complicate efforts to trace transactions and identify malicious actors. The intersection of cryptocurrency and cybercrime underscores the importance of global regulatory frameworks, law enforcement collaboration, and the development of tools to trace and mitigate illicit cryptocurrency transactions.

Emerging technologies, such as artificial intelligence (AI) and machine learning (ML), are both a boon and a potential threat in the evolving cybersecurity landscape. While AI and ML technologies enhance threat detection, automate response mechanisms, and analyze vast datasets for anomalies, they can also be exploited by adversaries to conduct more sophisticated attacks. Adversarial machine learning, wherein attackers manipulate AI models to generate misleading results, poses challenges for the reliability of automated security systems. As AI becomes integral to cybersecurity defenses, organizations must strike a balance between leveraging these technologies and addressing their vulnerabilities.

Quantum computing, while holding promise for transformative advancements, introduces potential risks to traditional encryption methods. Quantum computers, once sufficiently developed, could render current encryption algorithms obsolete, threatening the confidentiality of sensitive information. Post-quantum cryptography research aims to develop cryptographic techniques resistant to quantum attacks, highlighting the need for a proactive approach in preparing for the post-quantum era. As quantum computing matures, organizations must anticipate and adapt to the evolving landscape of cryptographic vulnerabilities.

The interplay between cyber threats and critical infrastructure poses significant risks to public safety, national security, and economic stability. Cyberattacks on energy grids, transportation systems, and healthcare facilities can have far-reaching consequences, disrupting essential services and compromising the integrity of critical infrastructure. The convergence of cyber and physical threats amplifies the need for comprehensive security measures, resilience planning, and cross-sector collaboration to safeguard critical infrastructure against evolving cyber threats.

In conclusion, the ever-evolving threat landscape in cybersecurity is characterized by a myriad of current and emerging challenges that demand adaptive and comprehensive responses. From the persistence of malware and the sophistication of ransomware to the nuances of social engineering, IoT vulnerabilities, and supply chain attacks, the threat landscape is dynamic and multifaceted. Addressing these challenges requires continuous innovation, collaboration, and a proactive mindset to stay ahead of cyber adversaries. As technologies advance and new threat vectors emerge, the cybersecurity community must remain vigilant, embracing a holistic approach to defense that encompasses technology, awareness, regulation, and international cooperation. Only through such collective efforts can organizations and individuals navigate the complexities of the evolving threat landscape and fortify their defenses against emerging cyber threats.

The significance of staying abreast of emerging trends for proactive security measures.

The significance of staying abreast of emerging trends in the ever-evolving landscape of cybersecurity cannot be overstated, as it forms the cornerstone for the development and implementation of proactive security measures. In a digital ecosystem characterized by rapid technological advancements and an escalating array of cyber threats, organizations and security professionals must maintain a proactive stance to anticipate, understand, and effectively counter emerging trends. By keeping abreast of the latest developments, whether they be in terms of technological innovations, attack methodologies, or regulatory changes, individuals and organizations can foster a dynamic and adaptive security posture that not only mitigates current risks but also prepares for the challenges of the future.

One of the primary reasons for staying informed about emerging trends is the relentless evolution of cyber threats. As threat actors continuously refine their tactics, techniques, and procedures (TTPs), staying ahead of these developments is paramount for effective defense. New malware variants, novel social engineering strategies, and sophisticated exploitation techniques are continually emerging, demanding a nuanced understanding of the evolving threat landscape. Proactive security measures that are informed by current trends enable organizations to preemptively address vulnerabilities, anticipate potential attack vectors, and fortify their defenses against the latest cyber threats.

Moreover, the proliferation of advanced persistent threats (APTs) and nation-state-sponsored cyber activities underscores the importance of staying abreast of geopolitical and threat intelligence trends. APT groups, characterized by their sophistication, persistence, and strategic targeting, often leverage zero-day vulnerabilities and conduct long-term campaigns with specific objectives. Understanding the geopolitical context and threat intelligence allows organizations to discern potential adversaries, their motivations, and the specific vulnerabilities they might exploit. Proactive security measures, informed by geopolitical insights, enable organizations to tailor their defenses to the specific threats that align with their industry, geography, or strategic interests.

The advent of new technologies, such as artificial intelligence (AI) and the Internet of Things (IoT), introduces both opportunities and challenges for cybersecurity. Staying abreast of emerging trends in these technologies is essential for recognizing potential security implications. AI and machine learning (ML) technologies, for example, offer enhanced capabilities for threat detection and analysis, but they also introduce new risks, such as adversarial machine learning, wherein attackers manipulate AI models. Understanding the nuances of these technologies enables organizations to harness their benefits while implementing proactive measures to mitigate associated risks effectively.

Similarly, the expanding attack surface presented by the IoT requires vigilant awareness of emerging trends. The growing number of connected devices introduces new entry points for cyber adversaries, making IoT security a critical consideration. Staying informed about the latest developments in IoT security enables organizations to implement proactive measures, such as robust device authentication, secure communication protocols, and continuous monitoring, to safeguard against potential vulnerabilities in this interconnected landscape.

Furthermore, the significance of staying abreast of emerging trends extends to the regulatory and compliance landscape. Governments and regulatory bodies are increasingly recognizing the importance of cybersecurity and enacting legislation to protect individuals' privacy and ensure the security of critical infrastructure. Proactive security measures must align with these regulatory frameworks, necessitating a thorough understanding of evolving compliance requirements. Staying informed about regulatory changes enables organizations to adapt their security policies, practices, and technologies to maintain compliance and minimize legal and financial risks.

The interconnected nature of the global digital ecosystem necessitates collaborative approaches to cybersecurity. Information sharing and collaboration within the cybersecurity community are crucial for collective defense against emerging threats. Staying abreast of trends in threat intelligence sharing platforms, industry alliances, and collaborative initiatives enables organizations to tap into a collective pool of knowledge. Proactive security measures benefit from shared insights, enabling organizations to leverage the experiences and expertise of the broader cybersecurity community to enhance their own defense strategies.

Moreover, the significance of staying informed about emerging trends extends to the realm of incident response and crisis management. As cyber threats evolve, incident response strategies must adapt to effectively detect, respond to, and recover from incidents. Keeping abreast of incident trends, such as the tactics employed by ransomware actors or the nuances of supply chain attacks, allows organizations to refine and enhance their incident response plans. Proactive security measures in incident response involve continuous improvement based on real-world scenarios and lessons learned from the evolving threat landscape.

In the context of the workforce, the dynamic nature of the cybersecurity landscape demands ongoing education and training. Security professionals must stay current with emerging trends, tools, and techniques to remain effective in their roles. Continuous professional development ensures that security teams are equipped with the latest knowledge and skills required to address evolving cyber threats. Proactive security measures in this regard involve investing in training programs, certifications, and awareness campaigns to empower the workforce with the expertise needed to navigate the complexities of the contemporary cybersecurity landscape.

The significance of staying abreast of emerging trends is particularly evident in the context of supply chain security. As supply chain attacks become more sophisticated and prevalent, organizations need to be proactive in understanding the latest tactics employed by threat actors to compromise the supply chain. Emerging trends in supply chain security involve robust vendor risk management practices, secure software development lifecycles, and heightened scrutiny of third-party dependencies. Organizations that stay informed about these trends can implement proactive measures to secure their supply chains effectively.

The COVID-19 pandemic has accelerated digital transformation initiatives, with remote work becoming a pervasive trend. This shift has implications for cybersecurity, as organizations need to secure remote access, address new attack vectors, and adapt to the evolving threat landscape. Staying abreast of these trends enables organizations to implement proactive security measures tailored to the challenges of remote work, encompassing secure connectivity, endpoint protection, and user awareness training.

In conclusion, the significance of staying abreast of emerging trends in cybersecurity cannot be overstated in the quest for proactive security measures. The relentless evolution of cyber threats, coupled with advancements in technology, regulatory changes, and shifts in the global landscape, demands a dynamic and adaptive approach to cybersecurity. Proactive security measures informed by current trends empower organizations to anticipate, prepare for, and effectively counter emerging threats, ensuring a resilient defense posture in the face of the ever-evolving challenges of the digital era. Continuous awareness, collaboration, and education form the pillars of a proactive cybersecurity strategy that not only addresses current risks but also positions organizations to navigate the uncertainties of the future.

Chapter 3: Securing Network Communication

Introduction to network security concepts within the operating system.

Network security within the operating system is a fundamental and intricate aspect of contemporary information technology landscapes, crucial for safeguarding the integrity, confidentiality, and availability of data in interconnected environments. The operating system serves as the foundational platform that facilitates communication and resource sharing among networked devices. As organizations increasingly rely on interconnected systems for seamless collaboration and data access, the significance of robust network security concepts within the operating system becomes paramount. This introduction explores key aspects of network security within the operating system, delving into the core principles, technologies, and challenges that define this critical domain.

At its essence, network security within the operating system revolves around the protection of data and communication channels from unauthorized access, malicious activities, and potential disruptions. The operating system acts as the intermediary between users, applications, and the underlying hardware, managing the flow of data within a networked environment. Ensuring the security of this data transmission and access is pivotal, considering the myriad of cyber threats that can exploit vulnerabilities in operating systems to compromise sensitive information, disrupt services, or gain unauthorized control. Network security within the operating system, therefore, encompasses a multifaceted set of principles and practices designed to mitigate these risks and create a resilient defense against evolving cyber threats.

Authentication and access control stand as foundational pillars within network security concepts in the operating system. Effective authentication mechanisms verify the identity of users and devices seeking access to the network or specific resources. Passwords, biometrics, multi-factor authentication, and other authentication protocols play a critical role in ensuring that only authorized entities can interact with the operating system and its associated network services. Concurrently, access control mechanisms define and enforce the permissions granted to users and processes, dictating their level of access to files, directories, and network resources. By implementing robust authentication and access control measures, the operating system establishes a secure foundation, limiting unauthorized entry points and reducing the risk of unauthorized data access or manipulation.

Encryption constitutes another pivotal element in the realm of network security within the operating system. The transmission of data over networks, whether local or remote, is susceptible to interception by malicious entities seeking to eavesdrop or manipulate the exchanged information. Encryption techniques, such as secure socket layer (SSL) or transport layer security (TLS) protocols, ensure that data is encrypted during transit, rendering it indecipherable to unauthorized parties. Within the operating system, encryption is applied not only to network communications but also to stored data, protecting files and sensitive information from unauthorized access. By incorporating encryption into network security strategies, the operating system plays a crucial role in safeguarding the confidentiality of data, even in the face of potential interception or data breaches.

Firewalls emerge as essential components in the network security arsenal within the operating system, acting as gatekeepers that monitor and control incoming and outgoing network traffic. These security mechanisms, whether implemented at the operating system level or through dedicated hardware devices, enforce predefined rules that govern the flow of data packets. Firewalls can be configured to filter traffic based on specific criteria, such as IP addresses, ports, or application types. They play a pivotal role in preventing unauthorized access, blocking malicious content, and detecting and thwarting potential cyber threats. Network security within the operating system is inherently tied to the effective implementation and configuration of firewalls, which serve as the first line of defense against external and internal threats.

Intrusion detection and prevention systems (IDPS) further augment the network security landscape within the operating system by actively monitoring for suspicious activities or potential security breaches. These systems employ sophisticated algorithms and rule sets to analyze network traffic patterns, identifying anomalies or known attack signatures. The operating system, as the nexus of network activities, integrates with IDPS to provide real-time insights into potential security incidents. When anomalous behavior is detected, the operating system can trigger alerts, initiate protective measures, or even block the malicious activity. The synergy between the operating system and IDPS enhances the overall security posture, enabling swift responses to emerging threats and minimizing the impact of potential security incidents.

Vulnerability management and patching are critical elements in maintaining a secure network environment within the operating system. As software vulnerabilities are discovered, operating system vendors release patches and updates to address these weaknesses. The timely application of these patches is essential for mitigating the risk of exploitation by malicious actors seeking to capitalize on known vulnerabilities. Network security within the operating system necessitates robust vulnerability management practices, including regular assessments, timely patching, and the implementation of security best practices. Failure to address vulnerabilities in a timely manner can expose the operating system and associated network to a range of cyber threats, underscoring the importance of proactive vulnerability management.

Network security within the operating system also extends to the domain of virtual private networks (VPNs), which play a crucial role in securing communications over public or untrusted networks. VPNs create secure, encrypted tunnels for data transmission, enabling users to connect to a network remotely while ensuring the confidentiality and integrity of the transmitted data. Operating systems often incorporate native VPN capabilities or support third-party VPN solutions to facilitate secure remote access. By integrating VPN technologies, the operating system contributes to the creation of secure communication channels, protecting sensitive data from interception during transmission over potentially insecure networks.

The concept of secure sockets layer (SSL) and its successor, transport layer security (TLS), encapsulates crucial principles within network security in the operating system. These cryptographic protocols ensure the secure transmission of data over the internet, facilitating secure communication between clients and servers. The operating system, as the intermediary between applications and the network stack, plays a pivotal role in supporting SSL/TLS implementations. These protocols are fundamental for securing web-based communication, online transactions, and various internet-connected services. By incorporating SSL/TLS support, the operating system contributes to the establishment of a secure communication framework, thereby safeguarding sensitive information exchanged over network connections.

An integral facet of network security within the operating system is the management of network protocols and services. Operating systems are equipped with a plethora of network protocols and services that facilitate communication and resource sharing. However, the diverse nature of these protocols can introduce potential vulnerabilities. It becomes imperative to judiciously manage and configure these protocols to minimize security risks. Protocols like the Transmission Control Protocol (TCP), Internet Protocol (IP), and Domain Name System (DNS) are foundational components of network communication within the operating system. Effective configuration and management ensure the secure and reliable functioning of these protocols, reducing the attack surface and enhancing overall network security.

The operating system's role in network security extends to the realm of network monitoring and logging. Continuous monitoring of network activities allows the operating system to detect anomalies, unauthorized access attempts, or potential security incidents. By leveraging logging mechanisms, the operating system can record critical events and activities, creating an audit trail for post-incident analysis and forensic investigations. Network security within the operating system is intimately tied to the effectiveness of monitoring and logging, providing insights into the health of the network, identifying potential threats, and facilitating the timely response to security incidents.

In conclusion, network security concepts within the operating system constitute a comprehensive framework designed to fortify the integrity, confidentiality, and availability of data in networked environments. Authentication, access control, encryption, firewalls, intrusion detection and prevention systems, vulnerability management, VPNs, SSL/TLS, protocol management, and network monitoring collectively shape the landscape of network security within the operating system. As organizations navigate the intricacies of interconnected digital ecosystems, the operating system stands as a linchpin in implementing and enforcing robust security measures. By embracing these principles and technologies, the operating system becomes a bastion of defense against the evolving array of cyber threats, ensuring the secure and resilient operation of networked infrastructures.

The relationship between OS security and secure network communication.

The relationship between operating system (OS) security and secure network communication is symbiotic and intricate, representing a critical nexus in the overarching framework of cybersecurity. The operating system serves as the foundational layer upon which secure network communication is built, and conversely, the integrity of the OS is intricately tied to the robustness of network security. This interdependence is rooted in the fact that the operating system, as the central hub managing hardware resources and facilitating communication between applications and networks, plays a pivotal role in enforcing security measures and protocols that govern the flow of data across interconnected systems.

Authentication, a cornerstone of OS security, establishes the identity of users, applications, and devices seeking access to the network. Secure network communication relies on the OS's ability to effectively authenticate entities, ensuring that only authorized entities can engage in data exchanges. User authentication mechanisms, such as passwords, biometrics, and multi-factor authentication, are fundamental components of OS security that extend their influence to the network layer. By verifying the identity of entities within the operating system, a secure foundation is laid for subsequent network interactions, establishing trust and preventing unauthorized access to network resources.

Access control, intimately tied to authentication, extends the OS's influence into the realm of secure network communication. The operating system defines and enforces access permissions, dictating the level of access granted to users and processes for files, directories, and network resources. Through meticulous access control mechanisms, the OS plays a crucial role in limiting privileges and mitigating the risk of unauthorized access or data manipulation within the network. This intersection between OS-level access controls and secure network communication ensures that entities interacting with the network adhere to predefined security policies, reducing the likelihood of data breaches or malicious activities.

Encryption, a linchpin of secure network communication, relies on the OS to implement and manage cryptographic protocols effectively. Whether encrypting data in transit or stored on disk, the operating system is tasked with seamlessly integrating encryption technologies into the network communication process. Protocols like Transport Layer Security (TLS) and Secure Sockets Layer (SSL) are often implemented at the OS level, ensuring that data exchanged between systems remains confidential and secure. The OS, by incorporating robust encryption methodologies, contributes significantly to safeguarding sensitive information during network transmissions, thereby fostering secure communication channels.

Firewalls, key components of network security, bridge the gap between OS security and secure network communication by monitoring and controlling incoming and outgoing network traffic. Operating systems often include built-in firewalls or support third-party firewall solutions that regulate the flow of data based on predefined rules. By functioning as gatekeepers at the OS level, firewalls enhance network security by filtering traffic, blocking malicious content, and preventing unauthorized access. This collaborative effort between the OS and firewalls establishes a proactive defense mechanism, ensuring that only legitimate and secure network communications are permitted while deterring potential cyber threats.

Intrusion Detection and Prevention Systems (IDPS), integral to the overall network security posture, rely on the OS for insights into system activities and behaviors. The OS provides a foundational layer for IDPS to monitor and analyze network traffic, system logs, and application behavior. By leveraging the information gathered at the OS level, IDPS can identify anomalies or potential security incidents, contributing to the timely detection and prevention of malicious activities within the network. The synergy between OS security and IDPS enhances the overall resilience of network communication by proactively identifying and mitigating emerging threats.

Vulnerability management and patching, critical elements of OS security, have a direct impact on the security of network communication. Operating systems are periodically updated to address vulnerabilities and weaknesses that could be exploited by malicious actors. The timely application of patches within the OS ecosystem is paramount to mitigating the risk of security breaches within networked environments. By actively managing vulnerabilities at the OS level, organizations enhance the security of network communication, minimizing the potential for exploitation and fortifying the overall resilience of interconnected systems.

Virtual Private Networks (VPNs), designed to establish secure communication channels over public or untrusted networks, rely on the OS for seamless integration and support. Whether native VPN capabilities within the operating system or third-party VPN solutions, the OS plays a central role in facilitating secure remote access and encrypted communication. By incorporating VPN technologies, the OS contributes to the creation of secure communication channels, safeguarding sensitive data from interception or unauthorized access during transmission over potentially insecure networks. This collaboration between OS security and VPNs underscores the holistic approach to securing network communication, especially in the context of remote access scenarios.

The secure management of network protocols and services within the operating system is paramount for mitigating security risks. Operating systems support a myriad of network protocols that facilitate communication and resource sharing. Effectively configuring and managing these protocols is an integral aspect of OS security, directly influencing the security of network communication. Protocols such as TCP/IP, DNS, and DHCP, managed by the OS, are foundational components of network communication. Secure configuration and management ensure the reliable functioning of these protocols, reducing the attack surface and enhancing the overall security of network interactions.

Network monitoring and logging, facilitated by the operating system, provide critical insights into network activities, security incidents, and potential threats. The OS records events and activities through logging mechanisms, creating an audit trail that is invaluable for post-incident analysis and forensic investigations. Network monitoring tools leverage the information gathered by the OS to detect anomalies, unauthorized access attempts, or unusual patterns within network traffic. This collaborative effort between OS security and network monitoring enhances the ability to identify and respond to security incidents promptly, thereby bolstering the overall security of network communication.

In conclusion, the relationship between OS security and secure network communication is deeply intertwined, constituting a synergistic partnership that underpins the broader landscape of cybersecurity. The operating system, as the linchpin in managing hardware resources and facilitating communication, establishes the foundation for secure network interactions. Authentication, access control, encryption, firewalls, IDPS, vulnerability management, VPNs, protocol management, and network monitoring collectively form an integrated framework where OS security and network security converge. This collaboration ensures that the principles and practices implemented at the OS level resonate throughout the network, fostering a secure environment where data integrity, confidentiality, and availability are paramount. As organizations navigate the complexities of interconnected systems, the symbiotic relationship between OS security and secure network communication emerges as a cornerstone in building resilient and robust cybersecurity postures.

The role of firewalls in filtering network traffic and preventing unauthorized access.

The role of firewalls in filtering network traffic and preventing unauthorized access is pivotal in establishing a robust defense against the myriad of cyber threats that permeate the digital landscape. A firewall, at its core, serves as a barrier between a trusted internal network and the untrusted external world, acting as a gatekeeper that carefully scrutinizes and regulates the flow of data packets. Its primary function is to analyze incoming and outgoing network traffic, making decisions based on predefined rules or security policies. By strategically filtering this traffic, firewalls play a crucial role in safeguarding the confidentiality, integrity, and availability of data, thereby forming an essential component of network security architectures.

One of the fundamental capabilities of firewalls lies in their ability to filter network traffic based on specific criteria, such as source and destination IP addresses, ports, and protocols. This granularity allows organizations to define rules that dictate which types of traffic are allowed or denied. For instance, a firewall can be configured to permit incoming traffic only on specific ports associated with authorized services, such as web or email servers, while blocking access to unused or unnecessary ports. This meticulous traffic filtering enables organizations to minimize the attack surface, reducing the likelihood of unauthorized access or exploitation of potential vulnerabilities within the network.

In the context of preventing unauthorized access, firewalls act as a first line of defense by establishing a perimeter that scrutinizes incoming connection requests. Network Address Translation (NAT) is a common technique employed by firewalls to conceal internal IP addresses from external entities, adding an additional layer of security. Firewalls utilize stateful inspection to track the state of active connections, distinguishing between legitimate outbound requests and potentially malicious inbound traffic. This stateful approach allows firewalls to make informed decisions based on the context of the communication, ensuring that only authorized connections are established and unauthorized access attempts are thwarted.

Firewalls are adept at enforcing access control policies, a critical aspect of preventing unauthorized access to network resources. Access control lists (ACLs) within firewalls define the rules governing which devices or users are granted access to specific services or data. These rules can be based on a variety of factors, including IP addresses, port numbers, and application protocols. By meticulously configuring access control policies, organizations can tailor their firewalls to align with their security requirements, limiting access to essential services and minimizing exposure to potential security risks. This proactive approach enhances the overall security posture, mitigating the risk of unauthorized access and potential breaches.

Intrusion Prevention Systems (IPS) integrated into firewalls extend their capabilities by actively monitoring and analyzing network traffic for signs of malicious activities or known attack patterns. In the event that the firewall detects anomalous behavior, such as a pattern indicative of a known exploit or intrusion attempt, the IPS component can take immediate action to block the malicious traffic. This dynamic response mechanism reinforces the preventative role of firewalls, allowing them to go beyond static rule-based filtering and actively mitigate emerging threats in real-time. The integration of IPS features further fortifies firewalls as a proactive defense against unauthorized access and potential security breaches.

The role of firewalls becomes particularly crucial in the context of distributed denial-of-service (DDoS) attacks, where malicious actors attempt to overwhelm a network or service with a flood of traffic. Firewalls are equipped with DDoS mitigation capabilities that enable them to identify and block malicious traffic patterns associated with such attacks. By distinguishing between legitimate and malicious traffic, firewalls act as a protective barrier, preventing the saturation of network resources and ensuring the continued availability of critical services. This resilience against DDoS attacks showcases the adaptive nature of firewalls in addressing diverse threats to network integrity.

Deep Packet Inspection (DPI) is a sophisticated feature employed by firewalls to analyze the content of data packets traversing the network. This granular inspection allows firewalls to scrutinize the payload of each packet, enabling the detection of malicious code, viruses, or other forms of malware embedded within seemingly benign traffic. DPI is instrumental in preventing unauthorized access by identifying and blocking malicious content before it can infiltrate the network. By incorporating DPI capabilities, firewalls enhance their effectiveness in detecting and thwarting advanced threats that may attempt to exploit vulnerabilities within the network.

Virtual Private Networks (VPNs), essential for establishing secure communication channels over public or untrusted networks, often leverage firewalls to enforce encryption and access control. Firewalls play a crucial role in VPN configurations by ensuring that only authorized users and devices can establish encrypted connections. Through the enforcement of VPN protocols and encryption standards, firewalls contribute to the creation of secure tunnels that protect sensitive data from interception during transit. This collaboration between firewalls and VPNs exemplifies their joint effort in preventing unauthorized access and securing communication channels, especially in scenarios involving remote access or connections over unsecured networks.

Logging and monitoring are integral components of the firewall's role in preventing unauthorized access. Firewalls maintain detailed logs of network traffic, connection attempts, and security events. By actively monitoring these logs, organizations gain insights into potential security incidents, unauthorized access attempts, or anomalous patterns within the network. The wealth of information provided by firewall logs enables security teams to conduct forensic analysis, investigate security events, and respond promptly to emerging threats. This proactive approach not only enhances the prevention of unauthorized access but also facilitates continuous improvement in security postures based on real-world insights and evolving threat landscapes.

Firewalls contribute significantly to the overall security of network communication by offering granular control over outbound traffic as well. Outbound filtering capabilities empower organizations to restrict access to specific websites, applications, or services, mitigating the risk of data exfiltration, and preventing communication with known malicious entities. By implementing outbound filtering policies, firewalls serve as a preventive measure against unauthorized data transfers and reinforce the organization's ability to enforce security policies consistently.

In conclusion, the role of firewalls in filtering network traffic and preventing unauthorized access is multifaceted, encompassing a range of sophisticated capabilities that collectively fortify the security posture of interconnected systems. From meticulous traffic filtering based on predefined rules to stateful inspection, access control enforcement, intrusion prevention, DDoS mitigation, deep packet inspection, VPN support, logging, and outbound traffic filtering, firewalls stand as the guardians of network integrity. Their proactive approach to identifying and thwarting potential threats, coupled with the ability to adapt to emerging security challenges, positions firewalls as indispensable components in the arsenal of cybersecurity defenses. As organizations navigate the complexities of the digital landscape, firewalls emerge as linchpins in the prevention of unauthorized access, safeguarding the confidentiality, integrity, and availability of data across diverse and interconnected networks.

How intrusion detection systems monitor and respond to potential security threats.

Intrusion Detection Systems (IDS) play a crucial role in safeguarding information technology infrastructures by actively monitoring and responding to potential security threats. These systems are designed to analyze network or system activities, identify patterns indicative of malicious behavior, and provide timely alerts or responses to mitigate the impact of security incidents. The intricate workings of IDS involve a combination of signature-based detection, anomaly detection, and, in some cases, behavioral analysis, all geared towards creating a comprehensive defense mechanism against a diverse range of cyber threats.

Signature-based detection, a foundational technique in intrusion detection, involves the comparison of observed network or system activities against known patterns or signatures of known threats. IDS equipped with signature databases can quickly identify and flag activities that match predefined signatures, effectively recognizing common attack patterns or malicious behaviors. This approach is particularly effective in detecting well-established threats, such as known malware or specific attack methodologies. However, its limitation lies in the inability to identify novel or previously unseen threats that lack identifiable signatures.

Anomaly detection represents another crucial facet of intrusion detection, focusing on identifying deviations from established baselines of normal behavior within the network or system. By establishing a profile of typical network traffic, user behavior, or system performance, anomaly detection mechanisms within IDS can detect unusual patterns or deviations that may indicate a potential security threat. This approach is particularly valuable in identifying previously unknown or zero-day attacks, as it does not rely on predefined signatures but rather on deviations from established norms. However, the challenge lies in distinguishing between genuine anomalies and legitimate variations in network or system behavior.

Behavioral analysis, often integrated into advanced IDS, takes anomaly detection a step further by focusing on the behavior of users, applications, or devices over time. By building behavioral models, IDS can identify patterns that deviate from expected behavior, even if the deviations are subtle or occur over an extended period. This approach is adept at recognizing sophisticated threats that may exhibit polymorphic or low-and-slow attack techniques designed to evade traditional signature-based detection. Behavioral analysis within IDS enhances the ability to detect insider threats, advanced persistent threats (APTs), and other subtle attacks that may go unnoticed by more traditional detection methods.

Network-based IDS (NIDS) and host-based IDS (HIDS) represent two primary deployment models for intrusion detection. NIDS are strategically positioned at key points within the network, actively monitoring the traffic that traverses those points. These systems analyze network packets, looking for patterns or behaviors that align with known attack signatures or anomalous activities. NIDS are well-suited for detecting threats that traverse the network, providing a centralized and comprehensive view of potential security incidents. HIDS, on the other hand, are deployed on individual hosts or endpoints, monitoring activities specific to the host system. This includes file system changes, log entries, and application behavior. HIDS are particularly effective in detecting threats that may originate or manifest within the host itself, offering a more granular and detailed perspective on potential security incidents.

The monitoring phase of IDS involves continuous observation of network or system activities in real-time. Network sensors within NIDS passively capture and analyze packets, while agents or sensors within HIDS actively monitor host activities. The collected data is then subject to analysis, with the IDS comparing the observed activities against predefined signatures, baselines, or behavioral models. In the context of NIDS, the analysis may include packet header inspection, payload analysis, and protocol validation. For HIDS, the analysis encompasses system logs, registry entries, file integrity checks, and application behavior analysis. This vigilant monitoring phase ensures that the IDS remains attentive to potential security threats as they unfold within the network or on individual hosts.

Upon detecting potential security threats, IDS initiate the alerting phase, generating notifications or alerts to inform security administrators or relevant personnel. Alerts are designed to convey critical information about the detected incident, including the type of threat, affected systems or network segments, and the severity of the incident. These alerts serve as an early warning mechanism, enabling security teams to respond promptly to potential security incidents. The effectiveness of alerting is contingent on the accuracy of the IDS in distinguishing between genuine threats and false positives. False positives, where benign activities are mistakenly identified as threats, can inundate security teams with alerts and undermine the efficiency of the IDS.

Response mechanisms within IDS are designed to take proactive actions to mitigate or contain the impact of potential security threats. Responses can range from simple alert notifications to more sophisticated actions, such as blocking or isolating malicious network traffic, quarantining compromised hosts, or initiating incident response protocols. The ability of IDS to respond effectively to security threats is contingent on the level of automation and integration with other security systems. Automated responses can help reduce the time between detection and mitigation, crucial in the context of rapidly evolving cyber threats. However, careful consideration must be given to the potential impact of automated responses on legitimate network activities to avoid inadvertent disruptions.

Correlation and aggregation of alerts represent advanced features in some IDS, facilitating a more comprehensive understanding of potential security incidents. Correlation involves analyzing multiple alerts in conjunction to identify patterns or relationships that may indicate a coordinated attack or a broader security event. Aggregation involves consolidating individual alerts into a unified view, providing security teams with a holistic perspective on the overall security posture. These features enhance the analytical capabilities of IDS, enabling security professionals to discern the larger context of potential security threats and respond strategically.

Intrusion Prevention Systems (IPS) represent an extension of IDS, incorporating the capability to actively block or prevent detected threats. While traditional IDS focus on detection and alerting, IPS take a more proactive stance by intervening to prevent malicious activities. IPS utilize a combination of signature-based detection, anomaly detection, and response mechanisms to identify and block potential security threats. The integration of IPS features within IDS exemplifies a shift towards a more preemptive approach to cybersecurity, where the system not only detects threats but also actively prevents their impact.

Continuous improvement and adaptation are integral aspects of IDS functionality. Regular updates to signature databases, baselines, and behavioral models are essential to ensure that the IDS remains effective against evolving threats. Threat intelligence feeds, which provide information on new vulnerabilities, attack techniques, and emerging threats, contribute to the ongoing refinement of IDS capabilities. Regular tuning and optimization based on historical data and lessons learned from previous incidents enhance the accuracy and efficiency of IDS in identifying and responding to potential security threats.

In conclusion, the multifaceted approach of intrusion detection systems encompasses signature-based detection, anomaly detection, and behavioral analysis, collectively working to monitor, detect, and respond to potential security threats within information technology infrastructures. The deployment models of NIDS and HIDS offer comprehensive visibility into network and host activities, respectively, while vigilant monitoring, alerting, and response mechanisms form the core functionalities of IDS. The integration of intrusion prevention features and the incorporation of advanced capabilities like correlation and aggregation contribute to the overall effectiveness of IDS in safeguarding against a diverse range of cyber threats. As organizations navigate the dynamic landscape of cybersecurity, intrusion detection systems emerge as critical components, providing a proactive defense against potential security incidents and contributing to the resilience of digital infrastructures.

Utilizing VPNs for secure and encrypted communication over networks.

Virtual Private Networks (VPNs) stand as an integral and versatile tool in the realm of cybersecurity, facilitating secure and encrypted communication over networks. At their core, VPNs create an encrypted tunnel between two endpoints, enabling the secure transmission of data over potentially insecure or public networks. The utilization of VPNs addresses the paramount concerns of confidentiality, integrity, and privacy in communication, making them indispensable in various scenarios, from remote work environments to safeguarding sensitive data during online transactions.

The foundational principle of VPNs revolves around encryption, where data is transformed into a secure, unreadable format as it traverses the network. Protocols like Secure Sockets Layer (SSL) and its successor, Transport Layer Security (TLS), play a pivotal role in establishing this encryption layer, ensuring that the information exchanged between connected devices remains confidential and resistant to interception by malicious entities. This encryption layer extends to various types of data, encompassing not only user credentials but also the entirety of the transmitted content, offering a comprehensive safeguard against eavesdropping and unauthorized access.

In the context of remote access scenarios, VPNs provide a secure bridge between users and corporate networks, especially in the era of widespread telecommuting. By encrypting the communication between an employee's device and the corporate network, VPNs allow remote workers to access internal resources, collaborate on sensitive projects, and conduct business transactions with confidence. The secure nature of VPNs ensures that even when employees connect to the corporate network from public Wi-Fi hotspots or other potentially insecure environments, the confidentiality and integrity of the transmitted data are maintained, reducing the risk of data breaches or unauthorized access.

Beyond remote access, VPNs play a pivotal role in securing communications over public Wi-Fi networks, which are inherently vulnerable to various forms of cyber threats. When users connect to public Wi-Fi in airports, coffee shops, or hotels, the unencrypted nature of the network leaves them susceptible to potential interception of their data by malicious actors. VPNs provide a robust solution by encrypting the data from the user's device to the VPN server, thereby creating a secure tunnel that shields sensitive information from prying eyes. This is particularly critical for safeguarding personal and financial data during online banking, shopping, or any other activity that involves transmitting sensitive information over public networks.

In the context of site-to-site communication, where multiple geographically dispersed locations need to securely exchange data, VPNs offer an efficient and cost-effective solution. By establishing encrypted connections between the networks of different sites, organizations can create a virtual private network that enables seamless and secure communication. This is especially relevant for multinational corporations or businesses with multiple branches, allowing them to share sensitive information, collaborate on projects, and access shared resources without compromising security. The versatility of VPNs in connecting disparate networks enhances organizational efficiency while maintaining the confidentiality of data transmitted between sites.

The concept of endpoint security within VPNs further fortifies their role in secure communication. VPN clients, installed on users' devices, create a secure connection to the VPN server, and through this connection, all data transmitted from the device is encrypted. This not only protects the data during transit but also ensures that the endpoint device remains shielded from potential threats lurking on the network. The encrypted tunnel created by the VPN client acts as a barrier, preventing unauthorized access to the device and mitigating the risk of malware infections or other forms of cyberattacks that often target vulnerable endpoints.

One of the key attributes that make VPNs an invaluable tool for secure communication is their ability to anonymize user identities and shield their online activities from surveillance. This is particularly relevant in an era where online privacy is a growing concern. VPNs achieve this by masking the user's IP address, substituting it with the IP address of the VPN server. As a result, the user's online activities become associated with the VPN server's IP address, adding an additional layer of anonymity. This is particularly valuable for users seeking to circumvent geographic restrictions, access region-restricted content, or simply maintain a higher level of privacy in their online interactions.

The role of VPNs in protecting against Man-in-the-Middle (MitM) attacks is noteworthy. In a Man-in-the-Middle attack, a malicious actor intercepts and potentially alters the communication between two parties without their knowledge. VPNs mitigate this risk by encrypting the data transmitted between the user's device and the VPN server. Even if a potential attacker manages to intercept the communication, the encrypted nature of the data renders it indecipherable, thwarting attempts to tamper with the information being exchanged. This resilience against MitM attacks enhances the overall security posture of VPNs, making them a reliable solution for secure communication.

The concept of split tunneling within VPNs allows users to selectively route their internet traffic through the VPN while maintaining direct access to local resources. This flexibility is particularly beneficial in scenarios where users need secure access to specific resources over the VPN while still requiring direct access to local services or the internet. By empowering users to define their routing preferences, split tunneling optimizes network performance and ensures that only the necessary traffic is transmitted through the encrypted VPN tunnel. This feature enhances the efficiency of VPN usage while catering to the diverse connectivity needs of users.

VPN security protocols, such as OpenVPN, IPSec, and L2TP/IPSec, contribute to the robustness of encrypted communication by defining the rules and mechanisms governing the establishment and maintenance of VPN connections. These protocols dictate the encryption algorithms, authentication methods, and key exchange processes used to secure the data transmission. The selection of an appropriate security protocol depends on factors such as the specific security requirements, the type of data being transmitted, and the balance between security and performance considerations. By offering a range of protocols, VPNs empower users and organizations to tailor their security configurations based on their unique needs.

The evolution of technology has given rise to innovations such as mobile VPNs, which extend the benefits of secure and encrypted communication to mobile devices. Mobile VPNs cater to the unique connectivity challenges posed by smartphones and tablets, allowing users to securely access corporate networks, browse the internet, and utilize mobile applications without compromising data security. Mobile VPNs play a critical role in addressing the vulnerabilities associated with mobile connectivity, including the risks posed by unsecured Wi-Fi networks and the need for seamless and secure access to organizational resources while on the go.

Despite the myriad benefits of VPNs, it is essential to acknowledge the challenges and considerations associated with their usage. Network latency, a common concern in VPN deployment, can impact the performance of real-time applications such as voice and video conferencing. The overhead introduced by encryption and the routing of traffic through VPN servers may lead to a slight delay in data transmission. Balancing the need for security with the requirements of performance is a delicate consideration in VPN deployment, requiring organizations to make informed decisions based on their specific use cases and priorities.

In conclusion, the utilization of Virtual Private Networks represents a linchpin in achieving secure and encrypted communication over networks, addressing a spectrum of cybersecurity concerns. From remote access scenarios to safeguarding against threats on public Wi-Fi networks, VPNs provide a versatile and robust solution. Their ability to establish encrypted connections, anonymize user identities, protect against various forms of cyber threats, and adapt to the evolving technological landscape makes them an indispensable tool in the arsenal of cybersecurity defenses. As organizations and individuals continue to navigate the complexities of the digital era, the role of VPNs in ensuring the confidentiality, integrity, and privacy of communication remains paramount.

Implementation and configuration of VPNs for enhanced OS security.

The implementation and configuration of Virtual Private Networks (VPNs) stand as a critical component in enhancing the security of operating systems (OS). VPNs play a pivotal role in securing communication over networks, and their proper integration into the

OS environment requires meticulous planning and configuration. At the forefront of this implementation is the selection of an appropriate VPN protocol, each with its unique strengths and considerations. Popular protocols like OpenVPN, IPSec, and L2TP/IPSec offer varying levels of security and performance, allowing organizations to align their VPN configurations with specific OS security requirements and network constraints. The choice of protocol often hinges on factors such as the desired balance between security and performance, compatibility with the OS, and adherence to industry standards.

The deployment of VPNs for enhanced OS security necessitates consideration of the encryption algorithms employed during data transmission. The selection of robust encryption algorithms is paramount to safeguarding sensitive information from potential eavesdropping or interception. Common encryption algorithms include Advanced Encryption Standard (AES), which is widely regarded for its security and efficiency, and Triple Data Encryption Standard (3DES). Striking the right balance between encryption strength and computational overhead is crucial, ensuring that the chosen encryption method aligns with the processing capabilities of the OS and the specific security requirements of the organization.

Authentication mechanisms form a vital aspect of VPN configuration, as they validate the identities of users and devices seeking access to the network. Implementing strong user authentication methods, such as username and password combinations, multi-factor authentication (MFA), or digital certificates, fortifies the access control measures within the VPN. The integration of MFA, involving additional verification steps beyond a simple password, adds an extra layer of security, mitigating the risk of unauthorized access even in the event of compromised credentials. Certificates, on the other hand, leverage public-key cryptography to verify the authenticity of users or devices, enhancing the overall security posture of the VPN.

In the realm of OS security, the role of VPN clients assumes paramount significance. VPN clients, installed on individual devices, establish secure connections to the VPN server, encapsulating and encrypting data during transmission. The configuration and management of VPN clients are integral aspects of the implementation process, requiring attention to detail in terms of compatibility with the OS, user-friendliness, and the ability to seamlessly integrate with existing network environments. Organizations often opt for VPN clients that offer a user-friendly interface, ensuring that end-users can easily connect to the VPN without requiring extensive technical expertise. Additionally, the ability to automatically update client software ensures that security patches and enhancements are promptly deployed across the OS environment.

The process of integrating VPNs with OS security often involves considerations for split tunneling, a feature that allows users to selectively route their internet traffic through the VPN while maintaining direct access to local resources. This flexibility addresses the diverse connectivity needs of users, enabling them to access specific resources securely over the VPN while still enjoying direct internet access for non-sensitive activities. Split tunneling optimizes network performance and conserves bandwidth by ensuring that only the necessary traffic traverses the encrypted VPN tunnel. However, careful configuration is required to strike the right balance between security and performance, as excessive split tunneling may expose users to potential security risks.

The implementation of VPNs for OS security extends to network-level considerations, with organizations often deploying VPN gateways strategically to regulate traffic entering and exiting the corporate network. VPN gateways serve as entry points for remote users or branch offices, and their configuration involves defining access policies, enforcing security protocols, and managing traffic effectively. The gateway acts as a control point, ensuring that only authorized and encrypted traffic is permitted to traverse the VPN tunnel. The configuration of VPN gateways requires attention to network topology, addressing schemes, and routing protocols to seamlessly integrate with the existing infrastructure while upholding security standards.

An aspect of VPN implementation crucial for OS security is the establishment of a robust and well-managed public key infrastructure (PKI) for the issuance and management of digital certificates. Digital certificates play a pivotal role in user authentication and the validation of VPN servers, contributing to the overall trustworthiness of the VPN environment. The configuration of a PKI involves the generation of cryptographic keys, the issuance of digital certificates to users and devices, and the implementation of certificate revocation mechanisms. PKI configuration is integral to the secure functioning of VPNs, ensuring that only authorized entities with valid certificates can establish encrypted connections.

The integration of VPNs with OS security protocols extends to the enforcement of access control policies within the VPN environment. Organizations configure access control lists (ACLs) to define rules governing which users or devices are granted access to specific resources or services over the VPN. This granular control ensures that only authorized entities can establish connections, mitigating the risk of unauthorized access or potential security breaches. The alignment of VPN access control policies with OS-level permissions and security groups enhances the overall security posture, creating a comprehensive and consistent framework for controlling access to network resources.

The logging and monitoring capabilities of VPNs play a pivotal role in the implementation of effective OS security measures. VPNs generate logs that capture critical information, including user login/logout details, connection timestamps, and security events. These logs provide a valuable audit trail for post-incident analysis, forensic investigations, and compliance requirements. The configuration of logging parameters, log storage, and log analysis tools contributes to the proactive monitoring of VPN activities. By continuously monitoring VPN logs, organizations gain insights into potential

security incidents, anomalous activities, or unauthorized access attempts, enabling prompt response and mitigation.

Regular updates and patch management are integral components of VPN implementation for enhanced OS security. VPN vendors regularly release updates to address vulnerabilities, improve security features, and ensure compatibility with evolving OS environments. Organizations need to establish a systematic process for updating VPN software, ensuring that the latest security patches are applied promptly to mitigate the risk of exploitation by malicious actors. The configuration of automatic update mechanisms within VPN clients and gateways streamlines the patch management process, reducing the window of exposure to potential security threats.

The implementation of VPNs for enhanced OS security necessitates a comprehensive understanding of the threat landscape and the evolving nature of cyber threats. Security teams should actively engage in threat intelligence gathering to stay abreast of emerging vulnerabilities, attack vectors, and new security risks. By incorporating threat intelligence into the VPN configuration process, organizations can proactively adapt their security measures to address evolving threats. This forward-looking approach enhances the resilience of the OS environment, ensuring that VPN configurations remain aligned with current security best practices and industry standards.

In conclusion, the implementation and configuration of Virtual Private Networks emerge as a pivotal strategy for enhancing the security of operating systems. This multifaceted process involves careful consideration of VPN protocols, encryption algorithms, authentication mechanisms, client configurations, split tunneling, gateway deployment, public key infrastructure, access control policies, logging, monitoring, patch management, and integration with threat intelligence. By systematically addressing these aspects, organizations can establish a robust VPN infrastructure that not only secures communication over networks but also fortifies the overall security posture of operating systems. As the digital landscape continues to evolve, the role of VPNs in OS security remains paramount, offering a versatile and proactive defense against a myriad of cyber threats.

Understanding the role of SSL and TLS in securing data transmission.

Secure Sockets Layer (SSL) and its successor, Transport Layer Security (TLS), play pivotal roles in safeguarding the confidentiality, integrity, and authenticity of data transmitted over the internet. These cryptographic protocols establish a secure communication channel between two entities, typically a client and a server, ensuring that sensitive information remains protected from malicious actors. The foundation of SSL/TLS lies in encryption, a process that transforms plaintext data into a ciphertext format that is indecipherable without the appropriate decryption key. This cryptographic mechanism prevents unauthorized access and eavesdropping, mitigating the risk of data interception during transmission.

One of the primary functions of SSL/TLS is to authenticate the communicating parties, verifying the identity of both the server and, in some cases, the client. This authentication process relies on digital certificates issued by trusted Certificate Authorities (CAs). These certificates serve as digital passports, confirming that the server (or client) is who it claims to be. The use of certificates helps establish a foundation of trust, as clients can validate the legitimacy of the server's identity before exchanging sensitive information. This authentication process is crucial in preventing man-in-the-middle attacks, where an adversary attempts to intercept and alter the communication between the client and server.

In addition to authentication, SSL/TLS protocols implement mechanisms for ensuring the integrity of the transmitted data. Hash functions, such as SHA-256, are employed to generate unique fingerprints, or checksums, of the data. These checksums are then included in the transmitted messages and verified by the recipient upon receipt. If the checksum matches, it indicates that the data has not been tampered with during transit. Any unauthorized modifications would result in a mismatch, signaling a potential security breach. This integrity check is vital for maintaining the reliability of transmitted information and preventing malicious alterations.

Furthermore, SSL/TLS protocols support the establishment of a secure communication channel through the use of key exchange mechanisms. The process involves the negotiation of cryptographic keys between the client and server, which are subsequently used to encrypt and decrypt the data. The widely adopted Diffie-Hellman key exchange and its elliptic curve variant enable secure key generation without exposing the keys during transmission. This key exchange mechanism ensures that even if an adversary intercepts the communication, they would not possess the necessary information to decrypt the exchanged data.

The evolution of SSL to TLS reflects ongoing efforts to address vulnerabilities and enhance security measures. TLS, the more modern and robust successor to SSL, introduces improvements in cryptographic algorithms, ciphersuites, and overall security mechanisms. The deprecation of outdated and insecure protocols, such as SSLv2 and SSLv3, underlines the commitment to maintaining a secure communication environment. As security threats continually evolve, the TLS protocol undergoes regular updates to address emerging vulnerabilities and strengthen its resistance against potential attacks.

Despite the robust security provided by SSL/TLS, it is essential to acknowledge potential challenges and considerations. The infamous POODLE (Padding Oracle On Downgraded Legacy Encryption) attack and vulnerabilities like Heartbleed highlight that even widely adopted security protocols are not immune to unforeseen threats. Prompt updates and patches, along with adherence to best practices, are crucial to mitigating risks and ensuring the ongoing effectiveness of SSL/TLS implementations.

The deployment of SSL/TLS extends beyond traditional web browsers, finding application in various protocols and services. Secure email communication, file transfers, and virtual private networks (VPNs) leverage SSL/TLS to establish secure connections. The prevalence of these protocols in diverse applications underscores their versatility and the critical role they play in securing data across the digital landscape.

In conclusion, SSL and TLS represent cornerstone technologies in ensuring the security of data transmission over the internet. Through encryption, authentication, integrity checks, and key exchange mechanisms, these protocols establish a secure communication channel, safeguarding sensitive information from unauthorized access and tampering. The continuous evolution of TLS underscores the commitment to addressing emerging threats and maintaining robust security standards. However, users and administrators must remain vigilant, implementing best practices and staying informed about potential vulnerabilities, to uphold the integrity and efficacy of SSL/TLS implementations in an ever-changing digital landscape.

Best practices for implementing and maintaining secure communication channels.

Implementing and maintaining secure communication channels is paramount in today's interconnected digital landscape. To achieve this, organizations and individuals must adhere to a set of best practices that encompass various aspects of security, ranging from encryption protocols to ongoing monitoring and updates. At the core of secure communication is the implementation of robust cryptographic protocols, such as SSL/TLS, which ensure that data remains confidential and tamper-proof during transmission. It is imperative to stay abreast of the latest cryptographic standards and avoid deprecated or vulnerable protocols, as the security landscape evolves continuously.

Authentication mechanisms play a pivotal role in establishing trust between communicating parties. Employing digital certificates issued by reputable Certificate Authorities (CAs) enhances the authentication process, verifying the identities of both servers and clients. Regularly updating and managing these certificates is essential to mitigate the risk of unauthorized access or impersonation. Additionally, organizations should consider implementing multi-factor authentication (MFA) for an added layer of security, requiring users to provide multiple forms of identification before gaining access to sensitive information.

Ensuring the integrity of transmitted data involves implementing hash functions and checksums. These mechanisms generate unique fingerprints of data, allowing the recipient to verify the data's integrity upon receipt. Regularly updating and strengthening hash algorithms helps maintain the reliability of the integrity checks, preventing malicious actors from tampering with the transmitted information. This practice becomes particularly crucial in scenarios where data integrity is of utmost importance, such as financial transactions or critical communications.

Key management is another critical aspect of secure communication. The use of robust key exchange mechanisms, like Diffie-Hellman or elliptic curve cryptography, ensures that cryptographic keys are securely negotiated between parties without exposing them during transmission. Regularly rotating and updating these keys adds an extra layer of security, preventing potential compromises that may arise from prolonged use of the same keys. Key management also involves protecting keys from unauthorized access, both in transit and at rest, to safeguard the entire cryptographic infrastructure.

Vigilant monitoring is indispensable for maintaining the security of communication channels. Implementing intrusion detection systems (IDS) and security information and event management (SIEM) solutions allows organizations to identify and respond promptly to any suspicious activities or potential security incidents. Continuous monitoring ensures that security teams can proactively address emerging threats and vulnerabilities, preventing unauthorized access or data breaches. Regularly reviewing and analyzing logs and alerts contributes to the overall resilience of the communication infrastructure.

Regular software updates and patch management are fundamental to addressing vulnerabilities in communication protocols and applications. Security patches provided by vendors often address known weaknesses and protect against emerging threats. Organizations should establish a systematic and timely process for applying these updates to all relevant components of the communication infrastructure, including servers, routers, and endpoints. Failure to keep systems up to date may expose vulnerabilities that malicious actors could exploit, compromising the security of communication channels.

Encryption extends beyond the transmission of data and should be implemented at rest as well. Encrypting stored data on servers, databases, and other storage devices adds an additional layer of protection, ensuring that even if unauthorized access occurs, the data remains unreadable without the appropriate decryption keys. This practice is particularly critical in environments where sensitive information is stored for extended periods, such as databases containing customer records or proprietary business data.

Establishing and enforcing strong security policies and access controls is crucial for maintaining secure communication channels. Clearly defined access levels, user roles, and permissions help prevent unauthorized access to sensitive information. Regularly reviewing and updating access policies in response to organizational changes or personnel adjustments is essential to maintaining a secure environment. Additionally, user education and awareness programs contribute to a security-conscious culture, empowering individuals to recognize and report potential security threats.

The deployment of firewalls and network segmentation enhances the security posture of communication channels. Firewalls act as a barrier between trusted internal networks and untrusted external networks, filtering and monitoring incoming and outgoing traffic. Network segmentation involves dividing a network into isolated segments, limiting the potential impact of a security breach. Combined, these measures provide an additional layer of defense against unauthorized access and mitigate the spread of threats within the network.

Regularly conducting security audits and assessments is instrumental in identifying and addressing potential vulnerabilities in communication channels. These assessments may include penetration testing, vulnerability scanning, and compliance audits. By proactively seeking and addressing weaknesses, organizations can strengthen their security posture and ensure compliance with industry regulations and standards. Additionally, these assessments contribute to a continuous improvement cycle, allowing organizations to adapt to evolving security threats.

In conclusion, implementing and maintaining secure communication channels requires a comprehensive and multifaceted approach. From robust cryptographic protocols and authentication mechanisms to vigilant monitoring, regular updates, and user education, organizations must adopt a holistic strategy to safeguard their digital communication infrastructure. By adhering to these best practices, individuals and organizations can mitigate the risk of unauthorized access, data breaches, and other security threats, fostering a secure and resilient communication environment in an ever-evolving digital landscape.

Security considerations for wireless networks in an operating system environment.

Securing wireless networks in an operating system environment is a complex and multifaceted task that requires a thorough understanding of potential vulnerabilities and the implementation of robust security measures. One of the foundational aspects of wireless network security is the authentication and authorization of devices attempting to connect. Employing strong authentication protocols, such as WPA3 (Wi-Fi Protected Access 3), ensures that only authorized users and devices can access the network. Implementing secure password policies and avoiding default credentials are essential steps in preventing unauthorized access, as weak or easily guessable passwords can be exploited by malicious actors attempting to compromise the network.

Encryption plays a pivotal role in protecting the confidentiality of data transmitted over wireless networks. The use of strong encryption protocols, such as WPA3's encryption suite, mitigates the risk of eavesdropping and unauthorized access to sensitive information. Additionally, organizations should avoid using deprecated and insecure encryption algorithms, opting for the latest and most robust options available to maintain a secure communication channel. Regularly updating encryption keys and rotating them in accordance with security best practices enhances the overall resilience of the wireless network.

The proper configuration of wireless routers and access points is crucial for minimizing potential security vulnerabilities. Disabling unnecessary services and features, such as WPS (Wi-Fi Protected Setup) or remote administration, helps reduce the attack surface and limit potential entry points for malicious actors. Organizations should also change default login credentials for routers and access points, as attackers often target devices with factory settings. Regularly updating firmware and applying security patches provided by the device manufacturers is imperative to address known vulnerabilities and enhance the overall security posture of the wireless network.

Network segmentation is a key strategy for enhancing the security of wireless networks within an operating system environment. Creating isolated segments for different types of devices or user groups limits the potential impact of a security breach. This segmentation can be achieved through the use of virtual LANs (VLANs) or other network segmentation technologies. By segmenting the network, organizations can contain and mitigate the spread of threats, reducing the overall risk associated with a potential security incident.

Continuous monitoring and intrusion detection are essential components of wireless network security. Implementing intrusion detection systems (IDS) and intrusion prevention systems (IPS) helps identify and respond to anomalous activities or potential security threats. Monitoring for unauthorized access attempts, unusual network traffic patterns, or the presence of rogue devices enhances the ability to detect and mitigate security incidents promptly. Regularly reviewing logs and alerts from wireless network devices provides valuable insights into potential vulnerabilities and emerging threats, contributing to a proactive security stance.

The use of virtual private networks (VPNs) adds an extra layer of security to wireless network communications, especially in environments where remote access is prevalent. VPNs encrypt data traffic between the user's device and the corporate network, protecting sensitive information from interception by malicious actors. Organizations should implement strong authentication mechanisms for VPN access, such as multi-factor authentication, to further enhance the security of remote connections. Regularly updating VPN software and ensuring compliance with industry standards are essential for maintaining the integrity and effectiveness of VPN security measures.

Security awareness and education programs are critical for fostering a security-conscious culture within an operating system environment. Users should be informed about the risks associated with connecting to unsecured or public Wi-Fi networks and educated on best practices for securing their wireless devices. Additionally, organizations should establish policies regarding the use of personal devices on corporate networks and provide guidelines for securing those devices to prevent potential security breaches.

Physical security considerations cannot be overlooked in the context of wireless network security. Securing physical access to wireless routers, access points, and other network infrastructure components is essential to prevent unauthorized tampering or interference. Physical security measures may include placing network devices in locked cabinets, restricting access to server rooms, and implementing surveillance systems to monitor and deter unauthorized access.

Regular security audits and vulnerability assessments are integral to identifying and addressing potential weaknesses in wireless network security. Conducting penetration tests and vulnerability scans helps organizations proactively identify and remediate security vulnerabilities before they can be exploited by malicious actors. These assessments should be conducted regularly to account for changes in the threat landscape and ensure that the wireless network's security measures remain effective over time.

In conclusion, securing wireless networks in an operating system environment requires a comprehensive and proactive approach. From robust authentication and encryption protocols to diligent network configuration, continuous monitoring, and user education, organizations must adopt a multifaceted strategy to mitigate the risks associated with wireless communication. By implementing these security considerations, organizations can create a resilient and secure wireless network environment that protects sensitive data and ensures the integrity and confidentiality of communications within the operating system landscape.

Strategies for securing Wi-Fi networks and protecting against unauthorized access.

Securing Wi-Fi networks and protecting against unauthorized access is a critical aspect of modern cybersecurity. One fundamental strategy is the implementation of strong authentication protocols. Wi-Fi Protected Access (WPA) and its latest iteration, WPA3, offer robust authentication mechanisms that ensure only authorized users can access the network. Employing secure and unique passwords for network access, coupled with the use of WPA3's Simultaneous Authentication of Equals (SAE) protocol, enhances the strength of authentication, mitigating the risk of unauthorized access through password-related vulnerabilities.

Encryption is another cornerstone of Wi-Fi network security. Utilizing strong encryption protocols, such as the Advanced Encryption Standard (AES) in WPA3, safeguards the confidentiality of data transmitted over the network. Encryption transforms data into an unreadable format during transmission, preventing eavesdropping and unauthorized access. Regularly updating encryption keys and avoiding deprecated encryption algorithms are crucial practices to maintain the effectiveness of the encryption measures over time.

Network segmentation plays a pivotal role in limiting the impact of unauthorized access. Creating separate segments or virtual LANs (VLANs) for different user groups or devices helps contain potential security breaches. In the event of unauthorized access, segmentation prevents lateral movement within the network, minimizing the exposure of sensitive information and critical resources. Additionally, segmenting the network allows for more granular control over access permissions and facilitates the implementation of targeted security measures for specific segments.

Rigorous password policies contribute significantly to Wi-Fi network security. Enforcing complex password requirements, including a combination of uppercase and lowercase letters, numbers, and special characters, enhances the resilience of authentication mechanisms. Regularly updating passwords and avoiding the use of default credentials for routers and access points are essential practices to prevent unauthorized access. Educating users on the importance of strong and unique passwords fosters a security-conscious culture within the organization.

Regular firmware updates and security patches are imperative for addressing vulnerabilities in Wi-Fi routers and access points. Manufacturers release updates to fix known security issues and enhance the overall security posture of network devices. Timely application of these updates ensures that potential entry points for unauthorized access are fortified against known vulnerabilities. Organizations should establish a systematic process for monitoring and applying firmware updates to maintain the integrity of their Wi-Fi network infrastructure.

Effective monitoring and intrusion detection mechanisms are crucial for identifying and responding to unauthorized access attempts promptly. Intrusion Detection Systems (IDS) and Intrusion Prevention Systems (IPS) can analyze network traffic patterns, detect anomalies, and alert administrators to potential security threats. Regularly reviewing logs and alerts provides valuable insights into the network's security status, enabling organizations to take proactive measures to prevent unauthorized access and respond swiftly to security incidents.

Rogue device detection is essential for preventing unauthorized access points from compromising network security. Deploying tools that can identify and locate unauthorized Wi-Fi devices helps organizations maintain control over their network infrastructure. This is particularly important in environments where bring-your-own-device (BYOD) policies are prevalent, as unapproved devices can introduce security vulnerabilities if not properly managed and monitored.

User education and awareness programs are integral components of a comprehensive Wi-Fi security strategy. Educating users about the risks associated with connecting to unsecured or public Wi-Fi networks helps them make informed decisions about network access. Training users to recognize social engineering tactics, such as phishing attempts or impersonation attacks, adds an additional layer of defense against unauthorized access attempts.

Implementing role-based access controls (RBAC) enhances Wi-Fi network security by assigning specific access privileges based on user roles. This ensures that users only have access to the resources and services necessary for their roles, minimizing the potential impact of unauthorized access. RBAC also simplifies the management of access permissions, making it easier to enforce security policies and respond to changes in user responsibilities.

Firewall deployment is crucial for securing Wi-Fi networks and preventing unauthorized access. Firewalls act as a barrier between the internal network and external threats, filtering incoming and outgoing traffic based on predetermined security rules. Configuring firewalls to block unauthorized access attempts and regularly reviewing firewall rules contribute to a robust defense against unauthorized access and potential security breaches.

Physical security measures are often overlooked but are essential for preventing unauthorized access to Wi-Fi network infrastructure. Securing physical access to routers, access points, and other network devices prevents tampering and unauthorized modifications. Placing network devices in locked cabinets or secure server rooms and implementing surveillance systems contribute to the overall physical security of the Wi-Fi network.

Regular security audits and vulnerability assessments are critical for identifying and addressing potential weaknesses in Wi-Fi network security. Conducting penetration tests and vulnerability scans helps organizations proactively discover and remediate security vulnerabilities before they can be exploited. These assessments should be performed regularly to adapt to changes in the threat landscape and ensure the ongoing effectiveness of security measures.

In conclusion, securing Wi-Fi networks and protecting against unauthorized access requires a comprehensive and layered approach. From strong authentication and encryption protocols to network segmentation, monitoring, and user education, organizations must adopt a multifaceted strategy to mitigate the risks associated with unauthorized access. By implementing these strategies, organizations can establish a resilient Wi-Fi network environment that safeguards sensitive data, maintains the confidentiality of communications, and prevents unauthorized access attempts in an ever-evolving cybersecurity landscape.

Chapter 4: User Authentication and Authorization

Overview of authentication methods, including passwords, biometrics, and multi-factor authentication.

Authentication methods form the bedrock of digital security, serving as the primary means to verify the identity of users and ensure that only authorized individuals gain access to sensitive information and systems. Passwords, the most traditional form of authentication, involve users providing a secret alphanumeric combination to confirm their identity. While passwords are ubiquitous, they come with inherent vulnerabilities, such as the risk of being forgotten, shared, or easily guessed. As a result, there has been a growing emphasis on enhancing authentication methods to bolster security.

Biometrics represent a revolutionary shift in authentication, relying on unique physical or behavioral characteristics for identity verification. Common biometric identifiers include fingerprints, retinal scans, facial recognition, and voice patterns. The advantage of biometrics lies in their inherent uniqueness and difficulty to replicate, providing a higher level of assurance compared to traditional passwords. However, challenges like privacy concerns, the potential for false positives or negatives, and the need for specialized hardware in some cases have prompted organizations to carefully consider the implementation of biometric authentication.

Multi-factor authentication (MFA) has emerged as a robust strategy to fortify digital security by combining multiple authentication methods. Typically, MFA involves the use of two or more of the following factors: something the user knows (knowledge-based factors, like passwords), something the user has (possession-based factors, like a smartphone or security token), and something the user is (biometric factors). The layered approach significantly enhances security by requiring attackers to compromise multiple factors for successful unauthorized access. MFA has become increasingly popular in mitigating the risks associated with password-based authentication alone.

Passwords, despite their limitations, remain a fundamental component of authentication systems. The best practices for password security include using complex combinations of letters, numbers, and symbols, avoiding easily guessable information, and regularly updating passwords. Additionally, the implementation of password policies, such as mandatory changes and restrictions on password reuse, contributes to overall security. However, the human factor remains a challenge, as users may still choose weak passwords or fall victim to phishing attacks that aim to trick them into revealing their credentials.

Biometric authentication methods leverage unique physiological or behavioral attributes to verify a user's identity. Fingerprint recognition, one of the most widely adopted biometric methods, analyzes the unique patterns of ridges and valleys on an individual's fingertip. Retinal and iris scans utilize the distinctive features of the eye, while facial recognition relies on mapping facial characteristics to confirm identity. Voice recognition analyzes the unique vocal patterns of individuals. While biometrics offer a high level of accuracy and convenience, concerns about privacy and the potential for data breaches have prompted careful consideration in their deployment. Biometric data, once compromised, cannot be easily changed, highlighting the need for secure storage and transmission methods.

Facial recognition technology, a subset of biometrics, has gained prominence in various sectors. It analyzes facial features, such as the distance between eyes or the shape of the nose and mouth, to create a unique facial template for each individual. Widely used in surveillance, border control, and mobile devices, facial recognition has faced scrutiny due to issues such as algorithmic bias, accuracy concerns—especially with different ethnicities—and privacy implications. Striking a balance between convenience and ethical considerations remains a challenge in the widespread adoption of facial recognition technology.

Voice recognition, another biometric authentication method, relies on capturing and analyzing unique vocal characteristics, such as pitch, tone, and speech patterns. While voice recognition provides a natural and convenient means of authentication, challenges include variations in voice due to illness, background noise, or intentional mimicry. The technology has found applications in voice-activated devices and telephone-based authentication systems, offering an additional layer of security beyond traditional methods.

Retinal and iris scans represent highly secure biometric methods, leveraging the unique patterns in the human eye for authentication. Retinal scans focus on the blood vessels at the back of the eye, while iris scans analyze the colored part of the eye. These methods are considered highly accurate and difficult to forge, but their adoption has been limited due to the need for specialized hardware, potential discomfort for users, and privacy concerns related to capturing detailed images of the eye.

Multi-factor authentication (MFA) stands out as a comprehensive approach to enhancing digital security. By requiring users to provide two or more factors for authentication, MFA adds layers of complexity for potential attackers. The combination of something the user knows (such as a password), something the user has (like a smartphone or security token), and something the user is (biometric data) significantly reduces the likelihood of unauthorized access. MFA has become increasingly prevalent across various industries, including finance, healthcare, and online services, as organizations recognize its effectiveness in mitigating the risks associated with single-factor authentication.

Knowledge-based authentication factors, such as passwords, often serve as the first layer in multi-factor authentication. The user provides information they know, typically a password, as the initial step in confirming their identity. To strengthen this layer, organizations often enforce password complexity requirements, regular updates, and additional security measures like account lockouts after multiple failed login attempts.

Possession-based authentication factors involve something the user possesses, beyond knowledge-based factors. Common methods include receiving a one-time code on a registered smartphone through SMS or mobile apps, using a hardware security token, or employing smart cards. Possession-based factors add an extra layer of security by requiring the user to have a physical or digital item in their possession for successful authentication.

Biometric factors contribute to the third layer of multi-factor authentication, involving something the user is. Combining biometrics, such as fingerprint or facial recognition, with other authentication factors creates a powerful and resilient security model. Biometric data is challenging to forge, adding a level of assurance to the authentication process. However, organizations must carefully address privacy concerns, data storage, and potential biases associated with biometric technologies.

While multi-factor authentication significantly enhances security, it is not without challenges. Usability concerns, potential costs associated with additional hardware, and the need for user education and support contribute to the complexity of implementation. Striking a balance between security and user experience is crucial to ensuring the widespread adoption and effectiveness of multi-factor authentication in various contexts.

In conclusion, the landscape of authentication methods encompasses a spectrum of techniques, each with its strengths and challenges. From traditional passwords to innovative biometrics and the layered approach of multi-factor authentication, organizations must carefully consider the context, user experience, and security implications when implementing these methods. As the digital landscape evolves, the ongoing quest for robust and user-friendly authentication solutions continues, with a focus on balancing convenience, privacy, and security in an interconnected and dynamic world.

The strengths and vulnerabilities associated with each authentication mechanism.

Authentication mechanisms, whether traditional or innovative, come with their distinct strengths and vulnerabilities, shaping the landscape of digital security. Traditional passwords, while ubiquitous, have notable weaknesses. Their primary strength lies in familiarity and ease of implementation, but vulnerabilities include the risk of weak password choices, reuse across multiple accounts, and susceptibility to phishing attacks. Users may opt for convenience over complexity, leading to easily guessable passwords. Moreover, the reliance on passwords alone provides a single point of failure, as compromised credentials can grant unauthorized access. Organizations must balance password complexity requirements with user convenience and implement additional security measures to mitigate these vulnerabilities.

Biometric authentication, leveraging unique physical or behavioral traits, introduces a higher level of security. Fingerprint recognition, for instance, provides a strong and distinctive identifier. The strength of biometrics lies in their inherent uniqueness and difficulty to forge, offering a more secure alternative to traditional passwords. However, vulnerabilities exist, including the potential for false positives or negatives, privacy concerns associated with the collection and storage of biometric data, and the risk of irreversible compromise if the biometric data is breached. Additionally, the accuracy of biometric systems may be influenced by factors such as variations in environmental conditions, injuries, or intentional mimicry, requiring careful consideration in deployment.

Facial recognition technology, a subset of biometrics, is characterized by its non-intrusive nature and wide range of applications. It is employed in surveillance, mobile devices, and access control systems. The strengths of facial recognition include its natural and convenient user experience, with no need for physical contact. However, vulnerabilities include concerns about algorithmic bias, accuracy issues, and the potential for unauthorized use or surveillance. Ethical considerations, privacy implications, and the risk of false positives or negatives with different ethnicities necessitate a thoughtful and transparent approach to the development and deployment of facial recognition technology.

Voice recognition, another biometric authentication method, relies on capturing and analyzing unique vocal patterns. The strength lies in its natural and convenient form of authentication, but vulnerabilities include variations in voice due to illness, background noise, or intentional mimicry. Additionally, the need for specialized hardware or microphone calibration may impact the widespread adoption of voice recognition. The privacy of voice data and the potential for unauthorized access to voiceprints are additional considerations in the deployment of this authentication mechanism.

Retinal and iris scans represent highly secure biometric methods, relying on the unique patterns of blood vessels in the retina or the colored part of the eye. The strengths include high accuracy and difficulty in forgery. However, vulnerabilities include the need for specialized hardware, potential user discomfort, and privacy concerns related to capturing detailed images of the eye. Striking a balance between the security benefits and user acceptance remains a challenge in the broader adoption of retinal and iris scans.

Multi-factor authentication (MFA), combining multiple authentication methods, addresses the limitations of single-factor authentication. The strength of MFA lies in its layered approach, requiring attackers to compromise multiple factors for unauthorized access. Knowledge-based factors, such as passwords, provide the first layer, possession-based factors involve something the user possesses (e.g., a smartphone), and biometric factors contribute an additional layer of assurance. MFA significantly enhances security but comes with challenges, including usability concerns, potential costs associated with additional hardware or software, and the need for user education and support. Striking a balance between security and user experience is crucial for successful MFA implementation.

In conclusion, each authentication mechanism brings its own strengths and vulnerabilities to the realm of digital security. Traditional passwords, while familiar, are susceptible to weaknesses such as weak choices and susceptibility to phishing. Biometrics offer enhanced security through unique physiological or behavioral characteristics, yet they face challenges related to privacy, accuracy, and potential compromise. Facial and voice recognition provide convenient alternatives, but ethical and privacy considerations must be carefully managed. Retinal and iris scans offer high security but come with practical and privacy-related challenges. Multi-factor authentication stands out for its layered approach, significantly boosting security but requiring careful consideration of usability and implementation challenges. As technology evolves, the quest for the most secure, user-friendly, and privacy-respecting authentication mechanisms continues, underscoring the dynamic nature of digital security in an interconnected world.

Understanding the concept of RBAC for user authorization.
Role-Based Access Control (RBAC) stands as a fundamental paradigm in the realm of user authorization, providing a structured and efficient approach to managing access to resources within an or-

ganization's digital environment. At its core, RBAC revolves around the concept of roles, which represent a collection of permissions or privileges associated with specific job functions or responsibilities within an organization. This approach contrasts with the more traditional discretionary access control methods, where individual users are directly assigned permissions. RBAC streamlines the complexity of managing user access by assigning roles to users based on their job responsibilities, facilitating more granular and systematic control over permissions.

One of the key strengths of RBAC lies in its ability to align access privileges with organizational roles. This alignment simplifies the process of assigning and revoking permissions, as changes to a user's responsibilities can be reflected by adjusting their role membership rather than individually modifying permissions. For instance, a finance manager might be assigned the 'Finance Manager' role, which includes permissions to access financial databases, generate reports, and perform financial transactions. Should the individual's responsibilities change, adjusting their role membership automatically updates their access privileges, ensuring a seamless and accurate reflection of their current role within the organization.

The concept of roles within RBAC introduces a hierarchical structure, allowing for the creation of nested or inherited roles. This hierarchy streamlines the administration of access control by establishing a logical relationship between roles, where certain roles inherit permissions from higher-level roles. This feature simplifies the assignment of access rights, as lower-level roles inherit the permissions of their parent roles. For example, a 'Supervisor' role might inherit permissions from both the 'Employee' and 'Team Leader' roles, aggregating access rights without the need for redundant assignments. This hierarchical approach enhances the manageability and scalability of access control in large organizations with diverse user roles and responsibilities.

Central to the RBAC model is the concept of permissions, representing the specific actions or operations that a user with a given role can perform on resources. Permissions define the boundaries of access control, ensuring that users only have the privileges necessary for their designated roles. RBAC distinguishes between various types of permissions, including read, write, execute, and delete operations, enabling fine-grained control over user interactions with resources. This precision in defining permissions contributes to a robust security posture, preventing unnecessary access and potential misuse of critical resources.

The RBAC model also introduces the concept of constraints, which are conditions or restrictions placed on the assignment of roles or permissions. Constraints allow organizations to tailor access control based on contextual factors, such as time of day, location, or specific user attributes. For instance, a constraint might limit access to sensitive data during non-working hours or restrict access to certain resources based on the geographic location of the user. Constraints add a layer of flexibility and adaptability to RBAC, enabling organizations to align access control with specific operational or security requirements.

RBAC provides a mechanism for separating the responsibilities of system administration and access control. The assignment of roles and management of role hierarchies typically falls within the purview of system administrators or security personnel. This separation of duties enhances security by reducing the risk of unauthorized modifications to access control settings. Regular users, in their respective roles, can benefit from the streamlined and consistent access control facilitated by RBAC without being burdened with the complexities of managing permissions or role assignments.

Scalability is a significant advantage of RBAC, particularly in large and complex organizational structures. As the number of users and roles grows, RBAC remains a scalable solution, offering a systematic and manageable approach to access control. This scalability is achieved through the abstraction of permissions into roles, allowing organizations to scale their access control infrastructure without resorting to an exponential increase in the number of individual user permissions. The hierarchical nature of RBAC further supports scalability by simplifying the management of roles and their relationships in large and dynamic environments.

While RBAC offers numerous advantages, it is not without its challenges. Role explosion, a phenomenon where the proliferation of roles becomes difficult to manage, is a common concern. Organizations must carefully design and maintain role hierarchies to avoid unnecessary complexity and ensure that roles align with actual job functions. Additionally, defining and updating roles accurately to reflect organizational changes requires a meticulous approach to prevent misalignments between roles and responsibilities.

Implementing RBAC necessitates a well-defined process for role engineering, which involves the creation, modification, and removal of roles based on organizational needs. Role engineering requires collaboration between system administrators, security personnel, and other stakeholders to ensure that roles accurately reflect the current organizational structure and job responsibilities. Regular reviews and audits of role assignments are essential to maintaining the integrity and effectiveness of RBAC over time.

In conclusion, Role-Based Access Control (RBAC) stands as a powerful and widely adopted model for user authorization, offering a structured and scalable approach to access control. By organizing permissions into roles and establishing hierarchical relationships, RBAC simplifies the administration of user access, enhances security, and aligns with organizational structures and job functions. The concept of roles, permissions, and constraints forms the foundation of RBAC, providing a flexible and adaptable framework for access control in diverse and dynamic digital environments. While challenges such as role explosion and the need for meticulous role engineering exist, the benefits of RBAC in terms of manageability, scalability, and precision in access control make it a cornerstone in the design and implementation of secure authorization systems.

Implementing RBAC to control user access based on roles and responsibilities.

Implementing Role-Based Access Control (RBAC) is a strategic endeavor aimed at enhancing the precision, efficiency, and security of user access within an organization. At the core of RBAC implementation is the meticulous process of role engineering, which involves defining, organizing, and assigning roles based on the responsibilities and job functions within the organization. The first step in this process is to conduct a thorough analysis of the organizational structure and the various job roles existing within the enterprise. This analysis serves as the foundation for identifying the distinct responsibilities associated with different positions, ensuring that roles accurately represent the access needs of individuals based on their job functions.

Once the roles are identified, the next step is to define the permissions associated with each role. Permissions, representing the specific actions or operations that users within a role are allowed to perform, must align closely with the responsibilities of the corresponding job function. This granular approach to defining permissions ensures that users are granted access only to the resources and actions necessary for the effective execution of their roles. This step demands collaboration between system administrators, security personnel, and other stakeholders to ensure a comprehensive understanding of the access requirements associated with each role.

Building upon the defined roles and permissions, RBAC introduces the concept of a role hierarchy, which establishes relationships between roles based on the organizational structure and job responsibilities. The hierarchy facilitates the inheritance of permissions from higher-level roles to lower-level roles, streamlining the assignment of access rights. For example, a 'Manager' role might inherit permissions from both the 'Employee' and 'Supervisor' roles, creating a logical and efficient structure that mirrors the reporting relationships within the organization. This hierarchical arrangement simplifies the administration of access control, especially in larger organizations with complex structures.

In practice, RBAC allows for the creation of roles that accurately mirror the job functions within the organization, such as 'Sales Representative,' 'Finance Manager,' or 'Human Resources Specialist.' Each role is associated with specific permissions relevant to the corresponding responsibilities, such as accessing customer data, financial records, or personnel files. The granularity of these roles ensures that individuals are granted access only to the resources and actions required for their designated tasks, minimizing the risk of unauthorized access.

Assigning roles to users constitutes a crucial aspect of RBAC implementation. Users are placed within roles based on their job responsibilities, and their access rights are determined by the permissions associated with those roles. This process requires close collaboration between the IT department, human resources, and department managers to ensure accurate role assignments that reflect the evolving responsibilities of individuals within the organization. Automated tools and identity management systems can streamline this process, ensuring that role assignments remain up-to-date as organizational changes occur.

An essential feature of RBAC is its support for dynamic role assignment and modification. As job responsibilities change or employees move between departments, the RBAC model allows for the dynamic adjustment of role assignments. This adaptability ensures that access privileges accurately reflect the current roles and responsibilities of individuals within the organization. For example, if an employee transitions from a sales role to a managerial role, their role assignment can be updated to reflect the change in responsibilities, granting or revoking access rights accordingly.

The RBAC model also introduces the concept of constraints, enabling organizations to tailor access control based on contextual factors. Constraints may include conditions or restrictions on role assignments or permissions, such as limiting access to certain resources during specific times or based on geographic locations. These constraints add a layer of flexibility to RBAC, allowing organizations to align access control with specific operational or security requirements. For instance, a constraint might restrict access to sensitive information only to employees within the corporate premises during business hours.

Regular reviews and audits are imperative components of RBAC implementation to ensure the ongoing accuracy and effectiveness of access control. Periodic assessments involve evaluating role assignments, permissions, and constraints to identify discrepancies and address any misalignments. These reviews may be triggered by organizational changes, compliance requirements, or security incidents. The goal is to maintain the integrity of the RBAC model and address any deviations promptly, ensuring that access control remains aligned with the evolving needs of the organization.

RBAC implementation is not without challenges. One common concern is the potential for role explosion, where the proliferation of roles becomes difficult to manage. To mitigate this risk, organizations must adopt a structured approach to role engineering, avoiding unnecessary complexity and ensuring that roles accurately reflect job functions. Role engineering involves ongoing collaboration between system administrators, security personnel, and department managers to refine and optimize the role hierarchy as the organization evolves.

To facilitate RBAC implementation, organizations often leverage specialized identity and access management (IAM) systems.

These systems provide a centralized platform for defining roles, managing role assignments, and enforcing access control policies. IAM systems also offer features such as role-based provisioning and de-provisioning, which automate the process of granting and revoking access based on role assignments. Additionally, these systems may include reporting and auditing capabilities to facilitate regular reviews and assessments of access control configurations.

In conclusion, implementing RBAC for user authorization is a strategic approach to access control that aligns user permissions with organizational roles and responsibilities. The process involves meticulous role engineering, defining permissions, establishing role hierarchies, and dynamically assigning roles based on user responsibilities. RBAC introduces a hierarchical structure that mirrors organizational reporting relationships, streamlining the administration of access control. Regular reviews and audits are essential to ensuring the accuracy and effectiveness of RBAC, while challenges such as role explosion necessitate a structured approach to role engineering. Leveraging IAM systems can enhance the efficiency of RBAC implementation, providing centralized control and automation features. Ultimately, RBAC stands as a powerful model for access control, offering a scalable, manageable, and precise approach to user authorization in dynamic organizational environments.

The benefits and challenges of implementing single sign-on solutions.

Implementing Single Sign-On (SSO) solutions presents a myriad of benefits and challenges, reflecting the complex landscape of modern digital environments. On the positive side, one of the most notable advantages of SSO is enhanced user convenience. By allowing users to access multiple applications and services with a single set of credentials, SSO streamlines the authentication process, reducing the burden of remembering and managing multiple passwords. This not only improves user experience but also contributes to increased productivity as users can seamlessly navigate through various systems without the need for repetitive login procedures. Furthermore, SSO significantly mitigates the risk of password fatigue and the subsequent security vulnerabilities that may arise from weak or reused passwords.

Security gains also constitute a substantial benefit of SSO implementation. With a centralized authentication system, organizations can enforce stronger password policies and multifactor authentication, bolstering overall security posture. The reduction in password-related issues, such as forgotten passwords or locked accounts, leads to decreased support costs and enhanced operational efficiency. Moreover, SSO facilitates quicker user provisioning and de-provisioning processes, ensuring that access privileges are promptly granted or revoked as employees join or leave the organization. This not only aligns with security best practices but also simplifies compliance with regulatory requirements.

Cost-effectiveness emerges as another advantage of SSO solutions. The streamlined authentication process reduces the workload on IT support teams, translating into lower operational costs. Additionally, SSO eliminates the need for users to invest time and effort in managing multiple credentials, further contributing to increased productivity. The economies of scale associated with centralized authentication systems can lead to long-term cost savings, particularly in large enterprises where managing numerous individual authentication processes can become resource-intensive.

However, the implementation of SSO is not without its challenges. One significant concern is the potential for a single point of failure. If the SSO system experiences a technical glitch or a security breach occurs, it could compromise access to multiple applications simultaneously, posing a severe risk to the organization's operations. Consequently, robust backup and recovery mechanisms are imperative to ensure uninterrupted access and mitigate the impact of potential outages.

Interoperability issues may also arise during the implementation of SSO, particularly when integrating with legacy systems or applications that do not support modern authentication protocols. The process of adapting existing infrastructure to seamlessly work with an SSO solution can be complex and time-consuming. Furthermore, ensuring compatibility with external partners or cloud-based services may present additional challenges, necessitating careful planning and coordination.

Security concerns constitute a dual-edged aspect of SSO implementation. While SSO enhances security through centralized control and enforcement of access policies, it also introduces a single point of attack for malicious actors. Successful compromise of the SSO system could grant unauthorized access to a plethora of applications, amplifying the potential damage. Therefore, robust security measures, such as encryption, continuous monitoring, and threat detection mechanisms, are crucial to safeguard the integrity of the SSO infrastructure.

Balancing security and user experience represents an ongoing challenge in SSO implementation. Organizations must strike a delicate equilibrium to ensure that security measures do not impede user convenience. Stricter security protocols, such as multifactor authentication, may be met with resistance from users seeking a frictionless experience. Achieving the right balance requires thoughtful design, user education, and ongoing communication to foster a security-conscious culture without compromising usability.

Another challenge lies in managing the transition to SSO within an organization. The migration process may disrupt existing workflows and necessitate comprehensive training for end-users. Resistance to change and potential pushback from employees accustomed to traditional authentication methods can pose obstacles. A well-thought-out change management strategy, including communication plans and training programs, is essential to smooth the transition and garner user acceptance.

In conclusion, the implementation of Single Sign-On solutions offers numerous benefits, ranging from improved user convenience and enhanced security to cost-effectiveness. However, organizations must navigate challenges such as the risk of a single point of failure, interoperability issues, and the delicate balance between security and user experience. Successful SSO implementation requires meticulous planning, robust security measures, and ongoing efforts to adapt to evolving technological landscapes. As organizations continue to embrace digital transformation, SSO remains a critical component in shaping a secure, efficient, and user-friendly authentication environment.

Integration of SSO to streamline user authentication across multiple systems.

The integration of Single Sign-On (SSO) represents a strategic initiative undertaken by organizations to streamline user authentication processes across a myriad of systems, fostering efficiency, security, and enhanced user experiences. At its core, SSO serves as a unifying mechanism, allowing users to access multiple applications and services with a single set of credentials. This consolidation of authentication not only alleviates the burden on users who would otherwise have to manage and remember multiple passwords but also optimizes the overall workflow within an organization. The seamless authentication experience enables users to navigate various systems without the hindrance of repetitive logins, promoting a more fluid and user-friendly computing environment.

One of the primary advantages of SSO integration is the substantial improvement in user convenience. Traditionally, users grapple with the challenge of remembering numerous passwords for different applications, leading to frustration and inefficiencies. With

SSO, this hurdle is effectively mitigated, as users only need to authenticate once to gain access to a multitude of systems. This enhanced convenience translates into time savings and a more positive user experience, contributing to increased productivity across the organization. The reduction in friction associated with authentication processes is particularly impactful in modern workplaces where employees engage with diverse applications to perform their tasks.

Security considerations stand as a pivotal driving force behind the adoption of SSO integration. By centralizing authentication processes, organizations gain the ability to enforce stronger security measures consistently across all applications. SSO facilitates the implementation of robust password policies, including requirements for complexity and regular updates, reducing the likelihood of security breaches resulting from weak or compromised passwords. Additionally, organizations can implement multifactor authentication more seamlessly, further fortifying their security posture. This centralized control not only enhances the organization's ability to safeguard sensitive information but also simplifies compliance with regulatory requirements regarding access controls and user authentication.

The cost-effectiveness of SSO integration emerges as another compelling factor motivating organizations to adopt this approach. The streamlined authentication process directly translates into reduced operational costs, as support teams spend less time addressing password-related issues and managing access credentials. The economies of scale associated with a centralized authentication system contribute to long-term cost savings, especially in large enterprises where the management of individual authentication processes can be resource-intensive. The optimized workflow and reduced support workload create an environment conducive to operational efficiency and financial sustainability.

However, the integration of SSO is not without its challenges. One notable concern is the potential vulnerability introduced by having a single point of authentication. If the SSO system encounters technical issues or, worse yet, becomes the target of a security breach, the consequences can be severe. A compromise of the SSO infrastructure could grant unauthorized access to a plethora of applications, significantly amplifying the potential impact of such an incident. To mitigate this risk, organizations must implement robust backup and recovery mechanisms to ensure continuity of access and minimize disruptions.

Interoperability issues pose another challenge during the integration of SSO, particularly when dealing with legacy systems or applications that do not support modern authentication protocols. The process of adapting existing infrastructure to seamlessly work with an SSO solution can be complex and time-consuming. Ensuring compatibility with external partners or cloud-based services may require meticulous planning and coordination to overcome potential hurdles, emphasizing the importance of a comprehensive integration strategy.

The dual nature of security concerns adds a layer of complexity to SSO integration. While the centralized control provided by SSO enhances security through consistent enforcement of access policies, it also introduces a single point of attack for malicious actors. Successfully compromising the SSO system could result in unauthorized access to a broad spectrum of applications, magnifying the potential damage. Therefore, organizations must implement stringent security measures, including robust encryption, continuous monitoring, and advanced threat detection mechanisms, to safeguard the integrity of the SSO infrastructure.

The delicate balance between security and user experience constitutes an ongoing challenge in the realm of SSO integration. Organizations must navigate this balance carefully, ensuring that security measures are robust enough to protect against potential threats while not impeding the seamless experience users expect. Stricter security protocols, such as multifactor authentication, may be met with resistance from users seeking a frictionless experience. Achieving the right equilibrium requires thoughtful design, user education, and ongoing communication to foster a security-conscious culture without compromising usability.

Managing the transition to SSO within an organization poses additional challenges. The migration process may disrupt existing workflows, and comprehensive training for end-users becomes essential. Resistance to change and potential pushback from employees accustomed to traditional authentication methods can pose obstacles. Therefore, a well-thought-out change management strategy, including communication plans and training programs, is imperative to smooth the transition and garner user acceptance.

In conclusion, the integration of Single Sign-On solutions offers a multifaceted approach to enhancing user authentication processes across diverse systems. While SSO brings undeniable benefits such as improved user convenience, heightened security, and cost-effectiveness, it is not without its complexities and challenges. Organizations embarking on the journey of SSO integration must carefully navigate the delicate balance between security and user experience, address potential interoperability issues, and implement comprehensive strategies to manage the transition effectively. As digital landscapes evolve, SSO remains a critical component in shaping a secure, efficient, and user-friendly authentication environment within organizations.

Utilizing access control lists to specify user permissions on resources.

Access control lists (ACLs) play a pivotal role in managing and defining user permissions on various resources within a computing environment. In the realm of information security, ACLs serve as a robust mechanism to regulate access and control over files, directories, networks, or any other system resource. These lists operate by associating specific permissions with individual users or groups, thereby dictating their level of interaction with the designated resources. ACLs essentially act as a gatekeeper, determining who can perform what actions on a given resource. This fine-grained control is crucial in safeguarding sensitive information and ensuring that only authorized individuals or entities can manipulate or access specific assets.

One of the fundamental aspects of ACLs is their flexibility in tailoring access permissions to the unique requirements of different users or groups. Each entry in the ACL typically consists of a combination of permissions, such as read, write, and execute, along with the associated user or group identifier. This granular approach allows administrators to craft a nuanced security framework, aligning precisely with the organizational structure and the nature of the tasks each user or group is entrusted with. For instance, a finance department might have read and write access to financial reports, while the marketing team might only have read access to the same files.

In the context of file systems, ACLs come into play when determining who can view, modify, or delete files and directories. These permissions extend beyond the basic owner, group, and other categorizations, enabling administrators to establish highly specific rules for access. In a multi-user environment, this capability becomes particularly valuable, as it empowers administrators to create tailored access policies for diverse user roles. Moreover, ACLs often offer the advantage of inheritance, allowing permissions to cascade down from parent directories to their subdirectories and files. This hierarchical approach streamlines the management of access controls, ensuring consistency and reducing the administrative burden.

Networks also benefit significantly from the implementation of ACLs. In this context, ACLs are commonly employed on routers and switches to regulate traffic flow and define which devices or users can communicate with specific network resources. By specifying rules within the ACLs, administrators can delineate which IP addresses, protocols, or ports are permitted or denied, effectively shaping the network's security posture. This meticulous control is instrumental in preventing unauthorized access, mitigating potential security threats, and optimizing network performance by managing bandwidth usage.

In addition to file systems and networks, ACLs are integral to database management systems (DBMS). In this domain, ACLs govern who can view, edit, or delete specific records or tables within a database. This level of control is invaluable in scenarios where different departments or teams share a common database but require distinct levels of access. For instance, a human resources department may need exclusive access to employee records, while a customer support team might only require read access to certain customer information. ACLs empower administrators to tailor these permissions, enhancing data security and confidentiality.

Furthermore, the concept of ACLs extends beyond the traditional realms of computing to encompass various technological ecosystems. Cloud computing, for example, leverages ACLs to manage access to cloud resources, such as virtual machines, storage, and databases. As organizations increasingly embrace cloud services, the role of ACLs becomes even more critical in ensuring that only authorized personnel can interact with sensitive data hosted in the cloud. Cloud service providers often offer sophisticated ACL management interfaces, allowing users to define and refine access controls in alignment with their specific requirements.

While ACLs are a powerful tool in the arsenal of security measures, their implementation requires careful consideration and ongoing management. A crucial aspect is the need for regular audits and reviews to validate that the assigned permissions align with the organization's evolving structure and operational demands. Over time, personnel changes, project requirements, and restructuring may necessitate adjustments to ACLs to maintain an optimal balance between security and operational efficiency. Administrators must also remain vigilant to potential security risks, such as privilege escalation, where users may gain unintended access by exploiting loopholes in the ACL configuration.

In conclusion, access control lists represent a cornerstone in the architecture of modern information security. Their ability to finely tune user permissions on diverse resources, including file systems, networks, and databases, makes them an indispensable tool for organizations seeking to safeguard their data and maintain operational integrity. The flexibility inherent in ACLs allows for the creation of tailored access policies that mirror the intricacies of an organization's structure, ensuring that users and groups only have the permissions necessary for their respective roles. As technology continues to advance and computing environments become increasingly complex, ACLs will likely continue to evolve, adapting to new challenges and providing administrators with the means to enforce robust access controls in an ever-changing landscape of digital security.

Fine-tuning access control through ACL configurations.

Fine-tuning access control through Access Control Lists (ACLs) is a critical aspect of information security, offering a nuanced approach to regulating user permissions across various resources within a computing environment. ACL configurations provide a versatile and granular method for administrators to exercise control over file systems, networks, databases, and other technological ecosystems. At the core of ACLs is the ability to specify precisely which actions, such as read, write, or execute, individual users or groups can perform on a given resource. This level of detail empowers organizations to tailor access policies according to their unique operational requirements, ensuring that users only possess the permissions essential to their specific roles.

In the realm of file systems, ACL configurations extend beyond traditional ownership and group permissions. They enable administrators to define access rights at a more detailed level, such as granting specific users or groups the ability to read or modify particular files and directories. This fine-grained control is particularly valuable in scenarios where diverse teams or departments share a common file repository, allowing administrators to craft access rules that align with the principle of least privilege. For example, while the marketing team may need read access to a shared folder containing promotional materials, the finance department could be granted read and write access to financial reports, reflecting their distinct responsibilities.

Networks benefit significantly from the meticulous control offered by ACL configurations. Routers and switches, for instance, use ACLs to regulate the flow of traffic based on predefined rules. Administrators can specify which devices or users are allowed to communicate with specific network resources by setting up rules within the ACL. This capability is crucial for enhancing network security, preventing unauthorized access, and optimizing performance by managing bandwidth effectively. ACLs in network configurations also play a pivotal role in safeguarding against potential security threats, as they enable administrators to control access based on criteria such as IP addresses, protocols, and ports.

Database management systems (DBMS) leverage ACL configurations to govern access to data stored within databases. In this context, ACLs define which users or groups have the authority to view, edit, or delete specific records or tables. This level of control is paramount in ensuring data security and confidentiality, especially in environments where multiple departments or teams interact with a shared database. For example, a human resources department may be granted exclusive access to sensitive employee records, while a customer support team might have read-only access to certain customer information. ACL configurations thus provide the flexibility needed to align access permissions with the diverse needs of different organizational units.

Cloud computing, with its dynamic and scalable nature, relies heavily on ACL configurations to manage access to cloud resources. Cloud service providers offer robust interfaces that allow users to define and refine ACLs for virtual machines, storage, databases, and other hosted services. The ability to fine-tune access controls in the cloud is crucial as organizations increasingly migrate their infrastructure to cloud environments. ACL configurations enable administrators to maintain a secure posture, ensuring that only authorized personnel can interact with sensitive data hosted in the cloud. This adaptability is essential in addressing the evolving landscape of cloud computing, where agility and security must coexist.

While ACL configurations provide a powerful means of access control, their implementation requires careful consideration and ongoing management. Regular audits and reviews are necessary to ensure that ACLs remain aligned with the organization's structure, personnel changes, and operational requirements. Administrators must stay vigilant to potential security risks, such as privilege escalation, where users may gain unintended access by exploiting vulnerabilities in the ACL configuration. As organizations evolve and technologies advance, the adaptability of ACL configurations becomes paramount in maintaining a robust and effective security posture.

In conclusion, fine-tuning access control through ACL configurations is a strategic imperative for organizations seeking to fortify their information security practices. The versatility and granularity offered by ACLs empower administrators to create tailored access policies that reflect the intricacies of their organizational structure and operational workflows. Whether applied to file systems, networks, databases, or cloud environments, ACL configurations provide a flexible and effective mechanism for controlling user permissions. As the digital landscape continues to evolve, the role of ACLs in ensuring security and access control is likely to become even more pronounced, underscoring their significance in the broader context of information technology and organizational resilience.

The role of biometrics in enhancing user authentication.

The role of biometrics in enhancing user authentication is a pivotal aspect of modern security frameworks, revolutionizing the way individuals gain access to various systems and sensitive information. Biometrics, as a field, encompasses the use of unique physiological or behavioral characteristics to verify and authenticate a person's identity. Unlike traditional authentication methods relying on passwords or tokens, biometric authentication leverages inherent and distinctive traits, adding an extra layer of security. The adoption of biometrics is driven by the need for robust and user-friendly authentication solutions in an era where cyber threats are increasingly sophisticated, and the vulnerabilities of traditional methods are more apparent.

Physiological biometrics involve the use of physical characteristics, such as fingerprints, facial features, iris patterns, or even DNA, to establish and confirm identity. Fingerprint recognition, perhaps one of the most widely recognized forms of physiological biometrics, relies on the unique ridge patterns and minutiae points on an individual's fingertips. Facial recognition, on the other hand, analyzes facial features, such as the distance between the eyes or the shape of the nose, to create a distinct biometric profile. Iris recognition focuses on the intricate patterns in the colored part of the eye, while DNA-based biometrics involve analyzing an individual's genetic code for unique markers. These physiological biometrics provide a high level of accuracy, as the probability of two individuals sharing identical traits is exceedingly low.

Behavioral biometrics, in contrast, capture patterns of behavior unique to an individual, such as keystroke dynamics, gait analysis, or voice patterns. Keystroke dynamics involve analyzing the typing rhythm and style of an individual, recognizing the subtle differences in how each person types. Gait analysis examines the distinct walking patterns of individuals, while voice recognition identifies and verifies individuals based on their unique vocal characteristics. Behavioral biometrics are particularly valuable in scenarios where continuous authentication is desired, as they can adapt to changes in an individual's behavior over time.

One of the key advantages of biometric authentication is its ability to provide a seamless and user-friendly experience. Unlike passwords or PINs that individuals may forget or lose, biometric traits are intrinsic and, for the most part, unalterable. This not only simplifies the authentication process for users but also reduces the risk associated with forgotten or easily guessable passwords. Additionally, the use of biometrics eliminates the need for individuals to remember multiple passwords for various accounts, addressing the common security concern of password reuse. The inherent nature of biometric traits adds a layer of convenience to the authentication process, fostering user acceptance and compliance.

Biometrics also enhances security by mitigating the risks associated with traditional authentication methods. Passwords and PINs are susceptible to various attacks, such as brute force attacks, where attackers systematically attempt to guess the correct password. Biometric traits, being unique to each individual, significantly raise the bar for unauthorized access attempts. Additionally, the physiological or behavioral characteristics used in biometric authentication are challenging to replicate or forge, providing a robust defense against impersonation or identity fraud. The use of multiple biometric factors for authentication, known as multimodal biometrics, further enhances security by requiring the verification of more than one biometric trait.

In the realm of financial transactions and online services, biometric authentication is increasingly being integrated to enhance security and prevent fraudulent activities. Mobile devices equipped with fingerprint sensors or facial recognition technology enable users to unlock their devices or authorize transactions with a simple touch or glance. This not only streamlines the user experience but also adds a layer of security that traditional methods struggle to match. Biometric authentication is particularly valuable in financial services, where the stakes are high, and the need for secure and seamless user identification is paramount.

The deployment of biometrics in border control and national security is another notable application. Airports and immigration checkpoints leverage facial recognition technology to verify the identity of travelers, enhancing the efficiency of the screening process while maintaining a high level of accuracy. This use of biometrics contributes to the broader goal of strengthening national security by ensuring that individuals entering or leaving a country are accurately identified and verified against government databases.

Despite the numerous advantages, the widespread adoption of biometric authentication is not without challenges and considerations. Privacy concerns are a significant factor, as the collection and storage of biometric data raise questions about the protection and potential misuse of such sensitive information. Establishing robust security measures for biometric databases and ensuring compliance with privacy regulations are crucial steps in addressing these concerns. Additionally, the potential for biometric data to be compromised or spoofed poses a continuous challenge, necessitating ongoing advancements in biometric technology to stay ahead of evolving threats.

In conclusion, the role of biometrics in enhancing user authentication represents a transformative shift in the landscape of digital security. The unique and intrinsic nature of biometric traits, whether physiological or behavioral, provides a robust and user-friendly means of verifying identity. From fingerprint and facial recognition to voice and gait analysis, biometrics offer diverse modalities for authentication, each with its strengths and applications. As technology continues to advance, and the need for secure and convenient authentication methods grows, biometrics is poised to play an increasingly central role in safeguarding digital identities across various domains, from personal devices and financial services to national borders and critical infrastructure. However, the ethical and privacy considerations associated with biometric data underscore the importance of responsible deployment and ongoing diligence in balancing security with individual rights and privacy protections.

Implementing biometric authentication systems for heightened security.

Implementing biometric authentication systems for heightened security represents a strategic and transformative approach in the realm of digital access controls. Biometrics, as a method of identity verification, relies on unique physiological or behavioral characteristics to authenticate individuals, offering a more robust and user-friendly alternative to traditional authentication methods. The process involves capturing and analyzing these distinctive traits, such as fingerprints, facial features, iris patterns, voice, or behavioral patterns like keystroke dynamics or gait, to create a unique biometric profile for each user. The integration of biometric authentication systems addresses the limitations of traditional methods, such as passwords or PINs, by leveraging features intrinsic to individuals, thus enhancing security while streamlining the user experience.

The implementation of biometric authentication systems begins with the selection of appropriate biometric modalities based on the specific security requirements and user scenarios. Fingerprint recognition, one of the most prevalent forms of biometrics, involves capturing and analyzing the unique ridge patterns and minutiae points on an individual's fingertips. Facial recognition technology, on the other hand, relies on capturing and comparing facial features, such as the distance between the eyes or the shape of the nose. Iris recognition focuses on the patterns in the colored part of the eye, while voice recognition analyzes unique vocal characteristics. The choice of biometric modality depends on factors like accuracy, ease of use, and the specific use case, with some applications benefiting from multimodal biometrics that combine multiple traits for enhanced security.

One of the key considerations in implementing biometric authentication systems is the integration of these technologies into existing infrastructure. Biometric systems are often deployed in conjunction with authentication servers, databases, and user management systems to facilitate the enrollment and verification processes. Enrollment involves capturing the biometric data of users and storing it securely in a centralized database. During verification, users' biometric traits are compared against the enrolled profiles to grant or deny access. Integration with existing systems requires careful planning to ensure compatibility and to minimize disruptions to established workflows. This integration extends to various domains, including personal devices, financial institutions, government agencies, and corporate environments.

In personal devices, the implementation of biometric authentication has become increasingly common, with smartphones and tablets incorporating features like fingerprint scanners or facial recognition sensors. These systems not only secure the device itself but also enable users to authorize transactions, access sensitive applications, or unlock encrypted data using their unique biometric traits. The seamless integration of biometrics into personal devices enhances the user experience, eliminating the need for cumbersome passwords and providing a more convenient and secure means of access.

Financial institutions have embraced biometric authentication systems to enhance security in online and mobile banking. Biometrics add an extra layer of protection to sensitive transactions, reducing the risk of unauthorized access or fraudulent activities. Fingerprint, facial, or voice recognition is often used to authenticate users during login or to authorize high-value transactions. The implementation of biometrics in the financial sector contributes to the overall security posture, protecting both individual users and the institution from cyber threats and identity fraud.

In government applications, biometric authentication plays a crucial role in border control, national security, and identity verification. Facial recognition technology, for instance, is employed at airports and immigration checkpoints to streamline the screening process by accurately verifying the identity of travelers against government databases. The implementation of biometrics in government systems contributes to the prevention of identity theft, enhances public safety, and supports law enforcement efforts by providing accurate and efficient means of identifying individuals.

Corporate environments deploy biometric authentication systems to secure physical access to premises, sensitive areas, or data centers. Fingerprint or iris recognition, for example, can replace traditional access cards or PIN-based systems, providing a more reliable and convenient method for employees to gain entry. Biometrics not only bolster security but also simplify access management for administrators, who can centrally control and monitor access permissions based on individual biometric profiles. This implementation is especially valuable in industries where the protection of sensitive information or assets is paramount.

The healthcare sector has also embraced biometric authentication systems to secure access to electronic health records, medical devices, and restricted areas within healthcare facilities. Fingerprint or palm vein recognition, for instance, provides healthcare professionals with a secure and efficient means of accessing patient data while ensuring compliance with privacy regulations. The implementation of biometrics in healthcare contributes to the protection of patient information, reduces the risk of unauthorized access, and enhances the overall efficiency of healthcare workflows.

Despite the benefits of biometric authentication, challenges and considerations must be addressed during implementation. Privacy concerns, particularly regarding the collection and storage of sensitive biometric data, necessitate the establishment of stringent security measures and compliance with privacy regulations. The potential for biometric data to be compromised or spoofed underscores the importance of ongoing advancements in biometric technology to stay ahead of evolving threats. Additionally, organizations must consider the scalability and interoperability of their biometric systems to accommodate growing user bases and evolving technologies.

The implementation of biometric authentication systems requires a comprehensive approach to user education and acceptance. Users need to understand the security benefits and the protection measures in place for their biometric data. Transparent communication regarding how biometric data is stored, processed, and protected fosters trust and encourages user acceptance. Educating users on the limitations and capabilities of biometric systems helps manage expectations and ensures a smoother transition from traditional authentication methods.

In conclusion, the implementation of biometric authentication systems represents a significant step towards achieving heightened security across various domains. The unique and intrinsic nature of biometric traits, coupled with their seamless integration into existing infrastructure, provides a robust and user-friendly solution to the challenges posed by traditional authentication methods. Whether securing personal devices, financial transactions, government applications, corporate environments, or healthcare systems, biometric authentication systems offer a versatile and effective means of enhancing security while enhancing the overall user experience. As technology continues to advance and the need for secure access controls intensifies, biometric authentication is poised to play an increasingly central role in safeguarding digital identities and sensitive information. Responsible implementation, addressing privacy concerns, and ongoing advancements in biometric technology are essential components of a successful and secure deployment, ensuring that the benefits of biometric authentication are realized without compromising individual privacy or system integrity.

Chapter 5: Data Encryption and Integrity

Overview of encryption algorithms used to secure data.

An overview of encryption algorithms used to secure data reveals the intricate and evolving landscape of cryptographic techniques designed to protect information from unauthorized access. Encryption serves as a fundamental pillar of modern cybersecurity, ensuring the confidentiality and integrity of sensitive data in a variety of contexts. Symmetric-key encryption, a foundational approach, involves the use of a single key for both encryption and decryption processes. Notable algorithms in this category include the Advanced Encryption Standard (AES), a widely adopted symmetric-key algorithm known for its efficiency and resilience against various attacks. AES operates on fixed-size blocks of data and supports key lengths of 128, 192, or 256 bits, providing a robust foundation for securing data in diverse applications.

Asymmetric-key encryption, or public-key cryptography, introduces the concept of two mathematically related keys: a public key for encryption and a private key for decryption. The RSA (Rivest–Shamir–Adleman) algorithm is a prominent example of asymmetric-key encryption widely used for secure communication and digital signatures. RSA relies on the difficulty of factoring large semiprime numbers, contributing to the security of the key pair. Public-key cryptography addresses some of the challenges associated with key distribution in symmetric-key systems, allowing secure communication between parties without a shared secret.

Elliptic Curve Cryptography (ECC) is another asymmetric-key encryption technique gaining popularity due to its efficiency and strong security properties. ECC leverages the mathematics of elliptic curves to provide the same level of security as traditional public-key algorithms with significantly shorter key lengths. This makes ECC particularly advantageous in resource-constrained environments, such as mobile devices or Internet of Things (IoT) devices, where computational efficiency is crucial.

Hash functions, while not encryption algorithms per se, are integral to data security by generating fixed-size output, or hash, from variable-size input. Cryptographic hash functions, such as SHA-256 (Secure Hash Algorithm 256-bit), are widely employed for integrity verification and password hashing. Hash functions should exhibit properties like collision resistance, ensuring that it is computationally infeasible to find two different inputs that produce the same hash value. As a result, even a minor alteration to the input data should yield a significantly different hash output, providing a robust means of verifying data integrity.

In the realm of securing data in transit over networks, the Transport Layer Security (TLS) protocol plays a crucial role. TLS, and its predecessor, the Secure Sockets Layer (SSL), employ a combination of symmetric and asymmetric encryption to establish secure communication channels over insecure networks. While various encryption algorithms can be used within TLS, commonly adopted ones include RSA for key exchange and authentication, and symmetric ciphers like AES for bulk data encryption. TLS ensures the confidentiality and integrity of data during transmission, safeguarding sensitive information exchanged between users and web servers.

Homomorphic encryption represents a groundbreaking approach that enables computations on encrypted data without decrypting it first. This innovation has significant implications for privacy-preserving computation, particularly in cloud computing scenarios where data owners may want to delegate computations without revealing the actual data. While homomorphic encryption is computationally intensive and comes with performance trade-offs, ongoing research and advancements aim to make it more practical for real-world applications.

Post-Quantum Cryptography (PQC) is gaining prominence as the field anticipates the advent of quantum computers capable of breaking widely used encryption algorithms, particularly those based on integer factorization or discrete logarithm problems. Lattice-based cryptography, hash-based cryptography, and code-based cryptography are among the post-quantum cryptographic approaches under consideration. These algorithms aim to withstand the computational power of quantum computers, ensuring that data encrypted using PQC remains secure even in the face of quantum threats.

Blockchain, the underlying technology of cryptocurrencies like Bitcoin, relies on cryptographic algorithms to secure the integrity and immutability of the distributed ledger. The SHA-256 hash function is a fundamental component in Bitcoin's proof-of-work consensus algorithm, contributing to the security of transaction blocks. Additionally, elliptic curve digital signatures (ECDSA) are employed to verify the authenticity of transactions, ensuring that only the legitimate owner of a private key can authorize a transfer.

In the context of password storage, key derivation functions (KDFs) are employed to transform user passwords into cryptographic keys. Argon2, scrypt, and bcrypt are examples of KDFs designed to slow down brute-force and rainbow table attacks by introducing computational intensity and memory requirements. By applying these functions to stored password hashes, organizations enhance the security of user credentials, protecting against unauthorized access even if the password hashes are compromised.

Quantum Key Distribution (QKD) represents an innovative cryptographic solution harnessing the principles of quantum mechanics to secure communication channels. QKD enables two parties to exchange cryptographic keys with the guarantee that any eavesdropping attempt will be detected. While QKD is in its early stages of practical implementation, it holds the promise of providing unconditionally secure key exchange, even in the face of quantum computing threats.

The selection of encryption algorithms is a nuanced process that requires consideration of various factors, including the specific use case, computational efficiency, key management, and resistance to known cryptographic attacks. As the field of cryptography continues to evolve in response to emerging technologies and threats, ongoing research focuses on developing algorithms that strike a balance between security, usability, and performance. The robustness of encryption algorithms remains paramount in safeguarding sensitive data across diverse applications, contributing to the resilience of digital communication, commerce, and information systems in an ever-evolving landscape of cybersecurity challenges.

Evaluating the strengths and suitability of different encryption methods.

Evaluating the strengths and suitability of different encryption methods is a complex undertaking that requires a comprehensive understanding of the diverse cryptographic techniques employed to secure digital data. Symmetric-key encryption, exemplified by the Advanced Encryption Standard (AES), stands out for its efficiency and versatility. With key lengths of 128, 192, or 256 bits, AES provides a robust foundation for securing data in various applications. Its strength lies in its ability to encrypt and decrypt data rapidly, making it well-suited for both small and large-scale implementations. However, the challenge with symmetric-key encryption lies in key management, as distributing and securely storing the key poses logistical concerns, particularly in scenarios involving multiple users.

Asymmetric-key encryption, also known as public-key cryptography, introduces the concept of two mathematically related keys: a public key for encryption and a private key for decryption. The RSA (Rivest–Shamir–Adleman) algorithm is a prominent example in this category, widely used for secure communication and digital signatures. RSA's strength lies in its reliance on the difficulty of factoring large semiprime numbers, providing a robust key pair. This method addresses the key distribution challenge inherent in symmetric-key systems, as users can freely share their public keys while keeping their private keys secure. However, RSA's computational intensity poses challenges in resource-constrained environments.

Elliptic Curve Cryptography (ECC), another asymmetric-key approach, leverages the mathematics of elliptic curves to offer robust security with shorter key lengths. ECC's strength lies in its efficiency and computational effectiveness, making it particularly advantageous in resource-constrained environments where bandwidth and processing power are limited. The shorter key lengths reduce the computational burden, enhancing performance without compromising security. ECC has gained prominence in securing communications and transactions on mobile devices and IoT devices, reflecting its suitability for scenarios with constrained resources.

Hash functions, while distinct from encryption, play a crucial role in data security. Cryptographic hash functions, such as SHA-256, generate fixed-size outputs, or hashes, from variable-size inputs. These functions are widely used for data integrity verification and password hashing. SHA-256's strength lies in its resistance to collisions — instances where different inputs produce the same hash value. This collision resistance ensures that even minor alterations to input data result in significantly different hash outputs, providing a reliable means of verifying data integrity. However, hash functions alone cannot recover the original data, limiting their applicability to specific security objectives.

In the context of securing data in transit over networks, the Transport Layer Security (TLS) protocol employs a combination of symmetric and asymmetric encryption. While various encryption algorithms can be used within TLS, RSA often features prominently in key exchange and authentication. RSA's strength in this context lies in its ability to establish secure communication channels over insecure networks, ensuring the confidentiality and integrity of data during transmission. However, the evolving landscape of cryptographic threats and the computational intensity of RSA has led to a shift towards more robust key exchange mechanisms, such as those based on elliptic curve cryptography.

Homomorphic encryption introduces a paradigm shift by enabling computations on encrypted data without the need for decryption. Its strength lies in its ability to preserve the privacy of data during computations, making it ideal for scenarios where data owners want to delegate computations without exposing sensitive information. However, homomorphic encryption is computationally intensive, impacting performance, and its practical adoption faces challenges related to scalability and efficiency. Ongoing research aims to enhance the feasibility of homomorphic encryption for real-world applications while addressing these computational challenges.

Post-Quantum Cryptography (PQC) arises from the recognition that quantum computers, when realized, could break widely used encryption algorithms based on integer factorization or discrete logarithm problems. Lattice-based cryptography, hash-based cryptography, and code-based cryptography are among the post-quantum cryptographic approaches. Their strength lies in their resilience against quantum attacks, offering a potential solution to the emerging threat posed by quantum computing. However, the field of post-quantum cryptography is still evolving, and standardization efforts are underway to establish widely accepted algorithms that balance security and efficiency.

Blockchain, the distributed ledger technology underlying cryptocurrencies like Bitcoin, relies on cryptographic algorithms to secure the integrity and immutability of the ledger. The SHA-256 hash function is a foundational component of Bitcoin's proof-of-work consensus algorithm, contributing to the security of transaction blocks. Additionally, elliptic curve digital signatures (ECDSA) verify the authenticity of transactions, ensuring that only the legitimate owner of a private key can authorize a transfer. The strength of these cryptographic methods lies in their ability to provide a decentralized and tamper-resistant system for recording and verifying transactions.

In password storage, key derivation functions (KDFs) play a critical role in transforming user passwords into cryptographic keys. Argon2, scrypt, and bcrypt are examples of KDFs designed to slow down brute-force and rainbow table attacks. Their strength lies in introducing computational intensity and memory requirements, making it more challenging for attackers to decipher passwords even if the hashed passwords are compromised. The choice of KDF depends on factors such as computational efficiency, memory usage, and resistance to emerging threats.

Quantum Key Distribution (QKD) represents a groundbreaking approach that uses quantum mechanics to secure communication channels. QKD's strength lies in its ability to detect eavesdropping attempts, providing an unconditionally secure key exchange method. However, practical challenges, such as the limited transmission distance and the need for specialized hardware, currently restrict its widespread adoption. As quantum technologies advance, QKD may play an increasingly significant role in securing communication against quantum threats.

In conclusion, evaluating the strengths and suitability of different encryption methods involves a nuanced consideration of factors such as security, computational efficiency, key management, and resistance to specific attacks. Each encryption method serves specific use cases and scenarios, addressing unique challenges in the evolving landscape of cybersecurity. The strengths of symmetric-key encryption, asymmetric-key encryption, hash functions, homomorphic encryption, post-quantum cryptography, blockchain, key derivation functions, and quantum key distribution highlight the diversity of cryptographic solutions available to safeguard digital data. As technologies continue to advance, the field of cryptography evolves to meet new challenges, emphasizing the ongoing need for robust and adaptable encryption methods in securing sensitive information across various domains.

Implementing file-level and disk-level encryption for data protection.

Implementing file-level and disk-level encryption represents a comprehensive approach to data protection, addressing the need for confidentiality and integrity across different layers of storage infrastructure. File-level encryption involves encrypting individual files, securing them with cryptographic algorithms to prevent unauthorized access. This method is particularly advantageous when granular control over access to specific files is necessary. The Advanced Encryption Standard (AES) is a widely adopted algorithm for file-level encryption due to its balance between security and efficiency. File-level encryption allows organizations to protect sensitive documents, ensuring that even if an unauthorized user gains access to the storage medium, the encrypted files remain indecipherable without the appropriate decryption key. This approach is commonly utilized in scenarios where specific files or directories require heightened security, such as in financial records, intellectual property, or personal information.

Disk-level encryption, on the other hand, focuses on encrypting entire disk volumes or partitions, providing a more encompassing layer of protection. Technologies like BitLocker for Windows or FileVault for macOS exemplify disk-level encryption solutions. Disk-level encryption safeguards all data stored on the disk, including the operating system and system files, making it a comprehensive defense against unauthorized access at the device level. The strength of disk-level encryption lies in its ability to protect against various attack vectors, including physical theft of the storage device. In enterprise environments, disk-level encryption is often applied to laptops and other mobile devices to mitigate the risk of data exposure in the event of device loss or theft.

File-level and disk-level encryption can coexist within a robust data protection strategy. A combination of both methods addresses different aspects of security and ensures a multi-layered defense against potential threats. In practice, organizations often deploy file-level encryption for specific sensitive documents or directories while implementing disk-level encryption for broader protection of entire storage volumes.

The implementation of file-level encryption typically involves the use of encryption software or tools that integrate with the operating system or file management systems. These tools provide user-friendly interfaces for encrypting and decrypting individual files or directories. Users are required to provide authentication credentials, such as passwords or cryptographic keys, to access the encrypted content. The encryption process occurs transparently in the background, ensuring minimal disruption to regular file operations. Additionally, some encryption tools allow for the creation of secure containers or virtual encrypted drives, enabling users to store sensitive files within an encrypted environment.

One notable advantage of file-level encryption is its flexibility in managing access controls. Administrators can assign different encryption keys or access permissions to specific users or groups, enabling fine-grained control over who can access certain files. This feature is valuable in collaborative environments where multiple users may need access to shared files, but not necessarily to all files within a storage medium. However, the decentralized nature of file-level encryption also requires careful key management to avoid the risk of losing access to important files if keys are misplaced or forgotten.

Disk-level encryption is often implemented at a lower level, directly interacting with the storage device or the file system. Operating system-integrated solutions like BitLocker or third-party tools like VeraCrypt offer disk-level encryption capabilities. The encryption process for disk-level solutions typically occurs during the initial setup or installation of the operating system. Users are required to provide authentication credentials during system boot to unlock the encrypted volume and gain access to the operating system and stored data. Disk-level encryption provides a more centralized approach to data protection, ensuring that all data on the disk is encrypted, regardless of the specific files or directories.

One of the key advantages of disk-level encryption is its ability to protect the entire system, including the operating system and system files. This comprehensive approach safeguards against various attack vectors, including attempts to bypass file-level encryption by targeting the underlying file system or gaining unauthorized access through system vulnerabilities. Disk-level encryption ensures that even if an attacker gains physical access to the storage medium, the encrypted data remains unreadable without the correct authentication credentials.

Furthermore, disk-level encryption is particularly beneficial for mobile devices, such as laptops, tablets, and smartphones, which are more susceptible to loss or theft. In the event of a device being misplaced, the encrypted data remains secure, mitigating the risk of unauthorized access to sensitive information. This is crucial for organizations with a mobile workforce or those handling sensitive data on portable devices.

The integration of file-level and disk-level encryption requires careful consideration of the specific security requirements, user workflows, and organizational policies. While both approaches contribute to a robust data protection strategy, their implementation involves trade-offs and considerations based on the unique needs of the environment.

Key management is a critical aspect of both file-level and disk-level encryption. Properly managing encryption keys ensures secure access to encrypted data while preventing unauthorized parties from decrypting it. Organizations must establish and enforce key management policies, addressing aspects such as key generation, distribution, storage, and rotation. Effective key management minimizes the risk of data loss due to forgotten or compromised keys and is essential for maintaining the integrity of the encryption implementation.

Usability and user education are important considerations in the successful implementation of encryption. Encryption solutions should be designed with user-friendly interfaces to minimize the impact on user workflows. Clear communication and training programs are essential to ensure that users understand the importance of encryption, the procedures for accessing encrypted data, and the consequences of mishandling cryptographic keys. User acceptance and compliance are crucial for the effectiveness of encryption strategies.

In addition to encryption, organizations must implement complementary security measures, such as access controls, authentication mechanisms, and regular security audits. These measures collectively contribute to a defense-in-depth strategy, enhancing the overall security posture of the organization. Regularly updating and patching software, including encryption tools, is imperative to address potential vulnerabilities and ensure the effectiveness of the implemented encryption solutions.

The regulatory landscape also plays a significant role in shaping encryption practices. Many industries, especially those handling sensitive or personally identifiable information, are subject to data protection regulations that mandate the use of encryption as a security safeguard. Compliance with these regulations not only ensures legal adherence but also demonstrates a commitment to protecting user privacy and sensitive information.

In conclusion, implementing file-level and disk-level encryption for data protection involves a strategic and multifaceted approach. File-level encryption provides granular control over specific files or directories, offering flexibility in access management. Disk-level encryption, on the other hand, provides comprehensive protection for entire storage volumes, safeguarding the entire system, including the operating system and system files. The integration of both encryption methods within an organization's security strategy offers a multi-layered defense against potential threats, addressing different aspects of data security. Careful consideration of key management, user education, usability, and regulatory compliance is essential for the successful implementation and effectiveness of encryption solutions. As organizations navigate the evolving landscape of cybersecurity threats, the judicious use of file-level and disk-level encryption remains a cornerstone in ensuring the confidentiality and integrity of sensitive data.

The impact of encryption on data integrity and access.

The impact of encryption on data integrity and access is profound, as encryption serves as a fundamental pillar in modern cybersecurity, influencing how data is protected, accessed, and maintained. Encryption, at its core, involves the use of cryptographic algorithms to transform data into a secure, unreadable format, rendering it indecipherable without the corresponding decryption key. One of the primary impacts of encryption on data integrity is its role in preventing unauthorized modifications or tampering of sensitive information. By encrypting data, organizations can ensure that only authorized individuals with the correct decryption keys can access and modify the information. This capability is particularly crucial in environments where data integrity is paramount, such as financial transactions, medical records, and legal documents.

The use of encryption also has a significant impact on data access, influencing who can read, modify, or interact with specific pieces of information. Access controls, often integrated with encryption, define and enforce the permissions granted to users or entities based on their roles, responsibilities, or specific cryptographic keys. This granular control over data access mitigates the risk of unauthorized users gaining entry to sensitive information, contributing to the overall security posture of an organization. Encryption ensures that even if an unauthorized entity gains access to the storage medium, the encrypted data remains incomprehensible without the corresponding decryption keys, thus safeguarding against unauthorized access and potential data breaches.

File-level encryption, as a specific application of encryption, impacts data integrity and access by securing individual files with cryptographic algorithms. This method allows organizations to selectively encrypt specific files or directories, offering flexibility in protecting sensitive information. File-level encryption is especially valuable in scenarios where different files may have varying security requirements, and the need for fine-grained access controls is crucial. The impact is notable in the assurance that even if an unauthorized user gains access to the storage medium, the encrypted files remain protected, preserving data integrity and restricting access to only those with the appropriate decryption keys.

Disk-level encryption, another manifestation of encryption, has a broader impact on data integrity and access by encrypting entire disk volumes or partitions. This approach provides a more encompassing layer of protection, ensuring that all data stored on the disk, including the operating system and system files, remains secure. Disk-level encryption is particularly impactful for devices with sensitive information, such as laptops or mobile devices, as it protects against unauthorized access in the event of physical theft or loss. The comprehensive nature of disk-level encryption extends its impact to both data integrity and access, offering a robust defense against various forms of unauthorized intrusion.

In the context of access controls, encryption plays a pivotal role in enforcing the principle of least privilege, ensuring that users or entities have only the necessary permissions to perform their specific tasks. This impact is crucial for preventing accidental or intentional data breaches that may occur when users have unnecessary access to sensitive information. By integrating encryption with access controls, organizations can tailor their security policies to align with specific data protection requirements, mitigating the risk of data exposure and ensuring that only authorized individuals can access sensitive data.

The impact of encryption on data integrity and access extends to data in transit over networks. The use of encryption protocols, such as Transport Layer Security (TLS) or its predecessor, Secure Sockets Layer (SSL), ensures the secure transmission of data between systems. This impact is particularly significant for online transactions, secure communication channels, and the protection of sensitive information during transit. The cryptographic protocols employed in data transport encryption contribute to the assurance that data integrity is maintained during communication and that only authorized parties can access the transmitted information.

Homomorphic encryption, a more advanced application of encryption, has a distinctive impact on data integrity and access by enabling computations on encrypted data without the need for decryption. This paradigm-shifting approach allows organizations to perform operations on sensitive data while it remains in an encrypted state. The impact of homomorphic encryption is particularly noteworthy in scenarios where privacy-preserving computation is paramount, such as in cloud computing environments. The ability to perform calculations on encrypted data without exposing the raw information offers a powerful means of maintaining data integrity while controlling access to sensitive computations.

Post-Quantum Cryptography (PQC), emerging as a response to the potential threat of quantum computers to existing encryption algorithms, has a significant impact on the long-term integrity and access to data. As quantum computers could potentially break widely used encryption methods, the development and adoption of post-quantum cryptographic algorithms become imperative. PQC aims to ensure that data encrypted using these algorithms remains secure even in the face of quantum threats. The impact of PQC lies in its proactive approach to preserving data integrity and access, offering a transition path to encryption methods that can withstand the computational power of quantum computers.

The impact of encryption on data integrity and access is not without challenges and considerations. Key management, a critical aspect of encryption, requires careful planning to ensure secure generation, distribution, storage, and rotation of cryptographic keys. Inadequate key management can undermine the effectiveness of encryption, potentially leading to data loss or exposure. Usability and user education also play a vital role in the impact of encryption, as organizations must strike a balance between robust security measures and user-friendly interfaces to encourage proper adoption and compliance.

Regulatory considerations, especially in industries dealing with sensitive or personally identifiable information, further shape the impact of encryption on data integrity and access. Compliance with data protection regulations often mandates the use of encryption as a security safeguard. The impact is evident in the legal and ethical obligation to protect user privacy and sensitive information, aligning encryption practices with industry standards and legal frameworks.

In conclusion, the impact of encryption on data integrity and access is far-reaching, influencing how organizations protect, control, and transmit sensitive information. Whether applied at the file-level, disk-level, or during data transport, encryption contributes to maintaining data integrity by preventing unauthorized modifications and ensuring that only authorized individuals can access encrypted information. The impact extends beyond traditional encryption methods to more advanced applications, such as homomorphic encryption and post-quantum cryptography, addressing emerging challenges in data security. As organizations navigate the dynamic landscape of cybersecurity threats, the judicious use of encryption remains a cornerstone in preserving the integrity of data and controlling access to sensitive information.

Understanding digital signatures as a means of ensuring data integrity.

Understanding digital signatures as a means of ensuring data integrity is paramount in the realm of digital communication, where the authenticity and unaltered state of data are crucial. Digital signatures employ cryptographic techniques to provide a verifiable and tamper-evident seal on digital documents, assuring recipients that the content has not been altered and that it originated from the claimed sender. The fundamental principle behind digital signatures lies in the use of asymmetric-key cryptography, which involves two mathematically related keys—a private key for signing and a public key for verification. The process begins with the sender generating a hash value, a fixed-size representation of the document's content, using a cryptographic hash function. The sender then encrypts this hash value with their private key, creating the digital signature. The recipient, armed with the sender's public key, can decrypt the signature and compare the resulting hash value with one generated from the received document. If the two hash values match, it verifies the document's integrity and the authenticity of the sender.

One of the key advantages of digital signatures in ensuring data integrity is their ability to detect even minor alterations to the signed data. The cryptographic hash function employed in the process is designed to produce a unique hash value for each unique set of data. Any change, no matter how small, to the original document results in a significantly different hash value. Thus, when the recipient uses the sender's public key to decrypt the digital signature, any inconsistency in the hash values becomes immediately apparent. This inherent tamper-evident quality makes digital signatures a robust tool for confirming the integrity of digital documents, providing a high level of assurance that the data has not been maliciously or inadvertently altered during transmission or storage.

The use of asymmetric-key cryptography in digital signatures contributes to their security and reliability. The private key, known only to the signer, is kept confidential and used exclusively for creating digital signatures. On the other hand, the public key is openly shared and can be distributed widely. This distinction ensures that while anyone can verify the digital signature using the public key, only the possessor of the private key can generate a valid signature. The security of digital signatures relies on the mathematical complexity of the underlying cryptographic algorithms, making it computationally infeasible for an adversary to forge a signature without access to the private key. This inherent asymmetry ensures the integrity of the data, as only the legitimate private key holder can produce a valid signature.

The deployment of digital signatures is widespread in various contexts, ranging from email communication to software distribution and financial transactions. In email communication, for instance, digital signatures provide a means for the sender to prove the authenticity of the message and its attachments. By signing an email with their private key, the sender assures the recipient that the content has not been altered in transit and that it indeed originated from the claimed sender. This application of digital signatures enhances data integrity, safeguarding against unauthorized modifications and ensuring the reliability of electronic communication.

In the realm of software distribution, digital signatures play a crucial role in verifying the authenticity and integrity of software packages. Software developers often sign their applications with a digital signature, allowing users to confirm that the software has not been tampered with or maliciously altered before installation. The digital signature serves as a trust anchor, offering users confidence that the software they are about to install has not been compromised during the distribution process. This practice enhances data integrity in the software supply chain, protecting end-users from the potential risks associated with corrupted or unauthorized software.

In financial transactions, digital signatures contribute significantly to the security and integrity of electronic transactions. Whether in online banking, digital contracts, or cryptocurrency transactions, the use of digital signatures ensures that financial data remains intact and unaltered. The application of digital signatures in financial transactions mitigates the risk of fraud and unauthorized access by providing a secure method for parties to verify the authenticity of electronic documents and transactions. This is particularly crucial in the era of online commerce and digital finance, where the integrity of financial data is paramount to building trust and ensuring the secure exchange of assets.

The concept of a Certificate Authority (CA) is integral to the widespread adoption and trustworthiness of digital signatures. A Certificate Authority acts as a trusted third party that verifies the identity of individuals, organizations, or entities wishing to use digital signatures. The CA issues digital certificates, which bind public keys to the identities of the certificate holders. When a recipient receives a digitally signed document, they can use the CA's public key to verify the authenticity of the signer's digital certificate. This chain of trust establishes a reliable link between the digital signature and the claimed identity of the signer, enhancing the overall integrity of the digital communication.

Public Key Infrastructure (PKI) further supports the deployment of digital signatures by providing a framework for managing digital keys and certificates. PKI facilitates the secure distribution and revocation of digital certificates, ensuring that only authorized individuals possess valid certificates for digital signing. The establishment of a robust PKI contributes to the scalability and reliability of digital signatures in large-scale applications, such as secure communication networks, where the integrity of data is a critical concern.

Despite the evident benefits of digital signatures, challenges exist, particularly concerning key management and the potential compromise of private keys. The security of digital signatures relies heavily on the secure storage and management of private keys, as a compromised private key could lead to unauthorized signature generation and a breach of data integrity. Key management practices, including the use of hardware security modules and secure key storage mechanisms, are essential to mitigating these risks. Additionally, the continuous evolution of cryptographic algorithms and the emergence of quantum computing pose considerations for the long-term security of digital signatures. Ongoing research and the adoption of post-quantum cryptographic algorithms are crucial to addressing these challenges and ensuring the continued effectiveness of digital signatures in maintaining data integrity.

In conclusion, digital signatures serve as a robust and widely adopted means of ensuring data integrity in the digital landscape. By leveraging asymmetric-key cryptography, digital signatures provide a tamper-evident seal on digital documents, assuring recipients of the unaltered state and authenticity of the data. The application of digital signatures spans various domains, including email communication, software distribution, and financial transactions, contributing to the security and reliability of electronic communication. The trustworthiness of digital signatures is further bolstered by the existence of Certificate Authorities and Public Key Infrastructure, which establish a chain of trust in verifying the identity of the signer. While challenges exist, particularly in key management and the potential impact of emerging technologies, the enduring significance of digital signatures in preserving data integrity underscores their pivotal role in the secure exchange of digital information.

The process of generating, verifying, and managing digital signatures.

The process of generating, verifying, and managing digital signatures is a multifaceted undertaking that relies on cryptographic principles to ensure the integrity and authenticity of digital documents. The generation of digital signatures begins with the use of asymmetric-key cryptography, involving two mathematically related keys—a private key for signing and a public key for verification. The sender, wishing to sign a digital document, first creates a hash value of the document's content using a cryptographic hash function. This hash value serves as a fixed-size representation of the document, unique to its content. The sender then encrypts this hash value with their private key, producing the digital signature. The resulting combination of the digital signature and the original document forms the signed digital document. This process ensures that the signature is unique to the document and can only be created by the possessor of the private key.

Verification of digital signatures is a complementary process that involves confirming the authenticity and integrity of a digitally signed document. The recipient, armed with the sender's public key, uses it to decrypt the digital signature and retrieve the hash value. Simultaneously, the recipient generates a new hash value of the received document using the same cryptographic hash function. If the decrypted hash value matches the newly generated hash value, the digital signature is deemed valid, confirming that the document has not been altered and that it indeed originated from the claimed sender. The public key serves as the verification mechanism, allowing anyone to verify the authenticity of the digital signature without requiring access to the sender's private key.

Key management is a critical aspect of the digital signature process, encompassing the secure generation, distribution, storage, and revocation of cryptographic keys. The private key, being the cornerstone of the digital signature generation, must be kept confidential and securely stored. In practice, this often involves the use of hardware security modules or secure key storage mechanisms to safeguard against unauthorized access or compromise. The public key, on the other hand, is distributed openly and may be included in a digital certificate issued by a trusted Certificate Authority (CA). Digital certificates, issued by CAs, bind the public key to the identity of the certificate holder, providing a chain of trust that enhances the reliability of digital signature verification. Proper key management practices are essential to the overall security of digital signatures, as the compromise of private keys could lead to unauthorized signature generation and a breach of data integrity.

The issuance and management of digital certificates fall under the broader framework of Public Key Infrastructure (PKI), which provides a systematic approach to key and certificate management. PKI establishes a trust infrastructure, ensuring that public keys are associated with their rightful owners and facilitating the secure distribution and revocation of digital certificates. The Certificate Authority (CA) plays a pivotal role within PKI, verifying the identity of certificate holders and vouching for the authenticity of their public keys. When a recipient verifies a digital signature, they rely on the associated digital certificate and the CA's public key to confirm the legitimacy of the signer. PKI contributes to the scalability and reliability of digital signatures in large-scale applications, ensuring that key and certificate management aligns with established security practices.

The generation, verification, and management of digital signatures find application in various domains, each with its unique requirements and considerations. In email communication, digital signatures provide a means for the sender to prove the authenticity of the message and its attachments. By signing an email with their private key, the sender assures the recipient that the content has not been altered in transit and that it indeed originated from the claimed sender. The use of digital signatures in emails enhances data integrity, safeguarding against unauthorized modifications and ensuring the reliability of electronic communication.

Software distribution represents another context where digital signatures play a crucial role in ensuring data integrity. Software developers often sign their applications with a digital signature, allowing users to confirm that the software has not been tampered with or maliciously altered before installation. The digital signature serves as a trust anchor, offering users confidence that the software they are about to install has not been compromised during the distribution process. This application of digital signatures enhances data integrity in the software supply chain, protecting end-users from potential risks associated with corrupted or unauthorized software.

In financial transactions, the generation and verification of digital signatures contribute significantly to the security and integrity of electronic transactions. Whether in online banking, digital contracts, or cryptocurrency transactions, the use of digital signatures ensures that financial data remains intact and unaltered. The application of digital signatures in financial transactions mitigates the risk of fraud and unauthorized access by providing a secure method for parties to verify the authenticity of electronic documents and transactions. This is particularly crucial in the era of online commerce and digital finance, where the integrity of financial data is paramount to building trust and ensuring the secure exchange of assets.

The process of managing digital signatures encompasses key life-cycle management, including key generation, distribution, rotation, and revocation. Key generation involves the creation of a secure pair of private and public keys, with the private key kept confidential and the public key openly distributed or included in a digital certificate. Distribution mechanisms ensure that public keys are available to those who need them for verification purposes. Regular key rotation, where new key pairs are generated and deployed, contributes to the long-term security of digital signatures by limiting the exposure of any single key pair over time. Key revocation becomes necessary when a private key is compromised or when the associated digital certificate needs to be invalidated. Proper key management practices, including secure storage mechanisms and secure channels for key distribution, are essential to maintaining the security and reliability of digital signatures.

Despite the evident benefits of digital signatures, challenges exist, particularly concerning key management and the potential compromise of private keys. The security of digital signatures relies heavily on the secure storage and management of private keys, as a compromised private key could lead to unauthorized signature generation and a breach of data integrity. Key management practices, including the use of hardware security modules and secure key storage mechanisms, are essential to mitigating these risks. Additionally, the continuous evolution of cryptographic algorithms and the emergence of quantum computing pose considerations for the long-term security of digital signatures. Ongoing research and the adoption of post-quantum cryptographic algorithms are crucial to addressing these challenges and ensuring the continued effectiveness of digital signatures in maintaining data integrity.

In conclusion, the process of generating, verifying, and managing digital signatures is foundational to the assurance of data integrity and authenticity in the digital realm. Through the use of asymmetric-key cryptography, digital signatures provide a tamper-evident seal on digital documents, assuring recipients that the content has not been altered and that it originated from the claimed sender. The principles of key management, digital certificates, and Public Key Infrastructure contribute to the security and scalability of digital signatures in various applications, including email communication, software distribution, and financial transactions. While challenges persist, the enduring significance of digital signatures underscores their pivotal role in the secure exchange of digital information and the preservation of data integrity.

The role of hash functions in maintaining data integrity.

The role of hash functions in maintaining data integrity is fundamental to modern cybersecurity, providing a robust mechanism for ensuring that data remains unaltered and authentic during transmission, storage, or processing. Hash functions are mathematical algorithms that take an input (or message) of any size and produce a fixed-size string of characters, often referred to as a hash value or hash code. The key characteristic of hash functions is their one-way nature, meaning that it is computationally infeasible to reverse the process and reconstruct the original input from the hash value. This irreversibility ensures that hash functions are suitable for creating unique fingerprints or digital signatures for data, facilitating the verification of data integrity.

A primary application of hash functions in maintaining data integrity is in the creation of digital fingerprints or checksums. When a piece of data is subjected to a hash function, it produces a fixed-size hash value that is unique to the specific input. Even a minor change in the input data, whether intentional or accidental, results in a significantly different hash value. This property enables the use of hash functions to detect alterations in data. By comparing the hash value of the original data with the hash value generated from the received or stored data, users can quickly determine whether the data has been tampered with. If the hash values match, it indicates that the data is likely unaltered, preserving data integrity.

Hash functions are extensively utilized in data verification processes, such as file integrity checks and digital signatures. In the context of file integrity, hash functions generate checksums for files, which are then published or stored separately. When users want to verify the integrity of a file, they recompute its hash value and compare it with the originally generated checksum. If the hash values match, it signifies that the file has not been modified since the checksum was generated, providing a high level of confidence in the file's integrity. This approach is widely used in software distribution, where users can verify the authenticity and integrity of downloaded files by comparing hash values.

Digital signatures also leverage hash functions to ensure the integrity of digitally signed documents. In this process, the sender creates a hash value of the document using a hash function and then encrypts this hash value with their private key to generate the digital signature. The recipient can then use the sender's public key to decrypt the digital signature and obtain the hash value. By independently computing the hash value of the received document and comparing it with the decrypted hash value, the recipient can verify the integrity of the document and confirm its authenticity. The role of hash functions in this context is crucial in providing a tamper-evident seal, safeguarding against unauthorized modifications and ensuring the reliability of digitally signed documents.

The collision-resistant property of hash functions is another significant aspect contributing to their role in maintaining data integrity. A collision occurs when two different inputs produce the same hash value. In cryptographic terms, a hash function is considered collision-resistant if finding two distinct inputs that result in the same hash value is computationally infeasible. This property ensures that the uniqueness of hash values is preserved, reinforcing the reliability of hash functions in data integrity applications. The collision-resistant nature of hash functions is essential for preventing attackers from creating manipulated data with the same hash value as the original data, thereby evading detection.

Hash functions play a pivotal role in the implementation of cryptographic protocols, including the creation and verification of digital signatures. The use of hash functions in digital signatures addresses the challenge of efficiently signing and verifying large amounts of data. Instead of signing the entire data set, which could be computationally expensive and impractical, a hash value of the data is signed. This not only reduces the computational burden but also provides an effective means of ensuring data integrity. The hash value serves as a compact representation of the data, making the signing and verification processes more efficient without compromising the security of the digital signature.

Beyond individual files and documents, hash functions contribute to the integrity of data structures and databases. In scenarios where large volumes of data need to be checked for integrity, hash functions are employed to generate hash values for data structures or database records. These hash values act as checksums or fingerprints for the corresponding data, allowing quick verification of data integrity. If the hash value of a data structure matches the precomputed hash value, it indicates that the data within the structure has not been altered. This approach is valuable in scenarios where the integrity of large datasets or databases needs to be regularly validated, ensuring that any tampering or corruption is promptly detected.

In the context of password security, hash functions are commonly employed for storing and verifying passwords securely. Instead of storing passwords in plaintext, systems store the hash values of passwords. During the authentication process, the system hashes the entered password and compares the resulting hash value with the stored hash value. If the hash values match, the entered password is considered valid. This hash-based approach enhances security by preventing exposure of plaintext passwords even if the hash values are compromised. The collision-resistant property of hash functions ensures that different passwords produce different hash values, reinforcing the security of password storage and verification systems.

While hash functions are robust tools for maintaining data integrity, it is essential to consider their vulnerability to brute-force attacks and advances in computing power. The effectiveness of hash functions in preserving data integrity relies on their resistance to collision attacks and preimage attacks. Cryptanalysts continually work to develop more efficient algorithms, and as computational capabilities evolve, the security of existing hash functions may be challenged. In response to this, the cryptographic community engages in ongoing research and standardization efforts to develop and adopt more secure hash functions and cryptographic protocols, mitigating the impact of potential vulnerabilities.

In conclusion, the role of hash functions in maintaining data integrity is foundational to the field of cybersecurity. Whether applied to file integrity checks, digital signatures, data structures, databases, or password security, hash functions provide a reliable and efficient means of creating unique fingerprints for data. Their one-way, collision-resistant nature ensures the integrity of data by enabling the detection of even minor alterations. As cryptographic protocols evolve and computing capabilities progress, the ongoing development and adoption of secure hash functions remain crucial to upholding the integrity and authenticity of digital information in an ever-changing digital landscape.

Selecting and implementing secure hash algorithms for various use cases.

Selecting and implementing secure hash algorithms for various use cases is a critical aspect of cybersecurity, influencing the integrity and authenticity of digital information. The choice of a hash algorithm depends on the specific requirements and characteristics of the use case, considering factors such as security, efficiency, and the potential impact of evolving technologies.

In many applications, cryptographic hash functions like SHA-256 (Secure Hash Algorithm 256-bit) are widely adopted due to their strength and collision resistance. SHA-256 produces a fixed-size hash value of 256 bits, providing a high degree of uniqueness for different inputs. This makes it suitable for scenarios where data integrity is paramount, such as in file integrity checks. Implementing SHA-256 for file integrity checks involves generating a hash value for a file and comparing it with a precomputed hash value. If the hash values match, it indicates that the file has not been altered, ensuring data integrity.

Similarly, when selecting a hash algorithm for password storage and verification, security is of utmost importance. In this context, using a key derivation function (KDF) with a salted hash, such as bcrypt or Argon2, is a recommended practice. These algorithms not only provide a one-way transformation of passwords into hash values but also introduce the concept of salting. Salting involves adding a unique and random value (salt) to each password before hashing, preventing attackers from using precomputed tables (rainbow tables) for password attacks. The use of bcrypt or Argon2, known for their resistance to brute-force and rainbow table attacks, enhances the security of password storage systems.

For digital signatures, hash algorithms are integral to the process of creating and verifying signatures. Commonly used hash functions in digital signature applications include SHA-256 and SHA-3. The choice often depends on the specific cryptographic standards or protocols in use. SHA-256, being widely adopted, ensures the creation of a unique hash value for the document being signed, contributing to the tamper-evident nature of digital signatures. As cryptographic standards evolve, the implementation of hash algorithms in digital signatures needs to align with current best practices and recommendations to maintain a high level of security.

In the realm of blockchain technology, which relies heavily on hash functions, SHA-256 is commonly employed for creating hash values of blocks. The uniqueness and collision resistance of SHA-256 contribute to the immutability and security of the blockchain. The cryptographic hash of each block includes the hash of the previous block, creating a chain that links the blocks together. This chaining mechanism ensures that altering the data in one block would require changing all subsequent blocks, providing a robust defense against tampering and preserving the integrity of the blockchain.

As quantum computing becomes a growing concern in the realm of cryptography, the selection of hash algorithms also needs to consider post-quantum security. Hash-based digital signatures, such as those based on the Lamport or Merkle-Damgård constructions, are considered quantum-resistant. These algorithms leverage the structure of hash functions to provide security against quantum attacks. The ongoing development of post-quantum cryptographic standards emphasizes the importance of considering the long-term security implications when selecting hash algorithms, especially in applications where data longevity is a critical factor.

In certain use cases, where performance and efficiency are paramount, implementing lighter hash algorithms may be preferable. For example, applications with limited computational resources, such as Internet of Things (IoT) devices, might benefit from hash functions like SHA-3 or BLAKE2b. These algorithms offer a balance between security and computational efficiency, making them suitable for resource-constrained environments. The selection process should consider the specific requirements of the use case, taking into account factors such as processing power, memory constraints, and the overall computational overhead.

When dealing with sensitive data in a compliance-driven environment, adherence to specific standards and regulations becomes crucial. For example, in the context of the Payment Card Industry Data Security Standard (PCI DSS), the selection of hash algorithms should align with the standards outlined by the PCI Security Standards Council. FIPS-compliant algorithms may be required in certain government or military contexts. Ensuring compliance with relevant regulations not only supports security objectives but also addresses legal and industry-specific requirements regarding the protection of sensitive information.

The implementation of hash algorithms should also consider the potential for side-channel attacks, where attackers exploit information leaked during the computation of the hash. Countermeasures, such as constant-time implementations and careful consideration of the platform's security characteristics, can mitigate the risk of side-channel attacks. Additionally, the choice of hash algorithm should account for any known vulnerabilities or weaknesses that may be discovered over time. Regular monitoring of the cryptographic landscape and prompt adoption of recommended updates or replacements for hash algorithms is essential to maintaining a secure implementation.

The deployment of hash algorithms in distributed systems, where data integrity and consistency are paramount, presents unique challenges. Consensus mechanisms, such as those used in blockchain or distributed databases, rely on hash functions for ensuring agreement among nodes. The hash values of data blocks play a crucial role in reaching consensus on the state of the distributed ledger. Selecting hash algorithms that align with the requirements of the consensus protocol and provide collision resistance is vital for the reliable operation of distributed systems.

In summary, selecting and implementing secure hash algorithms for various use cases necessitates a thorough consideration of the specific security, efficiency, and compliance requirements of each application. Whether securing passwords, ensuring file integrity, creating digital signatures, or supporting blockchain technology, the choice of hash algorithm influences the overall security posture. The evolving landscape of cryptographic research, emerging technologies, and the potential impact of quantum computing underscores the need for a thoughtful and adaptable approach to hash algorithm selection. As cybersecurity standards continue to evolve, organizations must stay informed, regularly reassess their cryptographic practices, and be prepared to transition to more secure hash algorithms when necessary to safeguard the integrity and authenticity of their digital assets.

Strategies for secure data backup and recovery.

Strategies for secure data backup and recovery are essential components of any comprehensive cybersecurity plan, ensuring the resilience and continuity of an organization's operations in the face of data loss or cyber threats. A robust backup strategy encompasses a combination of technical measures, procedural protocols, and strategic planning to safeguard critical data and facilitate efficient recovery processes.

One fundamental aspect of secure data backup involves the selection of appropriate backup mechanisms and technologies. Organizations often deploy a mix of full, incremental, and differential backups to optimize storage space and minimize backup duration. Full backups capture the entirety of data at a specific point in time, while incremental and differential backups focus on changes made since the last backup. Implementing a combination of these backup types allows organizations to balance storage efficiency with the granularity needed for quick recovery. Additionally, the use of disk-based backups, cloud storage, or tape backups as offsite solutions ensures geographical redundancy, protecting against localized disasters.

Encryption plays a pivotal role in securing data during the backup process. Encrypting data at rest, in transit, and during backup operations safeguards sensitive information from unauthorized access. Advanced Encryption Standard (AES) is commonly employed for encrypting backup data, providing a high level of security. Secure key management practices are crucial to ensure that only authorized personnel can access the decryption keys, preventing the compromise of encrypted backup data. Integrating encryption into the backup strategy adds an extra layer of protection, particularly when dealing with sensitive or regulated data.

Regular testing and validation of backup processes are integral to the efficacy of a secure backup strategy. Conducting periodic recovery tests ensures that backup systems are functioning correctly and that data can be successfully restored in the event of a disaster. These tests should encompass various scenarios, including complete data loss, specific file recovery, and system restoration. A well-documented and regularly rehearsed recovery plan helps minimize downtime in the event of an actual data loss or system failure, contributing to the overall resilience of the organization.

In the context of secure data backup and recovery, versioning mechanisms provide an additional layer of protection by retaining multiple iterations of files or data sets. Versioning allows users to roll back to a specific point in time, mitigating the impact of data corruption, accidental deletions, or ransomware attacks. Cloud-based backup solutions often offer built-in versioning capabilities, empowering organizations to restore data to a clean state before the occurrence of an incident. The implementation of versioning aligns with the principle of data integrity, ensuring that historical and unaltered versions of critical files are readily accessible for recovery purposes.

Effective access controls are paramount in securing backup infrastructure and preventing unauthorized access to backup data. Limiting access to backup systems, repositories, and management interfaces ensures that only authorized personnel can modify, delete, or recover data. Role-based access control (RBAC) mechanisms help define and enforce access permissions based on job roles and responsibilities, reducing the risk of insider threats or accidental data loss. Monitoring and auditing access logs contribute to the detection of any suspicious activities, facilitating timely intervention and maintaining the security of backup environments.

The concept of the 3-2-1 backup rule is widely endorsed as a best practice in secure data backup strategies. This rule dictates that organizations should maintain three copies of their data (original plus two backups), store the backups on two different media types, and keep one copy offsite. Adhering to the 3-2-1 backup rule provides a resilient framework that safeguards against various threats, including hardware failures, data corruption, natural disasters, and cyberattacks. Offsite backups, whether in geographically distant data centers or cloud repositories, protect against localized incidents that could impact onsite infrastructure.

Cloud-based backup solutions offer scalable and cost-effective alternatives to traditional backup methods, providing organizations with the flexibility to adapt to changing data volumes and operational needs. Cloud backups offer the advantage of offsite storage, automatic updates, and the ability to scale resources based on demand. Major cloud service providers implement robust security measures, including encryption, access controls, and redundancy, adding an extra layer of protection to backup data. However, organizations must carefully assess the security and compliance features of their chosen cloud backup service and implement additional measures as needed to meet their specific requirements.

Ransomware attacks pose a significant threat to data integrity, making ransomware-resistant backup strategies a critical consideration. Immutable backups, achieved through technologies like Write Once, Read Many (WORM) storage, prevent malicious actors from altering or deleting backup data. By creating a tamper-evident backup environment, organizations can maintain a secure repository that remains impervious to ransomware attempts. Regular audits of backup systems, coupled with proactive monitoring for signs of ransomware activity, contribute to the overall resilience of the backup strategy against evolving cyber threats.

Effective monitoring and alerting mechanisms are essential components of a secure data backup strategy. Continuous monitoring of backup processes, storage health, and access logs enables timely detection of anomalies or potential security incidents. Automated alerts provide immediate notification of any issues, allowing administrators to respond swiftly and mitigate risks. Monitoring should extend to both onsite and offsite backup environments, ensuring comprehensive coverage and rapid response capabilities. Regularly reviewing logs and conducting security assessments contribute to the ongoing refinement of the backup strategy and its alignment with emerging security challenges.

Data deduplication and compression technologies play a role in optimizing storage efficiency in backup solutions. These techniques reduce the amount of redundant data stored in backups, minimizing storage requirements and enhancing the overall cost-effectiveness of the backup strategy. While improving efficiency, organizations must ensure that these processes do not compromise the security or integrity of backup data. Balancing storage optimization with the preservation of data fidelity is essential to maintain the effectiveness of secure data backup solutions.

Integration with incident response and business continuity plans is crucial for a holistic approach to secure data backup and recovery.

In the event of a cybersecurity incident or data loss, the backup and recovery plan should seamlessly align with broader incident response strategies. This integration ensures that the restoration of critical systems and data is coordinated with incident containment and remediation efforts. Business continuity plans should incorporate the role of backup and recovery processes in minimizing downtime and restoring normal operations swiftly, contributing to the organization's overall resilience.

In conclusion, strategies for secure data backup and recovery are integral to an organization's cybersecurity posture, providing a safeguard against data loss, cyber threats, and operational disruptions. The selection of appropriate backup mechanisms, encryption practices, testing protocols, access controls, and monitoring mechanisms collectively contributes to the resilience and effectiveness of the backup strategy. Adherence to best practices, such as the 3-2-1 backup rule, ransomware-resistant techniques, and integration with broader cybersecurity frameworks, reinforces the security and reliability of data backup solutions. As the cybersecurity landscape evolves, organizations must continually reassess and refine their backup strategies to address emerging threats and ensure the ongoing protection of critical data assets.

Ensuring data integrity during backup processes and expedient recovery in case of data loss.

Ensuring data integrity during backup processes and expediting recovery in the event of data loss are critical imperatives in modern information technology landscapes. Data integrity, defined as the accuracy and consistency of data, is paramount for organizations to maintain trust, compliance, and operational continuity. The backup processes that organizations employ play a pivotal role in preserving data integrity, and the seamless recovery of data is equally crucial for minimizing disruptions and ensuring business resilience.

A foundational element in the pursuit of data integrity during backup processes is the use of cryptographic techniques. Encryption, in particular, serves as a robust safeguard during both backup and storage phases. Employing encryption mechanisms, such as the Advanced Encryption Standard (AES), ensures that data is secured against unauthorized access during transmission and while at rest in backup repositories. This cryptographic layer not only protects sensitive information from potential breaches but also establishes a secure foundation for maintaining data integrity throughout the backup lifecycle.

A critical consideration in the pursuit of data integrity is the implementation of validation mechanisms during backup processes. Hash functions, specifically designed to produce unique hash values for distinct data sets, serve as indispensable tools for verifying data integrity. Generating hash values before and after the backup operation allows organizations to detect any changes or corruption in the data during the backup process. If the hash values match, it indicates that the data has been faithfully backed up, contributing to the assurance of data integrity. These validation mechanisms serve as a proactive measure to identify potential issues before they compromise the integrity of the backup data.

The timing and frequency of backups also play a pivotal role in ensuring data integrity. Regular, scheduled backups reduce the risk of data loss by capturing the most recent version of the data. Organizations often adopt strategies involving incremental or differential backups in addition to full backups to strike a balance between storage efficiency and data granularity. Incremental backups capture only the changes made since the last backup, reducing the storage footprint and expediting backup processes. Differential backups, on the other hand, store the changes made since the last full backup, offering a compromise between efficiency and the granularity needed for a swift recovery. Employing a combination of these backup types ensures that organizations can recover data with minimal loss and maintain data integrity even in the face of frequent updates or changes.

While considering data integrity during backups, the importance of versioning cannot be overstated. Versioning mechanisms allow organizations to retain multiple iterations of files, creating a historical record that facilitates recovery to a specific point in time. This becomes particularly valuable in scenarios where data corruption or unwanted changes occur gradually and may go unnoticed for an extended period. Versioning provides a safety net, allowing organizations to roll back to a known good state, thereby preserving data integrity and minimizing the impact of data loss incidents.

The adoption of offsite or geographically dispersed backup repositories is a strategic move to enhance data integrity. In the face of disasters, whether natural or man-made, having backups stored in a different geographical location safeguards against localized incidents that could impact the primary data center. Cloud-based backup solutions, with their inherent redundancy and accessibility, offer a compelling option for offsite storage. Leveraging offsite backups ensures that organizations can recover their data even if the primary data center is compromised, contributing to a resilient data integrity strategy.

In the context of backup and recovery, the 3-2-1 backup rule emerges as a widely embraced best practice. This rule stipulates that organizations should maintain three copies of their data, with two copies stored on different media types and one copy kept offsite. Adhering to the 3-2-1 backup rule provides a robust framework for data integrity by creating redundancy and diversity in backup strategies. In the event of primary data loss, having multiple copies in different locations and formats ensures that organizations can swiftly initiate recovery processes, maintaining the integrity of their critical data.

Ransomware attacks pose a significant threat to data integrity, making ransomware-resistant backup strategies imperative. Immutable backups, achieved through technologies like Write Once, Read Many (WORM) storage, prevent malicious actors from altering or deleting backup data. By creating a tamper-evident backup environment, organizations can withstand ransomware attempts and maintain the integrity of their backup repositories. Regular audits of backup systems, coupled with proactive monitoring for signs of ransomware activity, contribute to the overall resilience of the backup strategy against evolving cyber threats.

Effective access controls are essential in safeguarding data integrity during backup processes. Limiting access to backup systems, repositories, and management interfaces ensures that only authorized personnel can modify, delete, or recover data. Role-based access control (RBAC) mechanisms help define and enforce access permissions based on job roles and responsibilities, reducing the risk of insider threats or accidental data loss. Monitoring and auditing access logs contribute to the detection of any suspicious activities, facilitating timely intervention and maintaining the security of backup environments.

A proactive stance towards monitoring and auditing backup processes enhances the overall data integrity strategy. Continuous monitoring of backup operations, storage health, and access logs enables timely detection of anomalies or potential security incidents. Automated alerts provide immediate notification of any issues, allowing administrators to respond swiftly and mitigate risks. Monitoring should extend to both onsite and offsite backup environments, ensuring comprehensive coverage and rapid response capabilities. Regularly reviewing logs and conducting security assessments contribute to the ongoing refinement of the backup strategy and its alignment with emerging security challenges.

Integration with incident response and business continuity plans is a strategic imperative for the expedient recovery of data in case of data loss. The backup and recovery plan should seamlessly align with broader incident response strategies to ensure coordinated and effective responses. Business continuity plans should incorporate the role of backup and recovery processes in minimizing downtime and restoring normal operations swiftly, contributing to the organization's overall resilience. The synergy between backup and recovery initiatives and broader incident response and business continuity frameworks ensures a cohesive and effective approach to data protection and recovery.

Data deduplication and compression technologies, while optimizing storage efficiency, should be implemented cautiously to ensure they do not compromise the security or integrity of backup data. While these techniques reduce the amount of redundant data stored in backups, minimizing storage requirements and enhancing overall cost-effectiveness, organizations must strike a balance between storage optimization and the preservation of data fidelity. Maintaining the effectiveness of secure data backup solutions involves continuously evaluating the impact of storage optimization techniques on data integrity and adjusting strategies accordingly.

A comprehensive backup and recovery strategy must consider the human element. Employee training and awareness programs play a crucial role in ensuring that personnel are well-informed about the importance of data integrity, secure backup practices, and the role they play in the organization's overall cybersecurity posture. Human error remains a significant factor in data loss incidents, and proactive education efforts contribute to a culture of security-conscious behavior, reducing the likelihood of inadvertent actions that could compromise data integrity.

In conclusion, ensuring data integrity during backup processes and expediting recovery in case of data loss demand a multifaceted and proactive approach. Employing cryptographic techniques, validation mechanisms, versioning, offsite storage, and adherence to best practices such as the 3-2-1 backup rule collectively contribute to a robust data integrity strategy. Addressing emerging threats, such as ransomware, requires a dedicated focus on immutable backups and proactive monitoring. Integration with incident response and business continuity plans ensures a coordinated and effective approach to recovery. As organizations navigate the complex landscape of data protection, the synergy of technological measures, procedural protocols, and a security-aware culture establishes the foundation for resilient and secure data backup and recovery strategies.

Chapter 6: Endpoint Security

The importance of securing endpoints such as computers and mobile devices.

Securing endpoints, encompassing computers and mobile devices, is paramount in today's interconnected digital landscape where the proliferation of technology has become ubiquitous. Endpoints serve as the frontline in the battle against cyber threats, playing a pivotal role in safeguarding sensitive information, critical systems, and personal privacy. As the gateway to vast networks, these devices are susceptible to an array of malicious activities that can compromise not only individual users but also entire organizations and their infrastructures.

The digital realm is rife with diverse and sophisticated threats, ranging from malware and ransomware to phishing attacks and zero-day vulnerabilities. Computers and mobile devices, being the primary conduits through which individuals access, share, and store information, are prime targets for cybercriminals seeking unauthorized access, data theft, or system disruption. As the digital landscape evolves, the interconnectedness of endpoints amplifies the potential impact of security breaches, making it imperative to fortify these entry points to the digital domain.

One of the foremost reasons for securing endpoints lies in the sheer volume and sensitivity of data stored on these devices. Whether personal, financial, or business-related, the information housed within computers and mobile devices is a valuable commodity for malicious actors. Unauthorized access to sensitive data can lead to identity theft, financial fraud, or corporate espionage. Additionally, the compromise of personal information can have far-reaching consequences, affecting not only individuals but also eroding trust in digital platforms and services.

Beyond data security, securing endpoints is crucial for maintaining the integrity and availability of critical systems. Cyberattacks, such as ransomware, can cripple entire organizations by encrypting data and demanding payment for its release. The consequences of such attacks extend beyond financial losses, encompassing operational disruptions, reputational damage, and legal ramifications. The interconnected nature of modern systems means that a security breach on one endpoint can potentially cascade through an entire network, amplifying the impact and underscoring the need for robust endpoint security measures.

Moreover, the pervasiveness of mobile devices in both personal and professional spheres adds another layer of complexity to endpoint security. With the advent of the Bring Your Own Device (BYOD) culture, where employees use personal devices for work-related tasks, the boundaries between personal and corporate data blur. This trend accentuates the need for comprehensive endpoint security strategies that can adapt to the dynamic nature of today's work environments. The compromise of a mobile device can lead to unauthorized access to corporate networks, compromising sensitive business information and intellectual property.

Endpoint security is not solely about protecting against external threats; it also involves mitigating risks arising from internal sources. Human factors, such as negligent or uninformed user behavior, pose a significant challenge to endpoint security. Employees may inadvertently download malicious files, fall victim to phishing attacks, or neglect basic security practices, creating vulnerabilities that can be exploited by attackers. Educating users about cybersecurity best practices and implementing robust endpoint protection mechanisms are essential components of a holistic security approach.

In addition to individual devices, securing endpoints becomes even more critical in the context of the Internet of Things (IoT), where a myriad of interconnected devices ranging from smart home appliances to industrial sensors form an extended network. The proliferation of IoT devices introduces new vectors for cyber threats, as these endpoints may have limited security measures in place. Compromised IoT devices can be leveraged as entry points to larger networks, emphasizing the need for a comprehensive and integrated approach to endpoint security that encompasses all connected devices.

As the threat landscape continues to evolve, the concept of endpoint security expands beyond traditional antivirus solutions to incorporate advanced technologies such as artificial intelligence and machine learning. These technologies enable proactive threat detection and response, helping to identify and neutralize emerging threats before they can cause harm. Endpoint security solutions are evolving to provide real-time monitoring, behavior analysis, and automated response mechanisms, empowering organizations to stay ahead of the rapidly evolving threat landscape.

The importance of securing endpoints extends beyond individual users and organizations; it is integral to the overall stability and security of the digital ecosystem. Cybersecurity incidents can have cascading effects, affecting not only the targeted entities but also impacting critical infrastructure, national security, and the global economy. The interconnectedness of digital systems implies that vulnerabilities in one part of the world can potentially be exploited to compromise systems on a global scale. Therefore, securing endpoints is not merely a matter of individual responsibility; it is a collective imperative that requires collaboration between individuals, businesses, and governments to create a resilient and secure digital environment.

In conclusion, the importance of securing endpoints, encompassing computers and mobile devices, cannot be overstated in the contemporary digital landscape. The vulnerabilities inherent in these devices make them prime targets for a diverse array of cyber threats, ranging from data breaches to system disruptions. The ramifications of security breaches extend beyond individual users to impact organizations, critical infrastructure, and the global digital ecosystem. A comprehensive and integrated approach to endpoint security is essential, incorporating advanced technologies, user education, and proactive measures to mitigate the ever-evolving threat landscape. As we navigate the complexities of an interconnected digital world, securing endpoints becomes a collective responsibility to ensure the confidentiality, integrity, and availability of information and systems that underpin our modern way of life.

Implementing endpoint protection solutions for comprehensive security.

Implementing robust endpoint protection solutions is a cornerstone in achieving comprehensive security in the ever-evolving landscape of cybersecurity threats. Endpoint protection goes beyond traditional antivirus measures, encompassing a holistic strategy that addresses the myriad challenges posed by diverse and sophisticated cyber threats. The complexity of the modern threat landscape necessitates a multifaceted approach that combines advanced technologies, user education, and proactive measures to fortify the vulnerabilities inherent in computers and mobile devices.

At the core of effective endpoint protection is the deployment of cutting-edge security technologies. Traditional antivirus solutions, while still essential, are no longer sufficient on their own to combat the evolving tactics of cybercriminals. Advanced solutions that leverage artificial intelligence (AI) and machine learning (ML) have become integral in detecting and mitigating emerging threats in real-time. These technologies enable proactive threat hunting by analyzing patterns, behaviors, and anomalies, allowing for the identification of potential threats before they can inflict damage. The dynamic nature of these technologies ensures that endpoint protection stays ahead of the curve, adapting to the ever-changing tactics employed by cyber adversaries.

Furthermore, endpoint protection solutions should incorporate endpoint detection and response (EDR) capabilities. EDR goes beyond traditional antivirus measures by providing continuous monitoring of endpoint activities and the ability to respond to security incidents in real-time. By analyzing endpoint events, behaviors, and network traffic, EDR solutions enhance threat visibility and facilitate a swift and effective response to potential security breaches. This proactive approach is crucial in minimizing the impact of cyber threats, preventing the lateral movement of attackers within a network, and reducing the time it takes to detect and neutralize malicious activities.

User education is another critical component of comprehensive endpoint protection. Human factors, such as social engineering attacks and negligent user behavior, remain significant contributors to security breaches. Educating users about cybersecurity best practices, the risks associated with phishing attacks, and the importance of adhering to security policies helps create a human firewall against potential threats. User awareness campaigns, simulated phishing exercises, and regular training sessions contribute to a security-conscious culture, empowering individuals to recognize and report potential security incidents.

Implementing a comprehensive endpoint protection strategy also involves securing mobile devices, given their ubiquitous presence in both personal and professional settings. Mobile endpoint security extends beyond traditional antivirus measures to include mobile device management (MDM) and mobile threat defense (MTD) solutions. MDM ensures the enforcement of security policies, such as device encryption and password requirements, while MTD focuses on detecting and mitigating threats specific to mobile platforms. With the increasing prevalence of Bring Your Own Device (BYOD) policies in workplaces, securing mobile endpoints becomes paramount to prevent unauthorized access to corporate networks and protect sensitive business information.

Integration is key to the effectiveness of endpoint protection solutions. A seamless integration of different security technologies, such as antivirus, EDR, MDM, and MTD, creates a unified defense mechanism that provides comprehensive coverage against a broad spectrum of cyber threats. This integrated approach facilitates centralized management, real-time monitoring, and coordinated incident response, ensuring a cohesive and efficient security posture. Moreover, integration with threat intelligence feeds enables organizations to stay informed about the latest threats and vulnerabilities, allowing them to proactively adapt their security measures to emerging risks.

Regular and timely software patching is a fundamental aspect of endpoint protection. Vulnerabilities in operating systems, software, and applications can be exploited by cybercriminals to gain unauthorized access to endpoints. Timely patch management ensures that known vulnerabilities are addressed promptly, reducing the attack surface and minimizing the risk of exploitation. Automated patch deployment tools can streamline the patching process, ensuring that endpoints are consistently up-to-date with the latest security patches and updates.

Endpoint protection solutions should also include mechanisms for controlling and securing the use of removable media and external devices. USB drives and external storage devices can serve as vectors for malware transmission. Implementing policies that restrict unauthorized access to external devices, coupled with regular scanning for potential threats, helps mitigate the risk of malware introduction through removable media. This control extends to endpoint security policies that govern the use of external peripherals, ensuring that only authorized and secure devices are connected to endpoints.

Additionally, a comprehensive endpoint protection strategy involves data encryption to safeguard sensitive information stored on endpoints. In the event of a device theft or loss, encrypted data remains inaccessible to unauthorized individuals, preserving the confidentiality of critical information. Full disk encryption and file-level encryption are common techniques employed to protect data at rest, complementing other security measures focused on preventing unauthorized access and data exfiltration.

Endpoint protection solutions should be complemented by robust incident response and recovery plans. Despite proactive security measures, no system is entirely immune to the possibility of a security incident. Having well-defined incident response plans ensures a coordinated and efficient response to security breaches. Regularly conducting tabletop exercises and simulations helps organizations test the effectiveness of their incident response processes, identify areas for improvement, and enhance the overall resilience of their security posture.

Regular security audits and assessments are essential to evaluate the effectiveness of endpoint protection measures. Conducting vulnerability assessments, penetration testing, and security audits identify potential weaknesses in the security architecture and allow organizations to address them before they can be exploited by malicious actors. Continuous monitoring of security metrics, such as threat detection rates, incident response times, and user compliance with security policies, provides insights into the overall health of the endpoint protection strategy.

In conclusion, implementing endpoint protection solutions for comprehensive security involves a multifaceted approach that combines advanced technologies, user education, and proactive measures. The dynamic nature of the modern threat landscape requires organizations to go beyond traditional antivirus measures and embrace solutions that leverage artificial intelligence and machine learning for real-time threat detection and response. User education plays a pivotal role in creating a security-conscious culture, while securing mobile devices, integrating different security technologies, and ensuring timely patch management contribute to a cohesive and effective endpoint protection strategy. Encryption, control over external devices, and robust incident response plans add layers of resilience, and regular security audits help organizations stay ahead of evolving threats. By adopting a comprehensive and integrated approach to endpoint protection, organizations can fortify their defenses, mitigate risks, and safeguard the confidentiality, integrity, and availability of their digital assets in an ever-changing cybersecurity landscape.

Evaluating the effectiveness of antivirus and anti-malware tools.

Evaluating the effectiveness of antivirus and anti-malware tools is a critical undertaking in the realm of cybersecurity, where the ever-evolving landscape of digital threats necessitates robust protection measures. Antivirus and anti-malware tools serve as the first line of defense against malicious software, including viruses, worms, Trojans, ransomware, and other forms of malware that pose a constant threat to the integrity and security of computer systems. The effectiveness of these tools is contingent upon their ability to detect, prevent, and remediate a wide array of malicious activities, all while minimizing false positives that could disrupt normal user activities.

A fundamental aspect of evaluating antivirus and anti-malware tools is assessing their detection capabilities. The efficacy of these tools hinges on their ability to identify and flag known malware signatures. Traditional signature-based detection relies on a database of predefined patterns that match known malware. While effective against well-established threats, this approach may falter in the face of rapidly evolving, polymorphic, or zero-day malware that lacks recognizable signatures. As such, the effectiveness of antivirus tools is often measured by their capacity to incorporate heuristic analysis and behavioral detection techniques, enabling them to identify suspicious patterns and activities indicative of malware even in the absence of specific signatures.

Moreover, the ability of antivirus tools to provide real-time protection is crucial in the dynamic landscape of cyber threats. Real-time protection involves continuous monitoring of system activities to promptly detect and block malicious processes or files. Effective antivirus tools employ proactive measures to prevent malware execution before it can compromise the system. This includes analyzing file behavior, scrutinizing network traffic for signs of malicious communication, and preventing the execution of code that exhibits characteristics associated with malware. The real-time component is pivotal in preventing the initial infection and subsequent spread of malware within a network.

Behavioral analysis plays a pivotal role in evaluating the effectiveness of antivirus and anti-malware tools. By scrutinizing the behavior of files and processes, these tools can identify anomalies that suggest malicious intent. Behavioral analysis goes beyond signature-based detection, offering a proactive approach to identify previously unknown threats based on their behavior. This is particularly crucial in the detection of polymorphic malware that can change its appearance to evade traditional signature-based defenses. Effective antivirus tools leverage behavioral analysis to detect malicious activities, such as unauthorized system changes, suspicious network communication, or attempts to exploit vulnerabilities, providing a layer of defense against emerging threats.

The efficiency of antivirus and anti-malware tools also relies on their ability to provide timely and accurate updates. Malware evolves rapidly, with new variants emerging regularly. Regular updates to the antivirus database, which includes new malware signatures, ensure that the tool remains current and capable of recognizing the latest threats. Additionally, updates may include improvements to the tool's detection algorithms, enhancing its overall effectiveness. The frequency and reliability of updates are crucial factors in evaluating the robustness of antivirus solutions, as a tool that lags behind in updates may leave systems vulnerable to newly discovered threats.

A critical aspect of assessing the effectiveness of antivirus tools is their impact on system performance. While the primary goal is to protect against malware, the tool should do so without unduly burdening the system's resources. Antivirus tools that introduce significant latency, cause system slowdowns, or interrupt normal user activities may lead to frustration and decreased productivity. Striking a balance between effective protection and minimal system impact is essential. Modern antivirus solutions leverage optimization techniques, such as cloud-based scanning and resource-efficient algorithms, to deliver robust protection without compromising the user experience.

In evaluating the efficacy of antivirus and anti-malware tools, it is imperative to consider their ability to adapt to the diverse range of devices and operating systems in use today. With the proliferation of mobile devices, including smartphones and tablets, effective endpoint protection must extend beyond traditional computers. Assessing how well antivirus tools cater to the security needs of a variety of platforms is crucial, ensuring that both Windows and non-Windows environments receive adequate protection. Furthermore, as organizations adopt diverse operating systems, including macOS and Linux, evaluating cross-platform compatibility becomes essential for a comprehensive security strategy.

The effectiveness of antivirus and anti-malware tools is closely tied to their ability to address emerging threats, such as ransomware, which has become a prevalent and sophisticated form of malware. Ransomware operates by encrypting files and demanding payment for their release, posing a significant threat to individuals and organizations alike. Antivirus tools should incorporate specialized ransomware detection mechanisms, behavioral analysis, and heuristics to identify and mitigate this specific type of threat. The capability to detect and prevent ransomware attacks is a crucial benchmark in evaluating the overall effectiveness of antivirus solutions.

Furthermore, the integration of additional security features into antivirus tools contributes to their overall effectiveness. Features such as firewall protection, email filtering, and web browsing security enhance the tool's capacity to prevent various attack vectors. Firewalls, for instance, provide an additional layer of defense by monitoring and controlling incoming and outgoing network traffic. Email filtering helps identify and block malicious attachments or links in emails, which are common vectors for malware distribution. A comprehensive antivirus solution should encompass these supplementary features to provide a holistic defense against a broad spectrum of threats.

User interface and ease of use are often overlooked but crucial elements in evaluating the effectiveness of antivirus and anti-malware tools. An intuitive and user-friendly interface simplifies the configuration, management, and monitoring of security settings. Clear and informative alerts help users understand the nature of threats and make informed decisions. A well-designed user interface contributes to the overall user experience, encouraging users to actively engage with the security tool and adhere to recommended best practices.

Interoperability with other security solutions and collaboration with threat intelligence sources are vital considerations in evaluating antivirus effectiveness. Integration with security information and event management (SIEM) systems, for example, enhances the overall security posture by providing a centralized view of security events across the organization. Collaboration with threat intelligence feeds enables antivirus tools to stay abreast of the latest threats and vulnerabilities, allowing for a more proactive and adaptive defense against emerging risks.

In conclusion, evaluating the effectiveness of antivirus and anti-malware tools is a multifaceted process that considers their detection capabilities, real-time protection mechanisms, behavioral analysis, timely updates, impact on system performance, cross-platform compatibility, ransomware defense, additional security features, user interface design, and interoperability. The dynamic nature of the cyber threat landscape requires these tools to evolve continually, incorporating advanced detection techniques and adapting to emerging risks. Striking a balance between robust protection and minimal impact on user experience is paramount. Ultimately, the effectiveness of antivirus tools is a key determinant in fortifying the digital realm against the persistent and ever-changing threat landscape, ensuring the confidentiality, integrity, and availability of computer systems and data.

Best practices for selecting, configuring, and maintaining these tools.

Selecting, configuring, and maintaining cybersecurity tools is a complex and vital undertaking in today's ever-evolving digital landscape. The effectiveness of these tools directly impacts an organization's ability to protect its sensitive information, maintain operational continuity, and thwart cyber threats. To embark on this journey, organizations must adhere to best practices that span the entire lifecycle of these tools, from initial selection to ongoing maintenance.

The first phase involves the meticulous process of selecting the right cybersecurity tools to suit the organization's specific needs and challenges. A foundational step is conducting a comprehensive risk assessment to identify potential threats, vulnerabilities, and the assets at risk. This risk assessment provides valuable insights into the organization's unique security requirements, guiding the selection of tools that align with its risk profile. When choosing tools, organizations should consider factors such as the type of threats they are likely to face, the nature of their IT infrastructure, and the regulatory compliance requirements that may govern their industry.

An essential aspect of tool selection is ensuring compatibility with the organization's existing technology stack. Cybersecurity tools should seamlessly integrate with other security solutions and systems, creating a cohesive and interoperable security architecture. This integration is crucial for streamlining workflows, centralizing threat intelligence, and providing a unified view of security events across the organization. Compatibility also facilitates effective incident response and enhances the overall efficiency of the cybersecurity ecosystem.

Once tools are selected, the next critical phase involves their configuration to maximize their effectiveness and align them with the organization's security policies. This requires a thorough understanding of the tool's capabilities, features, and configuration options. Organizations should tailor configurations to their specific needs, considering factors such as the organization's risk tolerance, the desired level of security, and the operational requirements of its users. Striking the right balance between security and usability is essential to avoid hindering legitimate user activities while maintaining a robust defense against cyber threats.

Configuration practices should encompass fine-tuning security parameters, defining access controls, and implementing incident response plans within the tool's framework. Regular updates and patch management are vital components of configuration, ensuring that the tools remain current and resilient against emerging threats. Moreover, organizations should establish configuration baselines and conduct periodic reviews to adapt to changing threat landscapes, technology environments, and business requirements.

Continuous monitoring is a cornerstone of effective cybersecurity, and configuring tools to provide real-time visibility into security events is paramount. Leveraging features such as intrusion detection and prevention systems, log analysis, and security information and event management (SIEM) tools allows organizations to detect and respond to threats promptly. These tools should be configured to generate actionable alerts, enabling security teams to investigate and mitigate potential incidents swiftly. Regularly reviewing and refining monitoring configurations ensures that the organization maintains situational awareness and can proactively address emerging threats.

A crucial aspect of maintaining cybersecurity tools is keeping them up-to-date through regular software updates and patches. Vendors release updates to address known vulnerabilities, enhance features, and adapt to the evolving threat landscape. Establishing a systematic approach to patch management, including testing patches in a controlled environment before deployment, helps prevent disruptions to critical systems and ensures that the organization benefits from the latest security enhancements. Automated patch deployment tools can streamline this process, reducing the window of vulnerability for potential exploits.

Organizations should also implement a robust backup and recovery strategy as part of maintaining cybersecurity tools. Regularly backing up critical data and configurations safeguards against data loss in the event of a security incident or system failure. Testing the restoration process periodically ensures that backups are reliable and can be quickly deployed when needed. An effective backup and recovery strategy is a crucial component of resilience, enabling organizations to recover swiftly from cyber incidents and minimize downtime.

User education and awareness play a pivotal role in the successful configuration and maintenance of cybersecurity tools. Training users on the proper use of security features, recognizing phishing attempts, and understanding the organization's security policies fosters a security-conscious culture. Users should be informed about the capabilities of cybersecurity tools and encouraged to report any suspicious activities promptly. Regular awareness programs and simulated phishing exercises help reinforce security best practices and empower users to become active participants in the organization's defense against cyber threats.

Regular audits and assessments of cybersecurity tools are essential to ensure that they continue to meet the organization's security objectives. Conducting vulnerability assessments, penetration testing, and security audits helps identify potential weaknesses in the configuration, deployment, or usage of these tools. These assessments also provide insights into emerging threats, allowing organizations to adapt their cybersecurity strategies proactively. Regular audits contribute to a continuous improvement cycle, where lessons learned from assessments are used to refine configurations, update policies, and enhance overall security posture.

Collaboration and information sharing within the cybersecurity community are integral to staying ahead of evolving threats. Organizations should actively participate in threat intelligence-sharing forums, industry collaborations, and information-sharing platforms. This collective approach helps organizations benefit from shared insights, indicators of compromise, and best practices. Integrating threat intelligence feeds into cybersecurity tools enhances their ability to identify and respond to emerging threats, providing an additional layer of defense.

Documentation is a foundational element of effective cybersecurity tool maintenance. Comprehensive documentation should cover the configuration settings, policies, and procedures associated with each tool. This documentation serves as a reference for administrators, facilitates knowledge transfer, and supports incident response efforts. It is crucial to keep documentation up-to-date, particularly after any changes to the tool's configuration or the introduction of new features.

In conclusion, selecting, configuring, and maintaining cybersecurity tools is a multifaceted process that demands careful consideration of an organization's unique risk profile, technology stack, and operational requirements. Best practices include conducting a thorough risk assessment, selecting tools that align with organizational needs, configuring tools to strike the right balance between security and usability, and maintaining an ongoing process of monitoring, updating, and refining configurations. User education, backup and recovery strategies, regular audits, collaboration within the cybersecurity community, and comprehensive documentation contribute to a holistic approach that enhances an organization's ability to defend against cyber threats. By adhering to these best practices, organizations can establish a resilient cybersecurity posture that safeguards their digital assets and ensures the confidentiality, integrity, and availability of critical information.

Strategies for controlling and managing connected devices.

Implementing effective strategies for controlling and managing connected devices is paramount in the era of the Internet of Things (IoT), where the proliferation of interconnected devices introduces new complexities and security challenges. Controlling and managing these devices involves addressing issues related to security, privacy, interoperability, and the overall governance of the expanding IoT ecosystem.

One fundamental strategy for managing connected devices is to establish a robust framework for device authentication and authorization. Ensuring that only authorized devices can connect to the network and access resources is crucial for preventing unauthorized access and potential security breaches. This involves implementing strong authentication mechanisms, such as secure certificates or biometric authentication, to validate the identity of each device. Authorization policies should be finely tuned to grant specific permissions based on the device's role and the required level of access.

Security updates and patch management play a pivotal role in maintaining the integrity and security of connected devices. Timely deployment of security patches is essential to address vulnerabilities that may be exploited by malicious actors. Establishing a systematic approach to patch management, including testing updates in controlled environments before deployment, helps mitigate risks associated with potential disruptions to device functionality. Automated patch deployment tools can streamline the update process, ensuring that devices remain resilient against emerging threats.

Network segmentation is another crucial strategy for controlling and managing connected devices. Segmenting the network isolates different categories of devices, such as IoT devices, from critical infrastructure and sensitive data. This segmentation helps contain potential security breaches, limiting the impact of a compromised device on the overall network. Implementing firewalls and access control lists further enhances network segmentation by regulating the flow of traffic between different segments and preventing unauthorized communication.

Encryption is a fundamental aspect of securing communications between connected devices and the broader network. Implementing strong encryption protocols safeguards data in transit, preventing eavesdropping and man-in-the-middle attacks. End-to-end encryption is particularly important for ensuring the privacy and confidentiality of data exchanged between devices. As the number of connected devices increases, encryption becomes integral to protecting sensitive information and maintaining the trust of users and stakeholders.

Establishing comprehensive policies for device management is essential for maintaining order and security in the IoT ecosystem. These policies should encompass device onboarding, configuration, monitoring, and decommissioning processes. Clear guidelines on the types of devices allowed on the network, the security requirements for each device, and the lifecycle management of devices contribute to a well-defined and organized approach to managing the diverse array of connected devices.

Implementing a device inventory and asset management system is a foundational step in gaining visibility and control over connected devices. Maintaining an accurate inventory helps organizations track the number and types of devices on their network, monitor their status, and enforce security policies consistently. Automated asset management tools can streamline this process, providing real-time insights into the state of the IoT ecosystem and facilitating proactive responses to potential security incidents.

Access control is a key strategy for managing connected devices and regulating the interactions between devices and users. Implementing role-based access control ensures that only authorized individuals have the necessary permissions to interact with specific devices or access certain functionalities. This approach minimizes the risk of unauthorized device manipulation or malicious actions by restricting user privileges based on their roles within the organization.

Behavioral analytics and anomaly detection play a crucial role in identifying potential security threats within the IoT ecosystem. By establishing baselines for normal device behavior, organizations can leverage analytics tools to detect deviations and anomalies that may indicate a security incident. This proactive approach allows for swift responses to abnormal activities, mitigating the impact of potential breaches and enhancing the overall security posture of the connected device environment.

Continuous monitoring and real-time visibility into the state of connected devices are essential components of effective device management. Monitoring tools should provide insights into device activities, network traffic, and security events. This visibility enables organizations to detect and respond to security incidents promptly, reducing the dwell time of threats within the network. Automated alerting mechanisms ensure that security teams are promptly notified of suspicious activities, enabling them to take immediate action.

Implementing privacy controls is vital, especially when dealing with connected devices that may collect and process sensitive information. Organizations must establish clear policies regarding the collection, storage, and use of data by connected devices, ensuring compliance with relevant privacy regulations. Integrating privacy features, such as data anonymization and user consent mechanisms, helps strike a balance between leveraging device data for operational insights and respecting individual privacy rights.

Secure software development practices are essential for building resilience into connected devices from the ground up. Manufacturers and developers should prioritize security in the design and coding phases, conduct thorough security assessments, and adhere to established security standards. By fostering a security-first mindset throughout the development lifecycle, organizations can minimize the risk of deploying vulnerable devices and reduce the likelihood of security incidents in the operational phase.

Collaboration and information sharing within the IoT ecosystem are critical for addressing emerging threats and vulnerabilities. Organizations, manufacturers, and industry stakeholders should actively participate in sharing threat intelligence, best practices, and security insights. This collective approach helps build a community-driven defense against evolving cyber threats, enabling the ecosystem to adapt and respond to new challenges collectively.

Regulatory compliance is a fundamental consideration in managing connected devices. Organizations must stay abreast of relevant regulations and standards governing the deployment and operation of connected devices in their industry. Ensuring compliance with these requirements not only mitigates legal and regulatory risks but also fosters a culture of responsible and ethical device management.

In conclusion, effective strategies for controlling and managing connected devices involve a multifaceted approach that encompasses security, privacy, network segmentation, encryption, policy development, access control, behavioral analytics, continuous monitoring, privacy controls, secure development practices, collaboration, and regulatory compliance. These strategies collectively contribute to building a resilient and secure IoT ecosystem. As the number and diversity of connected devices continue to grow, organizations must prioritize these strategies to ensure the confidentiality, integrity, and availability of data, as well as the overall security of the interconnected digital landscape.

Preventing unauthorized devices from compromising endpoint security.

Preventing unauthorized devices from compromising endpoint security is a critical aspect of maintaining a robust defense against cyber threats. Endpoint security, encompassing computers, laptops, and mobile devices, serves as the frontline defense against malicious activities. Unauthorized devices pose a significant risk, as they can introduce vulnerabilities, facilitate unauthorized access, and potentially lead to data breaches or system disruptions. Implementing effective strategies to prevent such unauthorized devices from compromising endpoint security involves a combination of technological controls, access policies, user education, and ongoing monitoring.

A fundamental step in preventing unauthorized devices is the implementation of robust access controls. Organizations should establish and enforce clear policies regarding which devices are allowed to connect to the network. Network access controls, such as port security, can be configured to allow only registered and authorized devices to connect. Implementing 802.1X authentication protocols adds an additional layer of security by requiring devices to provide valid credentials before gaining network access. This ensures that only authorized and properly configured devices can connect to the network, reducing the risk of unauthorized access.

Device identification and profiling are crucial elements in preventing unauthorized devices from compromising endpoint security. Network administrators should employ tools that can accurately identify and classify connected devices based on their characteristics, such as device type, manufacturer, and operating system. Network access control solutions can use this information to enforce policies that allow or deny access based on the device's compliance with security standards. This proactive approach helps organizations maintain visibility into the types of devices accessing the network and ensures that only authorized devices are granted entry.

Endpoint security solutions play a pivotal role in preventing unauthorized devices from compromising the overall security posture. Antivirus, anti-malware, and endpoint detection and response (EDR) tools should be configured to actively scan and monitor connected devices for any signs of malicious activity. These tools can detect and block unauthorized devices attempting to connect, providing an additional layer of defense against potential threats. Regular updates to endpoint security solutions are essential to ensure that they can effectively identify and respond to emerging threats and vulnerabilities.

Encryption is a key mechanism in preventing unauthorized devices from intercepting sensitive data during transmission. By encrypting communication between endpoints and the network, organizations can protect data from unauthorized interception and ensure the confidentiality and integrity of information. Secure protocols, such as SSL/TLS for web traffic and VPNs for remote access, add an extra layer of encryption, making it challenging for unauthorized devices to eavesdrop on communications. Encrypting data at rest on endpoints further fortifies security by safeguarding information even if a device is lost or stolen.

Implementing a comprehensive mobile device management (MDM) strategy is crucial for organizations dealing with the proliferation of mobile devices. MDM solutions enable organizations to enforce security policies, remotely manage device configurations, and control access to corporate resources. By defining and enforcing policies that specify which devices are allowed to connect to the corporate network and access sensitive data, organizations can prevent unauthorized devices from compromising endpoint security. MDM solutions also facilitate the remote wiping of data from lost or stolen devices, minimizing the risk of data breaches.

User education and awareness programs are integral components of preventing unauthorized devices from compromising endpoint security. Users should be informed about the risks associated with connecting unauthorized devices to the corporate network and the potential consequences for security. Training should emphasize the importance of adhering to security policies, avoiding the use of unauthorized devices, and reporting any suspicious activities promptly. Users should understand the potential impact of their actions on the overall security of the organization and be empowered to make informed decisions that prioritize security.

Network segmentation is an effective strategy to prevent unauthorized devices from compromising endpoint security. By dividing the network into segments and restricting communication between them, organizations can limit the potential impact of a compromised device. Even if an unauthorized device gains access to one segment, segmentation prevents lateral movement within the network, containing the threat and protecting critical resources. Implementing firewalls and access control lists (ACLs) at segment boundaries enhances network segmentation, allowing organizations to control the flow of traffic between different parts of the network.

Regular audits and assessments of endpoint security measures are essential to identify and address potential vulnerabilities. Organizations should conduct vulnerability assessments, penetration tests, and security audits to evaluate the effectiveness of existing security controls. These assessments help identify weaknesses that could be exploited by unauthorized devices and guide organizations in refining their security strategies. Regular audits contribute to a continuous improvement cycle, ensuring that security measures remain robust and adaptive to evolving threats.

Implementing device compliance checks is a proactive measure to prevent unauthorized devices from compromising endpoint security. Organizations can deploy tools that assess the compliance of connected devices with security policies and standards. These checks can include verifying the presence of up-to-date antivirus software, the application of security patches, and adherence to configuration standards. Non-compliant devices can be automatically quarantined or denied network access until they meet the specified security criteria. This approach ensures that only devices compliant with security policies are allowed to connect to the network, minimizing the risk of compromise.

Intrusion detection and prevention systems (IDPS) play a crucial role in preventing unauthorized devices from compromising endpoint security. These systems actively monitor network traffic for signs of malicious activity or behavior that deviates from normal patterns. By employing signature-based detection, anomaly detection, and heuristic analysis, IDPS solutions can identify and block unauthorized devices attempting to access the network. Regular updates to intrusion detection signatures and continuous monitoring enhance the effectiveness of these systems in preventing security incidents.

Collaboration with industry partners, threat intelligence providers, and cybersecurity communities can enhance an organization's ability to prevent unauthorized devices from compromising endpoint security. Sharing information about emerging threats, vulnerabilities, and best practices allows organizations to stay ahead of evolving risks. By participating in collaborative efforts, organizations can benefit from collective insights and leverage shared intelligence to strengthen their security posture. This collaborative approach creates a network effect, where the security community collectively contributes to a more resilient defense against unauthorized devices and other cyber threats.

In conclusion, preventing unauthorized devices from compromising endpoint security requires a multifaceted approach that incorporates access controls, device identification, encryption, endpoint security solutions, mobile device management, user education, network segmentation, compliance checks, intrusion detection, and collaboration. This holistic strategy aims to create a secure and resilient environment that mitigates the risks associated with unauthorized devices. As the threat landscape continues to evolve, organizations must remain vigilant, regularly reassess their security measures, and adapt their strategies to address emerging challenges in safeguarding endpoint security.

Implementing application whitelisting to control approved software.

Implementing application whitelisting is a powerful strategy for controlling approved software within an organization's IT environment. Application whitelisting is a security practice that involves creating a list of approved applications and allowing only those applications to execute on a system or network. This approach contrasts with blacklisting, where specific applications are identified as malicious and prohibited, leaving all others permitted by default. The primary goal of application whitelisting is to enhance security by restricting the execution of unauthorized and potentially malicious software, thereby minimizing the attack surface and mitigating the risks associated with unapproved applications.

To initiate the implementation of application whitelisting, organizations must start by defining a comprehensive inventory of approved applications. This process involves identifying the software applications essential for business operations, productivity, and security. By working closely with different departments and stakeholders, IT administrators can compile an exhaustive list of applications required for day-to-day tasks, specialized workflows, and critical functions within the organization. This collaborative approach ensures that the application whitelist accurately reflects the diverse needs of the organization and aligns with its business objectives.

Once the inventory of approved applications is established, organizations can leverage dedicated application whitelisting tools or built-in features within operating systems to create and enforce policies. These tools allow administrators to specify which applications are permitted to run on individual systems or across the entire network. Policies can be granular, enabling organizations to define rules based on various parameters, such as application name, file path, digital signatures, or cryptographic hashes. This granularity ensures a fine-tuned level of control over the approved software, enhancing security without unduly disrupting legitimate operations.

One key aspect of successful application whitelisting implementation is considering the dynamic nature of software environments. Updates, patches, and new releases are common occurrences in the software landscape, and organizations must establish procedures to review and update the application whitelist accordingly. Regularly reviewing and updating the whitelist ensures that it remains aligned with the organization's evolving software needs, addresses emerging security vulnerabilities, and accommodates changes in software versions or configurations. Automated tools can assist in this process, providing alerts for outdated or unauthorized software and facilitating streamlined updates to the whitelist.

Integrating application whitelisting into the organization's change management processes is essential for seamless operation and minimal disruption. This involves coordinating with IT, security, and other relevant teams to ensure that new software deployments, updates, or changes are appropriately reviewed and added to the whitelist before implementation. By incorporating application whitelisting into change management practices, organizations establish a proactive and standardized approach to maintaining control over their software environment, reducing the risk of unintentional security gaps or conflicts with existing policies.

Education and communication are critical components of a successful application whitelisting strategy. Users, particularly those accustomed to unrestricted software installations, should be informed about the reasons behind the implementation of application whitelisting and the benefits it brings to overall security. Clear communication helps build understanding and acceptance among users, reducing resistance and fostering a collaborative security culture within the organization. Training programs can also provide guidance on how to request the inclusion of new applications in the whitelist, ensuring a smooth process for adapting to changing business needs.

Organizations should conduct pilot programs or phased rollouts of application whitelisting to test its effectiveness and identify any potential issues before full-scale implementation. Pilots enable IT teams to assess the impact on different departments, user workflows, and specialized applications. Feedback from pilot participants can inform adjustments to policies, whitelists, or communication strategies, leading to a more tailored and effective implementation across the organization. This iterative approach allows organizations to fine-tune their application whitelisting strategy based on real-world usage and user feedback.

Continuous monitoring and auditing of application whitelisting policies are essential for maintaining an accurate and up-to-date control over approved software. Monitoring tools can provide insights into application usage patterns, detect anomalies, and generate alerts for any deviations from established policies. Regular audits, both automated and manual, help identify unauthorized or non-compliant applications that may have found their way into the environment. These audits contribute to the ongoing improvement of application whitelisting policies, ensuring that they align with the organization's evolving needs and the ever-changing threat landscape.

Collaboration with vendors and software developers is crucial for successful application whitelisting implementation. Organizations should engage with software vendors to obtain digital signatures or cryptographic hashes for their applications, enabling more robust verification of software integrity. Working closely with developers ensures a smoother integration of whitelisted applications and facilitates the inclusion of relevant information in the organization's application inventory. This collaborative approach strengthens the organization's ability to accurately identify and approve legitimate software, enhancing the effectiveness of the application whitelist.

In addition to preventing unauthorized or malicious software, application whitelisting can be leveraged to mitigate the impact of certain cyber threats, such as ransomware. By restricting the execution of unknown or unapproved applications, organizations can reduce the likelihood of ransomware infections and limit the ability of malicious software to propagate across the network. Application whitelisting provides an additional layer of defense against the unauthorized execution of scripts or executables commonly associated with ransomware attacks, enhancing the organization's overall cyber-security posture.

Integration with threat intelligence feeds enhances the proactive capabilities of application whitelisting by providing real-time information about emerging threats and vulnerabilities. Organizations can incorporate threat intelligence data into their whitelisting policies, allowing them to quickly adapt to new threats and prevent the execution of known malicious applications. This dynamic and intelligence-driven approach ensures that the application whitelist remains adaptive and responsive to the evolving cybersecurity landscape.

In conclusion, implementing application whitelisting to control approved software is a comprehensive and dynamic process that requires collaboration, communication, continuous monitoring, and adaptation. By defining an accurate inventory of approved applications, establishing granular policies, integrating with change management processes, educating users, conducting pilot programs, and collaborating with vendors, organizations can enhance their security posture and reduce the risk of unauthorized or malicious software compromising endpoint security. The iterative nature of this process, coupled with ongoing monitoring, auditing, and integration with threat intelligence, ensures that the application whitelist remains an effective and adaptive security control in the face of evolving cybersecurity challenges.

The role of blacklisting in preventing the execution of malicious applications.

The role of blacklisting is pivotal in the realm of cybersecurity as it pertains to preventing the execution of malicious applications. Blacklisting functions as a proactive defense mechanism by maintaining a comprehensive list of known malicious applications, file signatures, or behavior patterns. In contrast to whitelisting, which permits only approved entities, blacklisting operates on the premise of denying access or execution to known threats. This approach is instrumental in safeguarding computer systems, networks, and endpoints from the multitude of evolving and sophisticated malicious software that constantly seeks to exploit vulnerabilities, compromise data, or disrupt operations.

The foundation of blacklisting lies in the identification and categorization of malicious applications, which can include viruses, worms, trojans, ransomware, and other forms of malware. Security researchers and organizations compile extensive databases of known malicious signatures, patterns, or attributes associated with these threats. These databases serve as the basis for blacklists, enabling security systems to quickly identify and block the execution of files or processes that match the characteristics of recognized malicious entities. The dynamic nature of the threat landscape necessitates continuous updates to blacklists, reflecting the emergence of new threats and variants.

File-based blacklisting is a common approach, where specific file hashes, signatures, or patterns associated with malicious applications are identified and added to the blacklist. When a user attempts to execute a file, the system checks its hash or signature against the blacklist. If a match is found, the execution is denied, preventing the malicious application from running and potentially causing harm. This method provides a rapid and effective means of stopping known threats, especially those that have been previously analyzed and documented.

Behavior-based blacklisting expands the scope beyond specific file attributes to encompass the behavior exhibited by applications. Malicious applications often share common behaviors, such as attempting to modify system settings, establishing unauthorized network connections, or evading detection by altering their characteristics. Behavioral blacklisting focuses on identifying and blocking these patterns of activity, allowing security systems to detect and thwart previously unseen variants or mutations of known threats. This dynamic approach enhances the ability to counter emerging threats that may employ sophisticated evasion techniques.

Network-based blacklisting is another dimension of this defense strategy, focusing on blocking communication with known malicious domains or IP addresses. Many malicious applications rely on establishing connections to external servers for command and control, data exfiltration, or to download additional payloads. By maintaining a blacklist of known malicious network entities, organizations can prevent their systems from communicating with these sources, effectively neutralizing a significant avenue of attack. Network-based blacklisting is particularly relevant in the context of preventing the spread of malware and limiting its ability to connect with malicious infrastructure.

While blacklisting is a potent defense against known threats, it faces inherent challenges, particularly in dealing with zero-day vulnerabilities and new, undiscovered threats. Zero-day vulnerabilities refer to security weaknesses that are exploited by attackers before a patch or solution is available. Since blacklisting relies on recognizing known malicious entities, it may not be effective against threats that leverage previously undisclosed vulnerabilities. Attackers continuously evolve their tactics to bypass blacklists, employing techniques such as polymorphism, obfuscation, or encryption to alter the appearance of their malicious code and evade detection.

Furthermore, false positives represent a notable concern in blacklisting. A false positive occurs when a legitimate application is erroneously flagged as malicious and denied execution. This can result in disruptions to normal business operations, decreased productivity, and user frustration. Striking the right balance between a comprehensive blacklist and minimizing false positives requires careful curation and regular updates. Security administrators must continuously refine blacklists, taking into account new information, user feedback, and changes in the threat landscape to maintain efficacy without causing undue disruptions.

Blacklisting operates at different layers of the cybersecurity stack, ranging from endpoint protection to network security. Endpoint security solutions, such as antivirus software, leverage blacklists to scan files and processes on individual devices for known malicious attributes. Network security appliances utilize blacklisting to filter traffic and prevent communication with known malicious domains or IP addresses. These layers work in concert to create a multi-faceted defense, collectively mitigating the risks associated with a diverse range of malicious applications.

Automation is a critical component in the effectiveness of blacklisting, given the sheer volume and rapid evolution of threats. Automated systems can continuously update blacklists based on threat intelligence feeds, security research, and real-time analysis. Machine learning algorithms play a significant role in enhancing blacklisting capabilities by identifying patterns, anomalies, and new threat vectors. This enables security systems to adapt rapidly to changing circumstances and proactively identify previously unknown threats based on their behavior or attributes.

Collaboration within the cybersecurity community is integral to the success of blacklisting. Information sharing about newly identified threats, indicators of compromise, and emerging attack techniques allows organizations to collectively strengthen their blacklisting efforts. Industry collaborations, threat intelligence sharing platforms, and information-sharing forums facilitate a collective defense approach, enabling organizations to benefit from shared insights and collaboratively enhance their blacklisting capabilities.

The integration of blacklisting into a broader cybersecurity strategy is essential for a comprehensive defense posture. Blacklisting should be complemented by other security measures, such as application whitelisting, intrusion detection and prevention systems, vulnerability management, and user education. These components work together to create layers of defense, each addressing specific aspects of the threat landscape. The synergy between these strategies ensures a more resilient and adaptive security architecture that can effectively counter the diverse tactics employed by malicious actors.

In conclusion, the role of blacklisting in preventing the execution of malicious applications is fundamental to modern cybersecurity. By maintaining and leveraging blacklists of known malicious signatures, behaviors, or network entities, organizations can create a robust defense against a wide array of threats. Despite its efficacy, blacklisting faces challenges in addressing zero-day vulnerabilities, adapting to evolving threats, and managing false positives. The dynamic nature of the cybersecurity landscape requires continuous updates, automation, collaboration, and integration with other security measures to ensure that blacklisting remains a formidable component of a comprehensive cybersecurity strategy.

Guidelines for users and administrators to enhance endpoint security.

Enhancing endpoint security is a shared responsibility between users and administrators, requiring a combination of proactive measures, awareness, and collaboration to mitigate the evolving landscape of cyber threats. Users and administrators alike play crucial roles in fortifying the security posture of endpoints—computers, laptops, and mobile devices—that form the frontline defense against malicious activities. Guiding users and administrators through a comprehensive set of guidelines fosters a security-conscious culture, reduces vulnerabilities, and strengthens the overall resilience of the organization's digital environment.

Users are the first line of defense in maintaining endpoint security, and their actions significantly impact the overall security posture. Education and awareness are foundational elements for users, emphasizing the importance of security best practices and the potential risks associated with unsafe behaviors. Users should be encouraged to follow secure password practices, employing complex and unique passwords for each account, and enable multi-factor authentication whenever possible. Regular security awareness training empowers users to recognize phishing attempts, social engineering tactics, and other common methods used by attackers to compromise endpoints.

Maintaining updated software is paramount for users to enhance endpoint security. Regularly applying security patches, updates, and firmware upgrades ensures that known vulnerabilities are addressed promptly. Users should be educated on the significance of keeping operating systems, applications, and security software up to date, and organizations can implement automated tools to streamline the update process, reducing the risk of exploitation due to outdated software.

Users should exercise caution when interacting with emails, links, and attachments. Avoiding clicking on suspicious links or downloading attachments from unknown sources helps prevent malware infections. Organizations can reinforce these guidelines by implementing email filtering solutions that detect and quarantine malicious content. Users should be trained to verify the legitimacy of emails, especially those requesting sensitive information or financial transactions, and encouraged to report any suspicious emails to the IT department promptly.

Endpoint security is significantly strengthened by implementing robust access controls. Users should adhere to the principle of least privilege, only granting necessary permissions for their roles and responsibilities. Avoiding the use of administrator accounts for everyday tasks helps minimize the impact of potential security incidents. Organizations can enforce access controls through user account management and regularly review and update permissions based on changes in job roles or responsibilities.

The use of virtual private networks (VPNs) is an effective measure for users to enhance endpoint security, particularly when connecting to public Wi-Fi networks. VPNs encrypt internet traffic, safeguarding sensitive information from potential eavesdropping or interception by malicious actors on unsecured networks. Users should be encouraged to use VPNs, especially when accessing corporate resources or handling sensitive data remotely, contributing to a more secure communication channel.

Encryption is a vital component of endpoint security, and users should leverage encryption features provided by operating systems and applications. Encrypting data at rest and in transit helps protect sensitive information from unauthorized access. Users should enable full-disk encryption on their devices, ensuring that even if the physical device is lost or stolen, the data remains secure. Additionally, organizations can implement policies that mandate the use of encrypted communication channels, enhancing the overall confidentiality and integrity of data.

Backup practices are integral to users' resilience against data loss due to unforeseen events such as ransomware attacks or hardware failures. Users should regularly back up critical data to secure and offline storage solutions, preventing data loss in the event of a security incident. Automated backup tools can simplify this process, ensuring that users maintain up-to-date copies of their important files. Organizations can reinforce these guidelines by implementing and communicating backup policies to all users.

The use of endpoint security software is a proactive measure that significantly contributes to users' defense against a myriad of threats. Antivirus, anti-malware, and endpoint detection and response (EDR) tools provide real-time protection against known and emerging threats. Users should install and regularly update security software on their devices, conduct regular scans, and promptly report any security alerts or concerns to the IT department. Regularly updating security software ensures that users benefit from the latest threat intelligence and protection mechanisms.

User education about the risks associated with removable media, such as USB drives, is essential to prevent the introduction of malware through these vectors. Users should exercise caution when inserting unknown or untrusted USB drives into their devices, as they can potentially harbor malicious software. Organizations can implement policies that restrict the use of removable media or employ endpoint security solutions that scan and filter removable devices for potential threats before allowing access to the system.

Implementing strong authentication practices is imperative for users to secure their accounts and devices. Users should use complex passwords, avoid reusing passwords across multiple accounts, and consider the use of biometric authentication or multi-factor authentication (MFA) for an additional layer of security. Administrators can enforce MFA policies and educate users on the importance of these additional authentication measures in safeguarding their accounts and preventing unauthorized access.

Administrators play a pivotal role in shaping and maintaining the overall security infrastructure of an organization, including endpoint security. Ensuring that endpoint security policies are comprehensive, up to date, and effectively communicated to all users is a fundamental responsibility. Administrators should conduct regular risk assessments to identify potential vulnerabilities and adapt security policies accordingly. Collaborating with security teams, administrators can stay informed about emerging threats and incorporate new insights into their security strategies.

Endpoint security solutions should be deployed and configured by administrators to provide a layered defense against a spectrum of threats. These solutions may include antivirus software, firewalls, intrusion detection and prevention systems, and advanced endpoint protection tools. Administrators should configure these solutions to enforce security policies, conduct regular scans, and generate alerts for any suspicious activities. Regular updates to endpoint security solutions ensure that they remain effective against the latest threats and vulnerabilities.

Implementing network segmentation is a strategic approach for administrators to enhance endpoint security. By dividing the network into segments, administrators can isolate endpoints and limit the lateral movement of threats in the event of a security incident. Firewalls, access control lists, and network policies can be employed to regulate traffic between segments and prevent unauthorized access. Network segmentation complements endpoint security by adding an additional layer of defense, particularly in large or complex network environments.

Endpoint detection and response (EDR) tools are invaluable for administrators in monitoring, detecting, and responding to security incidents. EDR solutions provide real-time visibility into endpoint activities, enabling administrators to identify anomalous behavior, detect potential threats, and investigate security incidents promptly. These tools empower administrators to respond to incidents proactively, contain threats, and conduct post-incident analysis to enhance overall endpoint security.

Vulnerability management is a critical aspect of administrators' responsibilities in maintaining endpoint security. Regularly scanning endpoints for vulnerabilities, applying patches, and updating software are essential practices to address known weaknesses that could be exploited by attackers. Automated vulnerability scanning tools can streamline this process, providing administrators with insights into the security posture of endpoints and facilitating a timely and systematic approach to remediation.

Administrators should enforce the use of firewalls on endpoints to control inbound and outbound network traffic. Configuring firewalls to allow only necessary and authorized communication helps prevent unauthorized access and restricts the potential for malicious activities. Administrators can establish firewall policies based on the principle of least privilege, ensuring that only essential services and applications have network access.

Encryption of sensitive data on endpoints should be enforced by administrators as part of their security strategy. Full-disk encryption and encryption for data in transit contribute to the confidentiality and integrity of sensitive information. Administrators can implement policies that mandate the use of encryption features provided by operating systems or deploy additional encryption solutions to safeguard data against unauthorized access or theft.

Regular audits and assessments are essential for administrators to evaluate the effectiveness of endpoint security measures. Conducting vulnerability assessments, penetration tests, and security audits helps identify potential weaknesses, gaps, or misconfigurations

that could be exploited by attackers. These assessments provide valuable insights into the organization's security posture and inform administrators about areas that require attention, improvement, or additional safeguards.

Collaboration with users is a key aspect of administrators' efforts to enhance endpoint security. Administrators should foster a culture of open communication, encouraging users to report security incidents, concerns, or suspicious activities promptly. Collaboration enables administrators to gather insights from end-users, understand their security needs, and tailor security measures to align with the organization's overall objectives.

In conclusion, the guidelines for users and administrators to enhance endpoint security encompass a multifaceted approach that includes education, proactive measures, collaboration, and continuous improvement. Users and administrators are integral components of the collective defense against evolving cyber threats, and by adhering to these guidelines, organizations can establish a robust and resilient security posture for their endpoints. The synergy between users and administrators, coupled with a commitment to ongoing education and adaptation, contributes to a dynamic and effective endpoint security strategy in the face of an ever-changing threat landscape.

Periodic assessments and updates to fortify endpoint protection.

Periodic assessments and updates are fundamental pillars in the ongoing effort to fortify endpoint protection within an organization's cybersecurity strategy. As the digital landscape continues to evolve and cyber threats become increasingly sophisticated, the need for a dynamic and adaptive approach to endpoint protection is paramount. Periodic assessments serve as proactive measures, allowing organizations to evaluate the effectiveness of their existing endpoint security measures, identify potential vulnerabilities, and implement necessary updates to address emerging threats and reinforce defenses.

Regular vulnerability assessments are a cornerstone of periodic assessments for endpoint protection. These assessments involve the systematic scanning and analysis of endpoints to identify known security vulnerabilities that could be exploited by attackers. Automated tools can be deployed to conduct thorough scans of operating systems, applications, and configurations to detect weaknesses. The results of vulnerability assessments provide organizations with a comprehensive view of the security posture of their endpoints, enabling administrators to prioritize remediation efforts based on the severity and potential impact of identified vulnerabilities.

Penetration testing, another crucial element of periodic assessments, involves simulating real-world cyber-attacks to assess the resilience of endpoint security measures. Penetration testers, often external security experts, employ ethical hacking techniques to identify potential weaknesses in defenses, gaining insights into how adversaries might exploit vulnerabilities. The findings from penetration tests help organizations understand their vulnerabilities from an attacker's perspective and refine their security strategies accordingly. By periodically subjecting endpoints to simulated attacks, organizations can continuously improve their defenses and stay ahead of evolving threats.

Security audits are essential components of periodic assessments that evaluate the overall effectiveness of endpoint protection measures. These audits involve a comprehensive review of security policies, configurations, and user practices related to endpoint security. Security auditors assess adherence to established security guidelines, the robustness of access controls, and the effectiveness of security software deployed on endpoints. Regular security audits provide organizations with insights into the strengths and weaknesses of their endpoint security posture, guiding them in making informed decisions to enhance protection measures.

Continuous monitoring is a proactive approach within periodic assessments that involves real-time observation of endpoint activities. Monitoring tools analyze network traffic, system logs, and user behavior to detect anomalies, suspicious activities, or potential security incidents. By implementing continuous monitoring, organizations can identify and respond to security threats in a timely manner, reducing the dwell time of attackers within the network. Regular reviews of monitoring data during periodic assessments enable organizations to refine their detection capabilities and improve the overall responsiveness of endpoint protection measures.

Endpoint security software, including antivirus, anti-malware, and endpoint detection and response (EDR) solutions, requires regular updates to effectively combat evolving threats. Periodic assessments should include a thorough review and update of endpoint security software to ensure that it incorporates the latest threat intelligence, detection capabilities, and mitigation strategies. Administrators should verify that security software is configured correctly, conducts regular scans, and provides timely alerts for potential security incidents. Regular updates to endpoint security software contribute to the resilience of defenses by addressing emerging threats and enhancing the overall threat detection and response capabilities.

The importance of patch management in periodic assessments cannot be overstated. Patch management involves the systematic application of updates, patches, and security fixes to software, operating systems, and applications on endpoints. Vulnerability assessments often reveal known vulnerabilities for which patches are available. Periodic assessments should include a review of the patch management process to ensure that critical security patches are promptly applied. Automated patch deployment tools can streamline this process, reducing the window of exposure to known vulnerabilities and fortifying the security posture of endpoints.

Regular configuration reviews are essential in periodic assessments to evaluate the security configurations of endpoints. Security misconfigurations can introduce vulnerabilities that attackers may exploit to compromise endpoints. Periodic assessments should involve a comprehensive review of security configurations, including settings for firewalls, antivirus software, and other security controls. Organizations can employ automated tools to scan for and identify misconfigurations, ensuring that endpoints adhere to established security baselines. Regular configuration reviews contribute to the maintenance of a secure and standardized endpoint environment.

The human factor is a critical consideration in periodic assessments, necessitating ongoing education and awareness programs for end-users. Periodic security training sessions and awareness campaigns help users stay informed about the latest cyber threats, phishing tactics, and social engineering techniques. By periodically refreshing user knowledge and reinforcing security best practices, organizations empower users to become a proactive line of defense against various threats. Periodic assessments should include an evaluation of the effectiveness of these education programs and identify areas for improvement to enhance the human element in endpoint protection.

Incident response planning and testing are integral components of periodic assessments to ensure that organizations are well-prepared to handle security incidents involving endpoints. Periodic tabletop exercises or simulated incident scenarios allow organizations to test their incident response plans, assess the effectiveness of communication channels, and identify areas for improvement. By periodically rehearsing incident response procedures, organizations can enhance their ability to detect, respond to, and recover from security incidents, minimizing the potential impact on endpoint security.

Regular updates to security policies are essential for organizations to adapt to changes in the threat landscape, business requirements, and regulatory environments. Periodic assessments should include a review of existing security policies related to endpoint protection, ensuring that they align with current best practices and industry standards. Organizations should update policies based on lessons learned from incidents, changes in technology, and evolving compliance requirements. This iterative approach to policy development and refinement contributes to the resilience and relevance of endpoint protection measures.

Collaboration with external threat intelligence sources is a proactive strategy within periodic assessments to stay abreast of emerging threats and vulnerabilities. Organizations can subscribe to threat intelligence feeds, participate in information-sharing platforms, and collaborate with industry peers to gain insights into the latest cyber threats. Threat intelligence informs periodic assessments by providing organizations with contextual information about the specific risks and attack vectors relevant to their industry or sector. By leveraging external threat intelligence, organizations can enhance their ability to anticipate and mitigate potential threats to endpoint security.

Regular communication and collaboration between IT and security teams are crucial aspects of periodic assessments. IT administrators and security professionals should work in tandem to share insights, address vulnerabilities, and implement security updates effectively. Periodic assessments provide opportunities for cross-functional collaboration, allowing IT teams to align their activities with security priorities and ensuring that endpoint protection measures are integrated seamlessly into overall IT operations. This collaboration helps bridge the gap between security goals and operational realities, fostering a unified approach to endpoint security.

Documentation and reporting are essential components of periodic assessments, providing organizations with a record of activities, findings, and improvements. Comprehensive documentation includes details about vulnerability assessments, penetration test results, incident response exercises, and updates to security policies. Periodic reporting ensures that stakeholders, including executives and board members, are informed about the state of endpoint security, ongoing efforts to fortify defenses, and any notable changes in the threat landscape. Documentation and reporting contribute to transparency, accountability, and continuous improvement within the organization's cybersecurity program.

In conclusion, periodic assessments and updates are integral elements in the ongoing effort to fortify endpoint protection. By conducting regular vulnerability assessments, penetration tests, security audits, and continuous monitoring, organizations can identify and address potential vulnerabilities in a proactive manner. Regular updates to security software, patch management processes, and security policies contribute to the resilience of endpoint protection measures. The human factor, incident response planning, collaboration, and documentation further enhance the organization's ability to adapt to evolving threats and maintain a robust security posture. In a landscape where cyber threats are dynamic and persistent, the iterative and holistic approach of periodic assessments ensures that organizations remain vigilant and well-prepared to defend against emerging challenges to endpoint security.

Chapter 7: Patch Management and Updates

Understanding the significance of timely updates and patches.

The significance of timely updates and patches in the realm of cybersecurity cannot be overstated, as these measures serve as critical components in fortifying digital systems against evolving threats and vulnerabilities. Operating systems, software applications, and various technologies constitute the intricate fabric of the digital landscape, each layer susceptible to exploitation by malicious actors seeking to compromise the integrity, confidentiality, and availability of information. Timely updates and patches act as proactive measures, bridging the gap between identified vulnerabilities and robust defenses, thereby forming a crucial line of defense in the ongoing battle against cyber threats.

At the core of this significance lies the proactive nature of updates and patches. The digital environment is dynamic, constantly evolving with emerging technologies, changing user behaviors, and, unfortunately, the discovery of new security vulnerabilities. Developers and security experts tirelessly work to identify and address these vulnerabilities through updates and patches. The proactive release of these security measures enables organizations and individuals to stay ahead of potential threats, preventing attackers from exploiting known weaknesses to gain unauthorized access, execute malicious code, or compromise the confidentiality of sensitive information.

Timeliness is of the essence in the deployment of updates and patches, as cyber adversaries are known to exploit vulnerabilities rapidly once they become aware of them. The concept of a "zero-day" vulnerability, one that is actively exploited before a patch is available, underscores the urgency of swift action. Timely updates ensure that organizations and users can close the window of vulnerability promptly, reducing the risk of falling victim to attacks that leverage newly discovered weaknesses. The adage "time is of the essence" holds particularly true in the dynamic and relentless landscape of cybersecurity.

The role of updates and patches extends beyond merely addressing security vulnerabilities; they also contribute to the overall performance and stability of digital systems. Software developers regularly release updates that include enhancements, optimizations, and bug fixes. By staying current with these updates, users benefit not only from improved security features but also from a more reliable and efficient computing experience. Timely deployment of updates reflects a commitment to maintaining the health and functionality of digital systems, ensuring they operate optimally and meet the demands of an ever-changing technological landscape.

The significance of updates and patches is magnified in the context of widespread software usage. Operating systems, office suites, web browsers, and various applications serve as ubiquitous tools in daily computing activities. The widespread adoption of these technologies makes them lucrative targets for cybercriminals looking to exploit vulnerabilities on a large scale. Timely updates play a crucial role in mitigating the impact of potential large-scale attacks, as they allow organizations and users to quickly inoculate their systems against known vulnerabilities and fortify their digital defenses.

Beyond the realm of individual users, the importance of updates and patches is particularly pronounced in organizational settings. Enterprises, government agencies, and institutions rely on complex networks and systems to facilitate their operations, manage data, and deliver services. The interconnected nature of these environments amplifies the potential impact of a security breach. Timely updates become a strategic imperative for organizations, as they help maintain the security posture of entire networks, safeguard critical assets, and protect against the potentially devastating consequences of a successful cyberattack.

Compliance with regulatory requirements is another dimension of the significance of timely updates and patches, especially for organizations in sectors with stringent data protection standards. Regulatory frameworks often mandate the implementation of security measures, including the prompt application of updates, to ensure the confidentiality and integrity of sensitive information. Adhering to these compliance standards not only helps organizations avoid legal repercussions but also demonstrates a commitment to responsible and secure data management practices.

The interconnected nature of modern digital ecosystems introduces a chain reaction effect when it comes to cybersecurity. A vulnerability in one component can potentially impact the security of other interconnected systems. Timely updates and patches play a crucial role in breaking this chain, preventing the propagation of threats across networks and limiting the scope of potential damage. By addressing vulnerabilities promptly, organizations contribute to the collective security of the broader digital landscape, fostering a safer online environment for all users.

Cyber threats constantly evolve, and attackers often adapt their tactics to exploit the latest vulnerabilities. Understanding the significance of timely updates and patches requires recognizing the dynamic nature of the threat landscape. The continuous development of sophisticated attack methods, the discovery of new vulnerabilities, and the emergence of novel technologies underscore the need for a proactive and adaptive approach to cybersecurity. Timely updates enable organizations and individuals to keep pace with this ever-changing landscape, reducing the likelihood of falling victim to cyber threats that leverage the latest techniques and vulnerabilities.

The concept of the "patch cycle" is integral to the significance of timely updates, as it reflects a structured and systematic approach to maintaining the security and functionality of digital systems. The patch cycle involves a series of stages, including vulnerability discovery, patch development, testing, and deployment. Each stage contributes to the overall efficacy of the patching process. Timely adherence to the patch cycle ensures that organizations and users can benefit from the latest security measures without introducing unforeseen issues or disruptions to their systems.

Challenges and complexities arise in the practical implementation of timely updates and patches, especially in large-scale and diverse computing environments. Organizations often grapple with the need to balance security requirements with operational considerations, such as system uptime, compatibility, and potential disruptions to business processes. Effective patch management strategies address these challenges by prioritizing critical vulnerabilities, testing updates in controlled environments, and scheduling deployments during periods of minimal impact on operations.

The human element plays a crucial role in the success of timely updates and patches. Users, whether individuals or employees within an organization, are essential participants in the patching process. Education and awareness programs are instrumental in fostering a culture of cybersecurity consciousness, encouraging users to prioritize and promptly apply updates. Additionally, organizations must provide clear communication about the importance of updates, their role in maintaining security, and the potential risks associated with delaying or neglecting the patching process.

Automation emerges as a valuable ally in the quest for timely updates and patches. Automated patch deployment tools, vulnerability scanners, and update management systems streamline the process, reducing the manual effort required to keep systems current. Automation not only accelerates the patching cycle but also minimizes the risk of human error, ensuring that updates are applied consistently and comprehensively across diverse computing environments. Leveraging automation aligns with the principle of efficiency in cybersecurity operations, allowing organizations to stay agile in the face of evolving threats.

The cost of neglecting timely updates and patches can be severe, both in terms of financial implications and reputational damage. Cyberattacks that exploit known vulnerabilities can result in data breaches, financial losses, operational disruptions, and tarnished reputations. The aftermath of a successful cyberattack often involves extensive remediation efforts, legal consequences, and the need for reputation recovery. By contrast, the investment in timely updates and patches represents a proactive and cost-effective strategy to mitigate these risks and safeguard the long-term health of digital systems.

In conclusion, the significance of timely updates and patches lies at the core of effective cybersecurity. These measures act as proactive defenses against evolving threats, bridge the gap between vulnerability discovery and mitigation, and contribute to the overall performance and stability of digital systems. Whether in individual computing environments or large-scale organizational networks, timely updates play a pivotal role in maintaining the resilience of digital ecosystems. Recognizing the dynamic nature of the threat landscape, adhering to the patch cycle, addressing implementation challenges, involving the human element, leveraging automation, and understanding the potential consequences of neglect underscore the multifaceted significance of timely updates and patches in the ongoing quest for cybersecurity excellence.

The role of patch management in addressing vulnerabilities and enhancing system security.

The role of patch management in addressing vulnerabilities and enhancing system security is pivotal in the complex landscape of cybersecurity. Patch management refers to the systematic process of identifying, acquiring, testing, and deploying patches or updates to software, applications, and operating systems to address known vulnerabilities. As digital environments continuously evolve, so do the tactics of cyber adversaries seeking to exploit weaknesses for nefarious purposes. Patch management serves as a strategic and proactive approach to stay ahead of potential threats, minimizing the risk of security breaches, data compromises, and other cyber incidents that could compromise the confidentiality, integrity, and availability of information within systems.

At its core, patch management is a response to the persistent challenge of software vulnerabilities. Developers, in their ongoing efforts to create feature-rich and functional software, inevitably introduce code that may contain security flaws. These vulnerabilities, once identified, become potential entry points for cyber attackers. Patch management provides a structured framework to systematically address and mitigate these vulnerabilities, forming a crucial line of defense against the ever-evolving tactics employed by malicious actors.

The identification phase of patch management involves continuous monitoring and vulnerability assessments. Security researchers, vendors, and the cybersecurity community actively contribute to the discovery of vulnerabilities through ongoing analysis of software and systems. Automated tools and scanners aid organizations in identifying vulnerabilities within their environments. The information gathered during this phase serves as the foundation for the subsequent steps in the patch management process. Identifying vulnerabilities promptly is essential for staying ahead of potential exploits and ensuring that patches can be developed and deployed in a timely manner.

Once vulnerabilities are identified, the acquisition phase of patch management involves obtaining or creating patches to address these weaknesses. Software vendors play a crucial role in this phase by releasing official patches for their products. Security researchers may also contribute by developing and sharing unofficial patches for open-source software or applications that lack official support. The collaboration between the cybersecurity community and software vendors is integral in ensuring that patches are made available promptly and comprehensively for a wide range of software and systems.

Testing is a critical element in the patch management process, focusing on ensuring that patches do not inadvertently introduce new issues or disruptions to systems. Rigorous testing involves evaluating the compatibility of patches with existing software configurations, dependencies, and customizations within an organization's environment. Testing also assesses the impact of patches on system performance, stability, and functionality. The goal is to strike a balance between the need for security and the imperative to maintain operational continuity. Effective testing mitigates the risk of unintended consequences and instills confidence in the reliability of the patch deployment process.

The deployment phase of patch management is the point at which tested and verified patches are rolled out to the production environment. The deployment process should be carefully planned to minimize disruptions to operations. Organizations often use phased deployment strategies, targeting less critical systems first before applying patches to more critical or high-availability systems. Automated deployment tools can streamline this process, allowing patches to be applied efficiently across large and diverse computing environments. Ensuring that patches are deployed in a timely and systematic manner is essential to closing vulnerabilities and enhancing the overall security posture of systems.

Continuous monitoring and feedback mechanisms are integral to effective patch management. Even after deployment, organizations must remain vigilant, monitoring for any unexpected issues, system anomalies, or indications that a patch may not have been successful in addressing a vulnerability. Feedback loops contribute to the iterative nature of patch management, allowing organizations to adapt and refine their strategies based on real-world experiences. Monitoring also helps organizations identify any new vulnerabilities that may emerge over time, ensuring a proactive response to evolving threats.

The role of patch management extends beyond addressing vulnerabilities to encompass the broader goal of enhancing system security. A comprehensive patch management strategy contributes to the overall resilience of systems by reducing the attack surface available to potential adversaries. By promptly addressing known vulnerabilities, organizations limit the opportunities for attackers to exploit weaknesses and gain unauthorized access. This approach aligns with the principle of least privilege, minimizing the potential impact of security incidents and mitigating the risks associated with data breaches or system compromises.

Effective patch management is integral to regulatory compliance, particularly in industries where data protection and cybersecurity standards are stringent. Many regulatory frameworks mandate the implementation of security measures, including the timely application of updates and patches, to safeguard sensitive information. Organizations subject to regulatory requirements must demonstrate adherence to these standards through documented patch management processes. Compliance with regulations not only helps organizations avoid legal consequences but also contributes to a culture of responsible and accountable data management practices.

The holistic role of patch management is underscored by its contribution to incident prevention and response. Patched systems are inherently more resilient to common attack vectors, reducing the likelihood of successful exploitation. Moreover, in the event of a security incident, having up-to-date systems facilitates more effective incident response. Security teams can rely on the fact that known vulnerabilities are already addressed, allowing them to focus on detecting and mitigating novel or advanced threats. Patch management thus plays a crucial role in both proactive cybersecurity measures and reactive response strategies.

The scalability of patch management is a key consideration in modern computing environments. As organizations increasingly embrace cloud computing, virtualization, and diverse technology stacks, the ability to manage patches across a wide array of platforms and configurations becomes paramount. Automated and centralized patch management solutions help organizations address the challenges of scale, ensuring that patches are consistently applied to diverse systems, regardless of their location or underlying infrastructure. This scalability is essential for maintaining a unified and secure computing environment in the face of growing complexity and diversity.

Challenges in patch management arise from the delicate balance between security and operational considerations. Organizations often face pressures to maintain high system availability and minimize disruptions to critical operations. Balancing the need for timely patch deployment with the imperative to avoid downtime requires careful planning and coordination. Prioritizing patches based on risk assessments, criticality of vulnerabilities, and potential impact on operations helps organizations make informed decisions that align with both security goals and operational requirements.

The human element plays a crucial role in the success of patch management. End-users, system administrators, and IT staff all contribute to the effectiveness of the patch management process. User education and awareness programs foster a culture of cybersecurity consciousness, encouraging users to promptly apply updates and patches. System administrators play a central role in testing, deploying, and monitoring patches, ensuring that the process is executed in a manner that aligns with organizational objectives. Collaboration and communication between IT teams, security professionals, and end-users are integral to the success of patch management initiatives.

Automation emerges as a force multiplier in the realm of patch management. Automated tools and solutions streamline repetitive tasks, accelerate the patch deployment process, and reduce the risk of human error. Automation also facilitates the enforcement of patch management policies consistently across large and complex computing environments. By leveraging automation, organizations can enhance the efficiency of their patch management efforts, ensuring that patches are applied promptly, comprehensively, and with minimal manual intervention.

The economic impact of effective patch management is significant, especially when juxtaposed against the potential costs of security incidents. Investing in proactive patch management is a prudent financial decision, as it helps organizations avoid the financial repercussions associated with data breaches, legal consequences, and reputational damage. The long-term benefits of maintaining a secure and resilient computing environment far outweigh the costs associated with implementing robust patch management strategies.

In conclusion, the role of patch management in addressing vulnerabilities and enhancing system security is multifaceted and integral to modern cybersecurity. This systematic approach to identifying, acquiring, testing, and deploying patches plays a pivotal role in reducing the attack surface, preventing security incidents, and contributing to the overall resilience of digital systems. As the cyber threat landscape continues to evolve, effective patch management remains a cornerstone in the ongoing effort to fortify systems against potential exploits, ensuring that organizations can adapt and respond to emerging challenges in the dynamic world of cybersecurity.

Strategies for deploying patches without disrupting system operations.

Deploying patches without disrupting system operations is a complex and delicate process that demands a strategic and well-coordinated approach. Organizations face the challenge of maintaining the security of their systems by promptly applying updates and patches while simultaneously minimizing the potential impact on ongoing operations. Strategies for seamless patch deployment revolve around careful planning, risk assessment, communication, automation, and continuous monitoring. A key consideration is the need to strike a balance between the urgency of patching to address vulnerabilities and the imperative to avoid disruptions that may impact critical business processes.

A foundational strategy for deploying patches without disruption is the development of a comprehensive patch management plan. This plan outlines the organization's approach to identifying, acquiring, testing, and deploying patches systematically. It includes a detailed schedule that considers the criticality of patches, potential risks associated with vulnerabilities, and the impact of the deployment on different systems. A well-structured patch management plan serves as a roadmap, guiding organizations through the intricacies of the patching process and ensuring that each deployment is aligned with overall business objectives.

Prioritization is a central element of successful patch deployment strategies. Not all patches are created equal, and organizations must prioritize based on the severity of vulnerabilities, potential impact on operations, and criticality of the systems involved. A risk-based approach allows organizations to focus their efforts on addressing the most pressing security concerns first. Critical systems, those handling sensitive data or supporting essential business functions, should be prioritized to receive patches promptly, while less critical systems may follow a phased deployment schedule to minimize disruptions.

Testing patches in controlled environments before widespread deployment is a fundamental strategy to mitigate the risk of disruptions. Rigorous testing helps ensure that patches do not introduce new issues, conflicts with existing configurations, or negatively impact system performance. Organizations commonly use test environments that mirror their production systems to simulate real-world conditions. Testing allows IT teams to identify and address potential challenges before patches are deployed to the broader infrastructure, providing confidence in the stability and reliability of the patching process.

Phased deployment is a strategic approach that involves gradually rolling out patches across the organization rather than applying them universally and simultaneously. By adopting a phased deployment strategy, organizations can assess the impact of patches on a smaller scale before expanding to larger groups or critical systems. This incremental approach allows for early detection of any unexpected issues, enabling organizations to take corrective action and minimize disruptions. Phased deployment is particularly beneficial for large-scale environments where simultaneous patching may be logistically challenging.

Effective communication is a linchpin in deploying patches without disruption. Clear and timely communication helps manage expectations, informs stakeholders about the patching process, and outlines any potential impact on system availability. Providing advance notice to users, system administrators, and other relevant parties about scheduled patch deployments fosters awareness and allows for necessary preparations. Communication channels should remain open throughout the patching process to address any concerns, provide status updates, and promptly respond to unforeseen issues.

Automation plays a crucial role in streamlining the patch deployment process and reducing the potential for human error. Automated patch management tools can handle routine tasks, such as scanning for missing patches, downloading updates, and deploying patches to target systems. Automation not only accelerates the deployment timeline but also ensures consistency across diverse systems. By automating repetitive and time-consuming tasks, organizations can free up resources to focus on more complex aspects of patch management, contributing to a more efficient and error-resistant deployment process.

Creating system backups before deploying patches provides an additional layer of security and a fallback mechanism in case unexpected issues arise. Backups enable organizations to quickly restore systems to a known, stable state if the patching process results in disruptions or unintended consequences. Regular and verified backups serve as a safety net, offering a means to recover critical data and configurations in the event of unforeseen challenges during patch deployment. The ability to roll back changes provides a level of assurance and minimizes the potential impact on operations.

Rollback plans are integral components of patch deployment strategies, outlining the steps to revert changes in the event of disruptions or adverse effects. Despite thorough testing and preparation, unexpected issues can arise during the deployment process. A well-documented rollback plan allows organizations to respond promptly to disruptions, reverting systems to their pre-patch state while minimizing downtime and impact on operations. The existence of a rollback plan instills confidence in the patch deployment process and serves as a proactive measure to address unforeseen challenges.

Adopting a maintenance window or designated timeframe for patch deployment is a strategic measure to minimize disruptions during critical business hours. Organizations can schedule patch deployments during periods of lower system usage or during planned maintenance windows to reduce the impact on operations. Coordination with relevant stakeholders, including business units and IT teams, helps ensure that patch deployments align with operational considerations and do not conflict with essential business processes. The establishment of maintenance windows allows organizations to balance the need for security with the imperative to maintain system availability.

Continuous monitoring is an ongoing strategy that supports the deployment of patches without disruptions. Monitoring systems before, during, and after patch deployment enables organizations to promptly detect any anomalies, performance issues, or unexpected consequences. Real-time monitoring tools provide insights into system health, allowing IT teams to identify and address issues proactively. Continuous monitoring contributes to the overall resilience of systems by facilitating quick responses to emerging challenges, ensuring that organizations can adapt and refine their strategies in real-time.

Collaboration and coordination between IT teams, system administrators, and business units are essential strategies for successful patch deployment. Effective collaboration ensures that all relevant parties are informed, aligned, and prepared for the patching process. Engaging business units in the planning phase helps organizations understand the operational implications of patch deployment, allowing for adjustments to be made to minimize disruptions. Collaborative efforts enhance communication, streamline decision-making processes, and contribute to a unified approach to deploying patches without disrupting system operations.

The use of maintenance modes or failover mechanisms for critical systems is a strategic approach to maintain system availability during patch deployment. Organizations can implement maintenance modes for applications or systems that allow for continuous operation while patches are applied in the background. Failover mechanisms, such as redundant servers or clusters, ensure that critical services remain available even when individual systems are undergoing patching. These mechanisms contribute to high availability and minimize disruptions to essential business functions during the patch deployment process.

Ensuring that end-users are aware of and understand the importance of patch deployment is a crucial strategy for seamless implementation. User education and awareness programs foster a culture of cybersecurity consciousness, encouraging users to promptly apply updates and patches when prompted. Organizations can communicate the significance of patches in addressing security vulnerabilities, protecting sensitive data, and contributing to the overall resilience of the digital environment. Engaging end-users in the patching process fosters a collaborative and security-conscious culture, reducing the likelihood of delays in applying critical patches.

The role of risk assessment in patch deployment cannot be overstated. Organizations should conduct thorough risk assessments to evaluate the potential impact of patches on different systems and operations. Risk assessments help organizations make informed decisions about the timing and prioritization of patch deployment. Understanding the risk landscape allows organizations to balance the urgency of addressing vulnerabilities with the need to minimize disruptions. Risk assessments should consider factors such as the criticality of systems, business impact, and the potential consequences of delaying patch deployment.

In conclusion, deploying patches without disrupting system operations demands a holistic and strategic approach that encompasses careful planning, risk assessment, communication, automation, and collaboration. Organizations must prioritize patches based on risk, test them in controlled environments, and deploy them in a phased and incremental manner. Continuous monitoring, rollback plans, and collaboration between IT teams and business units contribute to the success of patch deployment strategies. Automation and user education further enhance the efficiency and effectiveness of the patching process. In the ever-evolving landscape of cybersecurity, deploying patches seamlessly is a dynamic and ongoing effort to balance security and operational considerations, ultimately contributing to the resilience of digital systems.

The importance of testing patches before widespread deployment.

Testing patches before widespread deployment is a critical aspect of maintaining a secure and stable computing environment. In the ever-evolving landscape of software and technology, patches are regularly released to address vulnerabilities, bugs, and performance issues in various applications and operating systems. While these patches aim to improve the overall functionality and security of the system, the potential risks associated with deploying untested patches can outweigh the benefits. The importance of a thorough testing process lies in its ability to identify and mitigate any adverse effects that may arise from the application of these patches.

One of the primary reasons for testing patches is to ensure compatibility with the existing software and hardware infrastructure. Organizations typically operate diverse IT environments with various applications, platforms, and configurations. A patch that works seamlessly in one environment may introduce compatibility issues in another. Through rigorous testing, IT teams can assess how patches interact with different components of the system, identifying any conflicts or unintended consequences that may arise. This proactive approach helps prevent disruptions to critical business processes and ensures a smooth transition when the patches are eventually deployed on a larger scale.

Moreover, testing patches provides an opportunity to evaluate the overall impact on system performance. While patches are designed to enhance functionality and address vulnerabilities, they may inadvertently introduce performance bottlenecks or resource utilization issues. Through systematic testing, organizations can measure the impact of patches on system resources, such as CPU and memory usage. This allows IT teams to gauge whether the benefits of the patch outweigh any potential negative effects, enabling informed decision-making regarding the deployment of the patch across the entire infrastructure.

Security is a paramount concern in the digital age, and patches are a crucial line of defense against emerging threats. However, deploying untested patches can inadvertently create new security vulnerabilities or exacerbate existing ones. Cybersecurity threats are constantly evolving, and malicious actors may exploit weaknesses introduced by poorly implemented patches. Thorough testing helps identify any unintended security gaps, allowing organizations to address these issues before exposing the system to potential threats. By prioritizing security in the testing process, organizations can maintain a robust defense against cyberattacks and protect sensitive data from unauthorized access.

In addition to technical considerations, testing patches also provides an opportunity to assess the user experience and functionality of the patched software. End-users interact with various applications and systems daily, and any disruptions or changes to the user interface can impact productivity and satisfaction. Testing allows organizations to gather feedback from users, ensuring that the updated software meets usability expectations and does not introduce confusion or frustration. This user-centric approach contributes to a positive overall experience and minimizes the risk of resistance to change among end-users.

Furthermore, the diversity of software and hardware configurations within an organization necessitates a comprehensive testing strategy. Testing patches in a controlled and representative environment helps uncover issues that may only manifest in specific setups.

For example, variations in operating systems, third-party software, and hardware peripherals can all influence the compatibility and performance of patches. By simulating different user scenarios and configurations during testing, organizations can uncover and address potential issues that might otherwise go unnoticed until widespread deployment, minimizing the likelihood of system-wide disruptions.

An essential aspect of patch testing is the establishment of a rollback plan. Even with the most thorough testing, unforeseen issues may arise once patches are deployed in a live environment. Having a well-defined rollback plan allows organizations to quickly revert to the previous state in the event of critical issues, reducing downtime and minimizing the impact on operations. The rollback plan should be an integral part of the testing process, ensuring that IT teams are well-prepared to address any unforeseen challenges that may arise during the deployment of patches.

Moreover, testing patches contributes to regulatory compliance and adherence to industry standards. In many sectors, organizations are required to comply with specific regulations and standards related to data security and privacy. Deploying untested patches without considering the potential impact on compliance can lead to violations and legal consequences. Thorough testing ensures that organizations can confidently demonstrate due diligence in maintaining the security and integrity of their systems, aligning with regulatory requirements and industry best practices.

The timing of patch deployment is also a crucial consideration, and testing plays a vital role in determining the optimal release schedule. Rushed deployments without adequate testing can lead to disruptions during critical business operations, causing financial losses and reputational damage. Testing allows organizations to plan and schedule patch deployments during periods of lower activity, minimizing the impact on daily operations and ensuring a more controlled rollout.

In conclusion, the importance of testing patches before widespread deployment cannot be overstated. It is a multifaceted process that encompasses compatibility assessment, performance evaluation, security scrutiny, user experience testing, and the creation of a robust rollback plan. Through comprehensive testing, organizations can identify and rectify issues before patches are applied across the entire infrastructure, mitigating the risk of system-wide disruptions, security vulnerabilities, and negative impacts on user satisfaction. The investment in thorough testing ultimately contributes to the overall stability, security, and reliability of IT systems, supporting the organization's ability to adapt to evolving technological landscapes while safeguarding critical data and operations.

Overview of automated patching tools for streamlined management.

Automated patching tools have emerged as indispensable assets in the realm of IT management, offering organizations streamlined and efficient methods for maintaining the security and functionality of their software ecosystems. These tools, designed to automate the process of identifying, testing, and deploying patches, address the perennial challenge of keeping systems up to date in the face of ever-evolving threats and vulnerabilities. One prominent feature of these tools is their ability to systematically scan the entire IT infrastructure, encompassing servers, workstations, and other devices, to identify missing patches and potential security gaps. This comprehensive scanning capability provides IT administrators with a holistic view of the patch status across the organization, allowing them to prioritize and address vulnerabilities based on criticality and potential impact.

The automation of patch deployment is a central facet of these tools, enabling organizations to expedite the implementation of patches without manual intervention. This automated process not only accelerates the patching cycle but also reduces the likelihood of human errors that may occur during manual deployments. By scheduling patch deployments during non-business hours or low-traffic periods, these tools minimize disruptions to regular operations, ensuring that critical systems remain available and functional. The ability to set predefined maintenance windows further enhances control over the timing of patch installations, aligning with organizational preferences and optimizing resource utilization.

Furthermore, automated patching tools often incorporate testing mechanisms that allow organizations to assess the compatibility and impact of patches before deployment. These testing features simulate real-world scenarios, enabling IT teams to evaluate how patches interact with various software configurations and hardware setups. By automating the testing process, organizations can identify potential conflicts or issues that may arise in specific environments, fostering a more informed decision-making process before deploying patches on a larger scale. This proactive approach contributes to the overall stability of IT systems and mitigates the risk of unintended consequences associated with patch deployment.

Another notable advantage of automated patching tools lies in their ability to generate detailed reports and logs, providing transparency into the patching process. These reports offer insights into the status of patches, highlighting successful deployments, failed installations, and any issues encountered during the process. This visibility not only aids in tracking the effectiveness of patch management but also supports compliance efforts by providing documentation of patching activities. Moreover, the reporting features enable organizations to demonstrate adherence to security best practices and regulatory requirements, essential for maintaining trust with stakeholders and meeting audit standards.

In addition to traditional software patching, some automated tools extend their capabilities to cover the patching of operating systems and firmware. This holistic approach ensures that the entire IT infrastructure, from application software to underlying system components, remains fortified against potential vulnerabilities. By automating the patching of diverse elements within the IT ecosystem, these tools contribute to a more robust and resilient security posture, reducing the attack surface and fortifying defenses against a multitude of potential threats.

Integration with vulnerability management systems is another hallmark of advanced automated patching tools. By leveraging vulnerability data, these tools can prioritize patches based on the severity and exploitability of identified vulnerabilities. This integration enhances the efficiency of patch management, directing resources towards addressing the most critical security risks first. The synergy between automated patching and vulnerability management aligns with a risk-based approach to cybersecurity, allowing organizations to allocate resources strategically and focus on mitigating the most pressing threats.

Moreover, many automated patching tools are designed with scalability in mind, accommodating the needs of organizations with diverse and complex IT infrastructures. These tools often support multi-platform environments, ensuring compatibility with various operating systems and software applications. The scalability of these tools becomes particularly relevant as organizations grow and evolve, providing the flexibility to adapt patching processes to the changing demands of an expanding IT landscape.

Despite the numerous advantages of automated patching tools, it is essential to acknowledge potential challenges and considerations associated with their implementation. The complexity of IT environments, variations in software configurations, and the need for specialized testing in certain industries may pose challenges to achieving seamless automation. Striking a balance between automation and human oversight is crucial to address these challenges effectively, ensuring that organizations can leverage the benefits of automated patching while maintaining the flexibility to address unique considerations within their IT ecosystems.

In conclusion, automated patching tools represent a paradigm shift in the management of software updates, offering organizations a potent and efficient means to enhance their cybersecurity posture. These tools streamline the patching process, from vulnerability identification to deployment, minimizing manual efforts and accelerating the response to emerging threats. The integration of testing, reporting, and scalability features further elevates the value of automated patching tools, making them essential components of modern IT management strategies. As organizations continue to grapple with an ever-changing threat landscape, the adoption of automated patching tools becomes not just a convenience but a strategic imperative to fortify digital defenses and safeguard against the evolving challenges of cybersecurity.

Implementing and configuring tools to automate the patching process.

Implementing and configuring tools to automate the patching process is a multifaceted endeavor that demands meticulous planning, strategic decision-making, and a comprehensive understanding of the organization's IT infrastructure. The first step in this process involves selecting the appropriate automated patching tool that aligns with the organization's needs and objectives. This decision hinges on factors such as the scale of the IT environment, the diversity of software and hardware components, and the specific requirements of the organization's industry and regulatory landscape.

Once a suitable automated patching tool is chosen, the implementation process begins with the installation and configuration of the tool within the IT infrastructure. This often entails deploying the tool on dedicated servers or utilizing cloud-based solutions, depending on the organization's preferences and existing infrastructure. Configuring the tool to integrate seamlessly with the organization's network, servers, and endpoints is crucial for ensuring a smooth and effective patching workflow. This integration may involve establishing connections with existing systems, such as configuration management databases (CMDBs) and vulnerability scanners, to enhance the tool's capabilities and align it with broader IT management processes.

The configuration of the automated patching tool extends to defining policies and rules that govern the patching process. These policies establish guidelines for patch prioritization, deployment schedules, and testing procedures. Considering the diverse nature of IT environments, these policies need to be flexible and adaptable to accommodate variations in software versions, operating systems, and criticality of systems. Striking the right balance between automation and human oversight is a key consideration during this configuration phase, as it influences the tool's decision-making capabilities and responsiveness to emerging threats.

Central to the success of automated patching is the establishment of a robust testing framework. Configuring the tool to conduct thorough testing of patches before deployment is essential for identifying potential conflicts, compatibility issues, or adverse effects on system performance. The testing framework should mirror real-world scenarios, encompassing different software configurations, user environments, and hardware setups to ensure comprehensive coverage. Configuring the tool to generate detailed reports and logs during the testing phase enhances transparency, providing insights into the success or failure of patch deployments, as well as any issues encountered during the testing process.

Furthermore, the implementation and configuration process should consider the organization's specific requirements regarding patch deployment schedules. Automated patching tools offer the flexibility to schedule deployments during non-business hours or low-traffic periods to minimize disruptions. Configuring maintenance windows and blackout periods aligns with the organization's operational preferences, ensuring that critical systems remain available during peak business hours while allowing for timely updates during periods of reduced activity.

Integration with existing vulnerability management systems is a critical aspect of configuring automated patching tools. Leveraging vulnerability data enables the tool to prioritize patches based on the severity and exploitability of identified vulnerabilities. Configuring this integration streamlines the patching workflow, directing resources towards addressing the most critical security risks first. The synergy between automated patching and vulnerability management supports a risk-based approach to cybersecurity, allowing organizations to prioritize and remediate vulnerabilities effectively.

As the organization's IT landscape evolves, scalability becomes a key consideration during the implementation and configuration of automated patching tools. Configuring the tool to scale seamlessly with the growing complexity of the IT infrastructure ensures that patch management remains efficient and effective. This scalability may involve accommodating additional endpoints, supporting new software applications, or expanding compatibility with different operating systems. A well-configured automated patching tool should be able to adapt to the changing needs of the organization, offering flexibility and scalability as the IT environment expands.

Security considerations play a pivotal role in the configuration process, particularly when dealing with sensitive data and critical systems. Configuring the automated patching tool to adhere to security best practices, encryption standards, and access controls helps safeguard the integrity of the patching process. Ensuring that the tool complies with industry regulations and standards is imperative for organizations operating in regulated sectors, where non-compliance may result in legal consequences and reputational damage.

Ongoing monitoring and optimization are integral components of the configuration process for automated patching tools. Configuring the tool to provide real-time monitoring and alerts enables IT administrators to stay informed about the status of patch deployments, potential issues, and overall system health. Continuous optimization involves fine-tuning policies, adjusting deployment schedules, and incorporating feedback from testing and deployment experiences. This iterative approach ensures that the automated patching tool remains aligned with the organization's evolving requirements and continues to deliver optimal results in the face of emerging cybersecurity challenges.

In conclusion, implementing and configuring tools to automate the patching process is a strategic undertaking that requires a holistic approach. The selection of a suitable automated patching tool, meticulous configuration to align with the organization's infrastructure, and the establishment of robust testing, scheduling, and monitoring frameworks are all critical elements. Balancing automation with human oversight, integrating with existing systems, and prioritizing security considerations contribute to the effectiveness of the automated patching workflow. As organizations navigate the complex landscape of cybersecurity threats, a well-implemented and properly configured automated patching solution becomes a cornerstone of proactive IT management, enhancing security, resilience, and overall operational efficiency.

Responding to critical vulnerabilities with emergency updates.

Responding to critical vulnerabilities with emergency updates is a pivotal aspect of cybersecurity, necessitated by the dynamic and ever-evolving threat landscape. When organizations become aware of vulnerabilities that pose severe risks to the security and integrity of their systems, the need for swift and decisive action becomes paramount. Emergency updates, often referred to as "patches," are a rapid and targeted response to identified vulnerabilities, aiming to mitigate the risk of exploitation by malicious actors. The urgency associated with critical vulnerabilities stems from the potential for significant and widespread damage, making the timely release and deployment of emergency updates a crucial element in the ongoing battle against cyber threats.

The first step in responding to critical vulnerabilities is the swift identification and assessment of the security risk. Security researchers, internal security teams, or external entities may discover vulnerabilities through various means, such as ethical hacking, routine security audits, or incident response investigations. Once a vulnerability is confirmed and its severity is determined, the organization must gauge the potential impact on its systems and data. The criticality of a vulnerability is often assessed based on factors such as the ease of exploitation, potential for unauthorized access, and the potential consequences if exploited. This initial assessment sets the stage for the subsequent emergency response efforts.

The decision to release an emergency update is not taken lightly, as it involves considerations of both the severity of the vulnerability and the potential disruption caused by the update. Organizations must carefully balance the need for swift remediation with the potential impact on the stability and availability of their systems. In cases where the risk of exploitation is deemed high, the organization may opt for an emergency update to address the vulnerability promptly and prevent potential security breaches. This decision-making process requires collaboration between security teams, IT administrators, and relevant stakeholders to ensure a well-informed and coordinated response.

Upon deciding to release an emergency update, the organization's development and release teams initiate a rapid response plan. This plan encompasses the development of the patch, quality assurance testing, and the establishment of a deployment strategy. The goal is to expedite the delivery of the update while maintaining the integrity and functionality of the affected systems. Collaboration between security and development teams is crucial during this phase to streamline the process and address any challenges that may arise. In some cases, organizations may leverage predefined incident response plans to facilitate a structured and efficient emergency update process.

Testing plays a pivotal role in the preparation of emergency updates. While the urgency of the situation may limit the depth of testing, it is essential to conduct thorough assessments to ensure that the emergency update does not inadvertently introduce new issues or disrupt critical system functionality. Testing may involve simulating real-world scenarios, evaluating compatibility with diverse system configurations, and conducting basic functionality checks. The goal is to strike a balance between the need for speed and the imperative to release a reliable and effective emergency update.

Communicating the existence of the critical vulnerability and the impending emergency update is a crucial component of the response process. Organizations must notify their user base, IT administrators, and relevant stakeholders about the security risk and the importance of applying the update promptly. Transparent and clear communication helps raise awareness, instills confidence in the organization's ability to address security issues, and encourages users to take prompt action. Additionally, organizations may provide guidance on the deployment process, potential impacts on system performance, and any interim measures users can take to mitigate the risk while awaiting the emergency update.

The deployment strategy for emergency updates is tailored to minimize disruptions and ensure widespread adoption. Organizations often prioritize the most critical systems, such as those handling sensitive data or critical business functions, in the initial wave of deployment. This targeted approach allows for a focused response to the most significant security risks. In cases where immediate deployment is not feasible for all systems, organizations may consider phased releases, scheduling updates during non-business hours, or utilizing automated deployment tools to streamline the process.

Post-deployment monitoring and validation are essential to confirm the effectiveness of the emergency update and identify any unforeseen issues. Continuous monitoring helps organizations assess the impact on system performance, user experience, and overall stability. In the event that issues arise post-deployment, organizations must be prepared to address them promptly, potentially through the release of subsequent updates or additional guidance to users. This iterative approach ensures that emergency updates not only address the immediate vulnerability but also maintain the overall reliability and functionality of the systems.

The aftermath of responding to critical vulnerabilities with emergency updates involves a comprehensive review of the incident response process. Organizations conduct post-mortem analyses to evaluate the effectiveness of their response, identify areas for improvement, and refine their incident response plans. This reflective process contributes to organizational learning, enhancing the ability to respond swiftly and effectively to future security incidents. Collaboration between security teams, IT administrators, and other relevant stakeholders is instrumental in this review, fostering a culture of continuous improvement in cybersecurity practices.

In conclusion, responding to critical vulnerabilities with emergency updates is a dynamic and multifaceted process that demands agility, collaboration, and a commitment to maintaining the security and resilience of IT systems. The swift identification of vulnerabilities, informed decision-making regarding the release of emergency updates, and a well-coordinated response effort are integral to mitigating the risks posed by emerging cyber threats. Through effective communication, thorough testing, strategic deployment, and post-incident analysis, organizations can not only address immediate security concerns but also strengthen their overall cybersecurity posture, contributing to a more resilient and secure digital environment.

Balancing the need for rapid patch deployment with thorough testing.

Balancing the need for rapid patch deployment with thorough testing represents a delicate equilibrium in the dynamic landscape of cybersecurity, where the urgency to address vulnerabilities competes with the imperative to ensure system stability and minimize disruptions. The pressing reality of ever-evolving cyber threats and the constant emergence of new vulnerabilities underscore the critical importance of swiftly deploying patches to fortify digital defenses. However, the potential risks associated with hasty deployments, such as unintended system outages, conflicts, or adverse impacts on critical operations, necessitate a cautious and meticulous testing process. This delicate balance between speed and thoroughness reflects the challenge faced by organizations seeking to maintain a secure and resilient digital infrastructure.

The need for rapid patch deployment is rooted in the relentless nature of cyber threats, where attackers exploit vulnerabilities at an accelerated pace. As vulnerabilities are discovered, the race against time begins, with organizations striving to apply patches swiftly to close potential entry points for malicious actors. The concept of "zero-day" vulnerabilities, those actively exploited before a patch is available, underscores the urgency of rapid deployment. In this context, timely patching becomes a proactive defense mechanism, akin to fortifying the gates of a castle before an impending siege. Organizations are compelled to keep pace with the threat landscape, deploy patches promptly, and minimize the window of opportunity for attackers to exploit vulnerabilities.

However, the need for speed must be tempered by the imperative of thorough testing to prevent unintended consequences that may result from hastily deployed patches. Thorough testing is the linchpin in ensuring that patches not only effectively address identified vulnerabilities but also do so without introducing new issues or disruptions to system operations. The complexity of modern digital environments, with diverse software configurations, interconnected systems, and unique organizational setups, accentuates the importance of meticulous testing. Rushed deployments can lead to compatibility issues, conflicts with existing software, and unforeseen consequences that may compromise the stability and functionality of critical systems.

One of the key challenges in balancing rapid deployment with thorough testing lies in the inherent tension between security needs and operational continuity. Organizations must navigate a path that acknowledges the urgency of addressing vulnerabilities while minimizing the risk of disrupting essential business processes. Striking this balance requires a nuanced understanding of the operational landscape, the criticality of systems, and the potential impact of patching on day-to-day operations. The challenge is to orchestrate a seamless integration of security measures without unduly hindering the flow of business operations, recognizing that the consequences of disruptions can be as detrimental as the vulnerabilities being addressed.

The concept of risk plays a pivotal role in navigating the balance between rapid deployment and thorough testing. Risk assessment becomes a guiding principle, informing decisions about the prioritization of patches, the extent of testing required, and the timing of deployments. Organizations must weigh the potential risks associated with a given vulnerability against the possible impact of deploying a patch without adequate testing. A risk-based approach enables organizations to tailor their patch management strategies, focusing resources on the most critical vulnerabilities and adjusting the level of testing based on the potential consequences of a security incident.

Phased deployment emerges as a strategic mechanism for mitigating risks and striking a balance between speed and thoroughness. Rather than deploying patches universally across all systems simultaneously, organizations can adopt a phased approach, gradually rolling out patches to subsets of systems or user groups. This incremental deployment allows organizations to assess the impact of patches on a smaller scale, identify any issues that may arise, and make adjustments before expanding the deployment to more critical or widespread environments. Phased deployment is particularly effective in large and complex infrastructures where the potential for unintended consequences is heightened.

Automated testing solutions play a crucial role in expediting the testing phase and supporting the balance between rapid deployment and thorough testing. Automated tools can quickly scan systems for compatibility issues, assess the potential impact of patches on existing configurations, and identify common issues that may arise during deployment. Automated testing helps organizations streamline the testing process, reduce the manual effort required, and accelerate the overall patch management lifecycle. By leveraging automation, organizations can achieve a more agile and responsive approach to testing, facilitating the timely deployment of patches without compromising on thoroughness.

Communication and collaboration are essential elements in achieving a balance between rapid deployment and thorough testing. Effective communication channels between security teams, IT personnel, and business units ensure that all stakeholders are aware of the patching process, its urgency, and the potential impact on operations. Collaboration becomes instrumental in aligning security goals with broader organizational objectives, allowing for a unified approach that considers both the need for speed and the necessity of thorough testing. Engaging business units in the testing process, obtaining their feedback, and understanding operational implications contribute to a more holistic and informed decision-making process.

The establishment of maintenance windows or designated time-frames for patch deployment represents a pragmatic strategy to reconcile the need for speed with the requirement for thorough testing. Organizations can schedule patch deployments during periods of lower system usage or planned maintenance windows to minimize the impact on critical business processes. By designating specific timeframes for patching, organizations can balance the urgency of addressing vulnerabilities with the imperative to avoid disruptions during peak operational hours. Maintenance windows provide a structured and predictable environment for testing and deployment, allowing organizations to navigate the delicate balance between speed and thoroughness.

User education and awareness programs contribute to the equilibrium between rapid deployment and thorough testing by fostering a culture of cybersecurity consciousness. Educated end-users are more likely to understand the importance of promptly applying patches and updates, reducing the risk of delays in the patching process. By raising awareness about the significance of patching in addressing security vulnerabilities, protecting sensitive data, and contributing to the overall resilience of the digital environment, organizations empower users to play an active role in the timely deployment of patches. User education complements technical measures by creating a collaborative and security-aware organizational culture.

The iterative nature of the patch management process itself contributes to the delicate balance between rapid deployment and thorough testing. Continuous monitoring and feedback mechanisms enable organizations to adapt and refine their strategies based on real-world experiences. Monitoring systems before, during, and after patch deployment provides insights into any unexpected issues, allowing organizations to respond proactively. Real-time feedback loops contribute to the ongoing optimization of patch management processes, ensuring that organizations remain agile and responsive to emerging challenges in the dynamic world of cybersecurity.

In conclusion, balancing the need for rapid patch deployment with thorough testing is a nuanced and multifaceted endeavor that requires organizations to navigate the complexities of the cybersecurity landscape. The urgency to address vulnerabilities and the potential risks associated with hasty deployments must be weighed against the imperative to ensure system stability and minimize disruptions. A risk-based approach, phased deployment strategies, automated testing solutions, effective communication, and collaboration with business units all contribute to achieving this delicate balance. In an environment where the threat landscape is dynamic and ever-evolving, organizations that can strike the right equilibrium between speed and thoroughness in their patch management practices are better positioned to maintain a secure, resilient, and operationally sound digital infrastructure.

The importance of user awareness in the update process.

The importance of user awareness in the update process cannot be overstated as users play a pivotal role in the overall security and effectiveness of system updates. Updates, whether they involve operating systems, applications, or security patches, are essential for addressing vulnerabilities, introducing new features, and ensuring the optimal performance of digital systems. However, the success of the update process is intricately tied to the awareness and actions of end-users. User awareness encompasses understanding the significance of updates, recognizing their role in maintaining cybersecurity, and actively participating in the timely application of updates. In a digital landscape where cyber threats are dynamic and persistent, user awareness serves as a crucial line of defense against potential exploits and contributes to the collective resilience of digital ecosystems.

At the core of the importance of user awareness in the update process lies the fundamental understanding of why updates are necessary. Users need to grasp that software, applications, and operating systems are not static entities but dynamic environments subject to continuous refinement and enhancement. Developers release updates to address security vulnerabilities that could be exploited by cybercriminals, fix bugs, and introduce new features. Users who are aware of the dynamic nature of software are more likely to appreciate the importance of staying current with updates to ensure their systems are equipped with the latest security measures and functionalities. This foundational awareness sets the stage for a proactive and security-conscious approach to the update process.

User awareness becomes particularly critical in the context of security updates and patches. Security vulnerabilities are a constant target for cyber attackers, who exploit weaknesses to gain unauthorized access, compromise data integrity, or execute malicious code. Users need to be aware that security patches are not merely optional improvements but urgent responses to identified vulnerabilities that could be actively exploited. Understanding the potential consequences of neglecting security updates, such as falling victim to cyberattacks, reinforces the importance of user engagement in the update process. In essence, user awareness serves as a powerful motivator for individuals to prioritize and promptly apply security patches to fortify their digital defenses.

Communication is a linchpin in fostering user awareness in the update process. Organizations must establish clear and transparent communication channels to convey the importance of updates, the reasons behind them, and the potential risks associated with neglecting them. Regular and accessible communication, whether through emails, notifications, or training sessions, helps demystify the update process for users. Clear communication should emphasize the role of updates in maintaining a secure digital environment, protecting sen-

sitive information, and contributing to the overall resilience of systems. Organizations that prioritize effective communication create
a culture of transparency, trust, and shared responsibility, laying the
groundwork for users to actively engage in the update process.

User education is a cornerstone of building robust awareness
in the update process. Training programs that empower users with
knowledge about the update lifecycle, the significance of security
patches, and the steps involved in applying updates contribute to
a more informed and security-conscious user base. User education
should cover not only the technical aspects of updates but also the
potential impact on system performance, the importance of staying
vigilant against social engineering tactics, and best practices for safely
navigating the update process. Well-informed users are more likely to
recognize the legitimacy of update prompts, understand the potential risks of delaying updates, and take proactive steps to ensure the
security of their digital environments.

Creating a sense of ownership and accountability among users is
another dimension of the importance of user awareness in the update
process. Users need to understand that their actions, or inaction, directly contribute to the overall security posture of the organization.
A culture of accountability fosters a proactive approach where users
take responsibility for keeping their systems up to date and play an
active role in the collective effort to fortify digital defenses. Organizations can encourage this sense of ownership by highlighting the
impact of individual actions on the broader cybersecurity landscape
and showcasing the role of users as integral components of the organization's cyber resilience.

User awareness extends beyond the understanding of updates as
a technical necessity to an appreciation of their role in enhancing the
user experience. Updates often bring improvements in performance,
usability, and features that can contribute to a more efficient and enjoyable computing experience. Users who are aware of the positive

aspects of updates are more likely to view the update process not as an inconvenience but as an opportunity to access new functionalities, enjoy a smoother user experience, and benefit from the latest innovations. This positive perspective contributes to a more cooperative and willing user base, facilitating smoother update deployments and minimizing resistance to the update process.

The importance of user awareness in the update process is accentuated by the prevalence of software in daily activities. Users interact with a myriad of applications and systems, ranging from operating systems and office suites to web browsers and mobile apps. The widespread adoption of these technologies makes users lucrative targets for cyber attackers seeking to exploit vulnerabilities on a large scale. User awareness becomes a collective defense mechanism, reducing the likelihood of successful attacks that leverage outdated software. A security-conscious user base acts as a force multiplier in the organization's efforts to stay ahead of potential threats and contributes to the creation of a resilient digital ecosystem.

Recognizing the diversity of users, organizations must tailor their awareness initiatives to different audiences. End-users with varying levels of technical expertise, responsibilities, and access to systems require targeted communication and education. Tailoring awareness programs acknowledges the diverse needs and challenges faced by different user groups, ensuring that the information provided is relevant, accessible, and meaningful. Organizations that adopt a nuanced and inclusive approach to user awareness enhance their ability to reach and engage users effectively, maximizing the impact of awareness initiatives across the entire spectrum of the user base.

Feedback loops and continuous engagement mechanisms are integral components of sustaining user awareness in the update process. Organizations should establish channels for users to provide feedback, seek clarification, and report any issues related to updates. A two-way communication model facilitates ongoing engagement, allowing organizations to address user concerns, refine communication strategies, and adapt awareness initiatives based on user input. Continuous engagement reinforces the importance of user awareness as an ongoing and evolving process, rather than a one-time effort, contributing to a culture of shared responsibility and collaboration in maintaining a secure digital environment.

User awareness also intersects with the concept of social engineering, where attackers manipulate human behavior to gain unauthorized access or extract sensitive information. Users who are aware of the tactics employed by cybercriminals, such as phishing emails, fake update prompts, or deceptive websites, are better equipped to discern legitimate update notifications from potential threats. Incorporating elements of social engineering awareness into user education programs enhances the overall effectiveness of user awareness in the update process. Users who can identify and report suspicious activities contribute to the organization's early detection and mitigation of potential cyber threats.

In conclusion, the importance of user awareness in the update process is a critical facet of cybersecurity that transcends the technical aspects of software maintenance. User awareness is a dynamic and multifaceted construct that involves understanding the necessity of updates, recognizing their role in security, and actively participating in the update process. Effective communication, user education, a sense of ownership, and positive framing contribute to building robust user awareness. In a digital landscape where cyber threats persist and evolve, users emerge as active participants in the collective effort to fortify digital defenses, creating a culture of cybersecurity consciousness that enhances the resilience of organizations against potential exploits and attacks.

Educating users on the significance of timely updates and their role in security.

Educating users on the significance of timely updates and their pivotal role in security is a multifaceted endeavor crucial for cultivating a cybersecurity-conscious user base. The foundation of this education lies in conveying a comprehensive understanding of why updates are essential components of digital hygiene. Users need to grasp that the software and systems they interact with, whether operating systems, applications, or security tools, are dynamic entities subject to continuous refinement. Updates are not mere inconveniences or technical nuances; they are integral to maintaining the health, functionality, and security of digital environments. By comprehending this dynamic nature of software, users can appreciate the urgency and importance of keeping their systems up to date.

Central to user education is the emphasis on security updates, which play a critical role in safeguarding digital assets from potential threats. Users must understand that security updates are not optional but rather imperative responses to identified vulnerabilities that could be exploited by malicious actors. The ever-evolving landscape of cyber threats necessitates a proactive and collective approach, and users become the first line of defense when it comes to applying security patches promptly. A clear understanding of the potential consequences of neglecting security updates, such as falling victim to cyberattacks, reinforces the significance of user engagement in the timely application of updates.

Effective communication becomes a linchpin in the educational process, serving as the conduit through which users receive information about updates and their security implications. Organizations must establish clear and transparent communication channels to convey the importance of updates, the reasons behind them, and the potential risks associated with neglecting them. Regular and accessible communication, whether through emails, notifications, or educational campaigns, helps demystify the update process for users. Clear communication should highlight the role of updates in maintaining a secure digital environment, protecting sensitive information, and contributing to the overall resilience of systems. By demystifying the update process, organizations can create a culture of transparency and trust, fostering a sense of shared responsibility for cybersecurity.

User education should not only focus on the technical aspects of updates but also on the broader context of cybersecurity. Users need to be aware of the evolving threat landscape, understanding that cybercriminals actively seek to exploit vulnerabilities for unauthorized access, data breaches, or other malicious activities. The educational process should delve into real-world examples of security incidents stemming from outdated software and showcase the tangible impact on individuals and organizations. By grounding the significance of updates in concrete and relatable scenarios, user education becomes more impactful, resonating with users on a personal and organizational level.

Highlighting the connection between individual actions and the broader cybersecurity landscape contributes to the sense of ownership and accountability among users. Users must recognize that their adherence to timely updates directly influences the overall security posture of the organization. A culture of accountability fosters a proactive approach where users take responsibility for keeping their systems up to date, understanding that their actions contribute to the collective effort to fortify digital defenses. Organizations can reinforce this sense of ownership by showcasing the impact of individual actions on the broader cybersecurity landscape and emphasizing the role of users as integral components of the organization's cyber resilience.

User education becomes particularly effective when it addresses the potential benefits of timely updates beyond just security. Updates often bring enhancements in performance, usability, and features that can contribute to a more efficient and enjoyable computing experience. Users who understand the positive aspects of updates are more likely to view the update process not as a burdensome task but as an opportunity to access new functionalities, enjoy a smoother user experience, and benefit from the latest innovations. This positive perspective contributes to a more cooperative and willing user base, facilitating smoother update deployments and minimizing resistance to the update process.

Creating a culture of continuous learning is vital for sustaining user education on the significance of timely updates. The digital landscape is dynamic, with new threats and technologies constantly emerging. User education should be an ongoing and evolving process, keeping pace with the changing nature of cybersecurity. Organizations can implement regular training sessions, webinars, or awareness campaigns to provide users with updates on the latest security threats, best practices for staying secure, and insights into the evolving landscape of cyber risks. Continuous learning fosters a sense of adaptability and resilience among users, empowering them to navigate the ever-changing terrain of cybersecurity with confidence.

User awareness is not a one-size-fits-all proposition, considering the diversity of users with varying levels of technical expertise, responsibilities, and access to systems. Tailoring educational initiatives to different audiences ensures that the information provided is relevant, accessible, and meaningful to diverse user groups. Organizations can adopt a nuanced and inclusive approach to user education, recognizing the diverse needs and challenges faced by different user segments. Tailored education programs cater to the specific concerns and priorities of different user groups, ensuring that the educational content resonates with each audience and maximizes its impact.

Incorporating elements of social engineering awareness into user education programs enhances the overall effectiveness of educating users on timely updates. Users who are aware of the tactics employed by cybercriminals, such as phishing emails, fake update prompts, or deceptive websites, are better equipped to discern legitimate update notifications from potential threats. Social engineering is a prevalent vector for cyberattacks, and user education should emphasize the importance of skepticism, verification, and reporting any suspicious activities. By integrating social engineering awareness into the educational curriculum, organizations empower users to be proactive in identifying and mitigating potential cyber threats.

Feedback loops and continuous engagement mechanisms are integral components of sustaining user education on timely updates. Organizations should establish channels for users to provide feedback, seek clarification, and report any issues related to updates. A two-way communication model facilitates ongoing engagement, allowing organizations to address user concerns, refine communication strategies, and adapt educational initiatives based on user input. Continuous engagement reinforces the importance of user education as an ongoing and evolving process, rather than a one-time effort, contributing to a culture of shared responsibility and collaboration in maintaining a secure digital environment.

In conclusion, educating users on the significance of timely updates and their role in security is a multifaceted and ongoing process that requires a holistic approach. Users are integral components of the collective defense against cyber threats, and their awareness is pivotal in ensuring the overall resilience of digital ecosystems. Effective communication, user education, a sense of ownership, positive framing, and continuous learning contribute to building robust user awareness. In a digital landscape where cyber threats persist and evolve, organizations that prioritize user education empower their users to be proactive contributors to the cybersecurity posture, fostering a culture of awareness, responsibility, and collaboration.

Chapter 8: Security Best Practices and Future Trends

Defining and implementing security policies to guide user behavior.

Defining and implementing security policies to guide user behavior is a critical component of a comprehensive cybersecurity strategy aimed at safeguarding digital assets and sensitive information. Security policies serve as the foundation for establishing a secure and resilient organizational environment, providing a framework that outlines acceptable behaviors, responsibilities, and expectations for users. These policies are instrumental in mitigating risks, preventing security incidents, and fostering a culture of awareness and compliance within an organization.

The process of defining security policies begins with a thorough understanding of the organization's unique risk landscape, industry regulations, and the specific nature of its digital assets. This involves conducting a comprehensive risk assessment to identify potential vulnerabilities, threats, and compliance requirements. The gathered insights lay the groundwork for crafting policies that are tailored to address the specific security needs and challenges faced by the organization.

A well-defined set of security policies encompasses a range of aspects, including access controls, data protection, incident response, acceptable use of technology resources, and compliance with regulatory requirements. Access control policies, for instance, outline the procedures for granting and revoking user access to sensitive systems and information, ensuring that only authorized individuals have appropriate permissions. Data protection policies establish guidelines for handling, storing, and transmitting sensitive data, safeguarding it against unauthorized access, disclosure, or manipulation.

The implementation of security policies involves a strategic and collaborative effort across various organizational levels. Communication is paramount during this phase, as employees need to be made aware of the policies that govern their behavior. This involves the development of clear and concise documentation that articulates the policies, their purpose, and the potential consequences of non-compliance. Organizations often conduct training sessions or awareness campaigns to ensure that users understand the significance of these policies and their role in maintaining a secure environment.

A key aspect of security policy implementation is the establishment of roles and responsibilities. Designating individuals or teams responsible for overseeing policy adherence, enforcement, and periodic reviews ensures accountability and a structured approach to policy management. This may involve appointing a Chief Information Security Officer (CISO) or a security team tasked with monitoring and enforcing security policies. The collaboration between IT personnel, security teams, and other relevant stakeholders is vital to align policy implementation with broader organizational objectives.

Access control policies, a fundamental component of security frameworks, dictate how users interact with digital resources. These policies define user privileges, password requirements, and mechanisms for granting or revoking access. By clearly outlining access control rules, organizations can restrict unauthorized access, reduce the risk of data breaches, and protect sensitive information. Implementation may involve deploying identity and access management (IAM) solutions to automate user provisioning, authentication, and authorization processes, thereby streamlining access control enforcement.

Data protection policies play a crucial role in safeguarding sensitive information throughout its lifecycle. These policies dictate how data is classified, encrypted, and shared, ensuring that it is handled in a manner commensurate with its sensitivity. Implementation often involves the deployment of encryption technologies, data loss prevention (DLP) tools, and secure communication protocols. Regular audits and assessments are integral to verifying compliance with data protection policies and identifying areas for improvement.

Incident response policies are essential for preparing organizations to effectively manage and recover from security incidents. These policies outline the procedures for reporting incidents, the roles of incident response teams, and the steps to be taken in the event of a security breach. Implementation involves creating an incident response plan, conducting drills and simulations, and establishing communication protocols to ensure a coordinated and efficient response to security incidents. Incident response policies contribute to minimizing the impact of incidents, preserving evidence for forensic analysis, and facilitating a swift return to normal operations.

Acceptable use policies delineate the permitted and prohibited uses of technology resources within an organization. These policies set boundaries on activities such as internet usage, email communication, and the installation of software. Implementation involves communicating these policies to users, often through an acceptable use agreement, and utilizing technologies such as web filtering and email monitoring to enforce compliance. Clear and consistently enforced acceptable use policies contribute to the prevention of security incidents, the protection of network resources, and the promotion of a secure computing environment.

Regulatory compliance policies are essential for organizations operating within specific industries or jurisdictions subject to legal and regulatory frameworks. These policies ensure that the organization aligns with relevant laws and standards, avoiding legal repercussions and potential financial penalties. Implementation involves staying abreast of evolving regulatory landscapes, conducting regular audits, and collaborating with legal and compliance teams to ensure ongoing adherence. Regulatory compliance policies provide a structured approach to meeting legal requirements, protecting sensitive data, and maintaining the trust of customers and stakeholders.

Continuous monitoring and periodic reviews are integral to the effectiveness of security policies. The dynamic nature of cybersecurity threats and the evolving organizational landscape necessitate regular assessments to ensure that policies remain relevant and effective. Implementation involves establishing a framework for continuous monitoring, conducting regular risk assessments, and adapting policies in response to emerging threats or changes in the organizational environment. Periodic reviews enable organizations to identify gaps, assess the impact of policy changes, and refine security measures in alignment with the evolving threat landscape.

Technology solutions, such as Security Information and Event Management (SIEM) systems, play a crucial role in supporting the implementation and enforcement of security policies. These tools provide real-time monitoring, analysis, and reporting of security events, enabling organizations to detect and respond to potential threats promptly. Implementation involves integrating SIEM solutions into the organization's infrastructure, configuring them to align with security policies, and leveraging their capabilities to gain insights into user behavior, system vulnerabilities, and potential security incidents.

Effective communication and training programs are vital components of security policy implementation. Users must be aware of the policies that govern their behavior and understand the rationale behind them. Organizations often conduct regular training sessions, workshops, or awareness campaigns to educate users on security policies, best practices, and the consequences of non-compliance. Implementation involves developing engaging and informative training materials, conducting interactive sessions, and fostering an ongoing culture of awareness and education. Communication channels, such as internal newsletters, intranet portals, and email notifications, are utilized to reinforce key messages and keep users informed about updates to security policies.

Integration with organizational culture is a critical aspect of successful security policy implementation. Policies should align with the values, goals, and operational practices of the organization to ensure a seamless integration into daily activities. Implementation involves fostering a culture of security consciousness, where users understand the shared responsibility for maintaining a secure environment. This may involve recognizing and rewarding adherence to security policies, incorporating security considerations into performance evaluations, and promoting a positive and collaborative approach to cybersecurity within the organizational culture.

A comprehensive and well-implemented security policy framework contributes to a robust cybersecurity posture, fostering a secure, resilient, and compliant organizational environment. Security policies provide a structured foundation for guiding user behavior, defining access controls, protecting sensitive data, and responding effectively to security incidents. The success of security policy implementation relies on ongoing communication, user education, technology integration, and alignment with organizational culture. By establishing and enforcing security policies, organizations can proactively mitigate risks, protect critical assets, and navigate the dynamic landscape of cybersecurity with confidence.

The role of security policies in shaping a secure operating environment.

The role of security policies in shaping a secure operating environment is pivotal, serving as the cornerstone of a comprehensive cybersecurity strategy aimed at mitigating risks, safeguarding assets, and fostering a culture of awareness and compliance. Security policies are the linchpin that defines the rules, procedures, and expectations governing user behavior, system configurations, and overall security practices within an organization. At the heart of this role is the establishment of a structured framework that delineates the organization's stance on security, aligning it with industry best practices, regulatory requirements, and the unique risk landscape specific to the organization.

One of the fundamental roles of security policies lies in providing clear and unambiguous guidelines for access controls. These policies define the parameters for granting, modifying, or revoking access to digital resources, ensuring that only authorized individuals have the appropriate privileges. By outlining the principles governing user authentication, authorization, and accountability, access control policies contribute to the establishment of a secure operating environment where the principle of least privilege prevails. Users are granted access only to the resources necessary for their roles, minimizing the potential for unauthorized access and limiting the impact of security incidents.

Data protection policies, another critical facet of security frameworks, play a central role in shaping a secure operating environment. These policies govern the handling, storage, and transmission of sensitive data, outlining measures to safeguard information against unauthorized access, disclosure, or manipulation. By categorizing data based on sensitivity and implementing encryption, data loss prevention (DLP), and secure communication protocols, organizations can create a resilient defense against data breaches. Data protection policies ensure that information is treated in accordance with its level of sensitivity, fostering a secure operating environment where the confidentiality and integrity of data are paramount.

Incident response policies, a key component of security frameworks, define the organization's approach to managing and recovering from security incidents. These policies establish procedures for reporting incidents, the roles and responsibilities of incident response teams, and the steps to be taken in the event of a security breach. The role of incident response policies is to shape a proactive and coordinated approach to security incidents, minimizing their impact and facilitating a swift return to normal operations. By outlining communication protocols, incident categorization, and mitigation measures, incident response policies contribute to the creation of a secure operating environment resilient to the challenges posed by evolving cyber threats.

Acceptable use policies are instrumental in guiding user behavior and defining the permissible use of technology resources within an organization. These policies set boundaries on activities such as internet usage, email communication, and the installation of software. By clearly articulating the rules and expectations for technology usage, acceptable use policies contribute to the prevention of security incidents stemming from misuse or exploitation of technology resources. The role of these policies is to foster a secure operating environment by promoting responsible and compliant use of technology, reducing the likelihood of security breaches resulting from negligent or malicious user actions.

Regulatory compliance policies are essential for organizations operating within specific industries or jurisdictions subject to legal and regulatory frameworks. These policies ensure that the organization adheres to relevant laws, standards, and industry-specific regulations. The role of regulatory compliance policies is to shape a secure operating environment by providing a structured approach to meeting legal requirements, protecting sensitive data, and maintaining the trust of customers and stakeholders. Compliance with these policies not only safeguards the organization from legal repercussions but also contributes to the overall resilience and credibility of the operating environment.

Continuous monitoring and periodic reviews are integral to the role of security policies in shaping a secure operating environment. The dynamic nature of cybersecurity threats and the evolving organizational landscape necessitate regular assessments to ensure that policies remain relevant, effective, and aligned with the organization's objectives. Continuous monitoring establishes a proactive stance, allowing organizations to detect potential threats in real-time, assess the effectiveness of existing policies, and adapt security measures in response to emerging challenges. Periodic reviews provide an opportunity to identify gaps, assess the impact of policy changes, and refine security measures, ensuring that the operating environment remains resilient in the face of evolving cyber threats.

The implementation of security policies involves a strategic and collaborative effort across various organizational levels. Communication is paramount during this phase, as employees need to be made aware of the policies that govern their behavior. This involves the development of clear and concise documentation that articulates the policies, their purpose, and the potential consequences of non-compliance. Organizations often conduct training sessions or awareness campaigns to ensure that users understand the significance of these policies and their role in maintaining a secure environment.

Access control policies, a fundamental component of security frameworks, dictate how users interact with digital resources. These policies define user privileges, password requirements, and mechanisms for granting or revoking access. By clearly outlining access control rules, organizations can restrict unauthorized access, reduce the risk of data breaches, and protect sensitive information. Implementation may involve deploying identity and access management (IAM) solutions to automate user provisioning, authentication, and authorization processes, thereby streamlining access control enforcement.

Data protection policies play a crucial role in safeguarding sensitive information throughout its lifecycle. These policies dictate how data is classified, encrypted, and shared, ensuring that it is handled in a manner commensurate with its sensitivity. Implementation often involves the deployment of encryption technologies, data loss prevention (DLP) tools, and secure communication protocols. Regular audits and assessments are integral to verifying compliance with data protection policies and identifying areas for improvement.

Incident response policies are essential for preparing organizations to effectively manage and recover from security incidents. These policies outline the procedures for reporting incidents, the roles of incident response teams, and the steps to be taken in the event of a security breach. Implementation involves creating an incident response plan, conducting drills and simulations, and establishing communication protocols to ensure a coordinated and efficient response to security incidents. Incident response policies contribute to minimizing the impact of incidents, preserving evidence for forensic analysis, and facilitating a swift return to normal operations.

Acceptable use policies delineate the permitted and prohibited uses of technology resources within an organization. These policies set boundaries on activities such as internet usage, email communication, and the installation of software. Implementation involves communicating these policies to users, often through an acceptable use agreement, and utilizing technologies such as web filtering and email monitoring to enforce compliance. Clear and consistently enforced acceptable use policies contribute to the prevention of security incidents, the protection of network resources, and the promotion of a secure computing environment.

Regulatory compliance policies are essential for organizations operating within specific industries or jurisdictions subject to legal and regulatory frameworks. These policies ensure that the organization aligns with relevant laws and standards, avoiding legal repercussions and potential financial penalties. Implementation involves staying abreast of evolving regulatory landscapes, conducting regular audits, and collaborating with legal and compliance teams to ensure ongoing adherence. Regulatory compliance policies provide a structured approach to meeting legal requirements, protecting sensitive data, and maintaining the trust of customers and stakeholders.

Continuous monitoring and periodic reviews are integral to the effectiveness of security policies. The dynamic nature of cybersecurity threats and the evolving organizational landscape necessitate regular assessments to ensure that policies remain relevant and effective. Implementation involves establishing a framework for continuous monitoring, conducting regular risk assessments, and adapting policies in response to emerging threats or changes in the organizational environment. Periodic reviews enable organizations to identify gaps, assess the impact of policy changes, and refine security measures in alignment with the evolving threat landscape.

Technology solutions, such as Security Information and Event Management (SIEM) systems, play a crucial role in supporting the implementation and enforcement of security policies. These tools provide real-time monitoring, analysis, and reporting of security events, enabling organizations to detect and respond to potential threats promptly. Implementation involves integrating SIEM solutions into the organization's infrastructure, configuring them to align with security policies, and leveraging their capabilities to gain insights into user behavior, system vulnerabilities, and potential security incidents.

Effective communication and training programs are vital components of security policy implementation. Users must be aware of the policies that govern their behavior and understand the rationale behind them. Organizations often conduct regular training sessions, workshops, or awareness campaigns to educate users on security policies, best practices, and the consequences of non-compliance. Implementation involves developing engaging and informative training materials, conducting interactive sessions, and fostering an ongoing culture of awareness and education. Communication channels, such as internal newsletters, intranet portals, and email notifications, are utilized to reinforce key messages and keep users informed about updates to security policies.

Integration with organizational culture is a critical aspect of successful security policy implementation. Policies should align with the values, goals, and operational practices of the organization to ensure a seamless integration into daily activities. Implementation involves fostering a culture of security consciousness, where users understand the shared responsibility for maintaining a secure environment. This may involve recognizing and rewarding adherence to security policies, incorporating security considerations into performance evaluations, and promoting a positive and collaborative approach to cybersecurity within the organizational culture.

A comprehensive and well-implemented security policy framework contributes to a robust cybersecurity posture, fostering a secure, resilient, and compliant organizational environment. Security policies provide a structured foundation for guiding user behavior, defining access controls, protecting sensitive data, and responding effectively to security incidents. The success of security policy implementation relies on ongoing communication, user education, technology integration, and alignment with organizational culture. By establishing and enforcing security policies, organizations can proactively mitigate risks, protect critical assets, and navigate the dynamic landscape of cybersecurity with confidence.

Implementing continuous monitoring tools for real-time threat detection.

Implementing continuous monitoring tools for real-time threat detection is a critical imperative in the contemporary cybersecurity landscape, marked by evolving and sophisticated cyber threats. Continuous monitoring represents a proactive approach to cybersecurity, emphasizing real-time visibility into an organization's digital environment to promptly identify and respond to potential security incidents. The implementation of such tools is underpinned by the recognition that traditional, periodic security assessments are insufficient in a rapidly changing threat landscape. Instead, continuous monitoring introduces a dynamic and ongoing process that leverages automated solutions to scrutinize network activities, system behaviors, and user interactions, providing a comprehensive and real-time understanding of the organization's security posture.

The essence of continuous monitoring lies in its capacity to offer a persistent and pervasive view of the organization's digital ecosystem. Unlike traditional point-in-time assessments, continuous monitoring tools operate in the background, continuously collecting and analyzing data from various sources across the network. This data encompasses a multitude of parameters, including network traffic, system logs, user activities, and application behaviors. By amalgamating these diverse data points, continuous monitoring tools create a holistic representation of the organization's digital footprint, enabling security teams to discern patterns, anomalies, and potential indicators of compromise in real-time.

One of the primary benefits of implementing continuous monitoring tools is their capacity to enhance threat detection capabilities. Traditional security measures often rely on predefined signatures and static rules to identify known threats. Continuous monitoring, however, goes beyond these static methods, employing advanced analytics, machine learning, and behavioral analysis to identify deviations from normal patterns. By establishing a baseline of normal behavior for networks, systems, and users, continuous monitoring tools can rapidly detect abnormal activities indicative of potential security threats, including advanced persistent threats (APTs), insider threats, and zero-day exploits.

The implementation of continuous monitoring tools is particularly pertinent in the context of the evolving sophistication of cyber threats. As attackers continuously refine their tactics, techniques, and procedures (TTPs), organizations must deploy equally adaptive and intelligent defenses. Continuous monitoring tools contribute to this adaptability by evolving alongside the threat landscape. Machine learning algorithms enable these tools to recognize new patterns and anomalies, enhancing their ability to detect previously unknown or novel threats. This capability is crucial in an era where signature-based detection methods often lag behind the rapid emergence of new and polymorphic malware.

The real-time nature of continuous monitoring tools is instrumental in reducing the "dwell time" of cyber threats within an organization's network. Dwell time refers to the duration a threat actor remains undetected within an environment before being identified and mitigated. By providing immediate visibility into potential threats, continuous monitoring tools significantly shrink dwell time, enabling security teams to respond promptly and mitigate the impact of security incidents. Rapid threat detection is especially critical in preventing data breaches, unauthorized access, and the exfiltration of sensitive information.

The implementation of continuous monitoring tools also addresses the challenge of alert fatigue faced by security teams. Traditional security measures often generate a plethora of alerts, overwhelming security analysts with false positives and noise. Continuous monitoring tools, however, apply contextual analysis and correlation to prioritize alerts based on their relevance and potential impact. By contextualizing alerts within the broader security landscape and correlating data across various sources, these tools empower security teams to focus on actionable intelligence, improving the efficiency and effectiveness of incident response.

In addition to threat detection, continuous monitoring tools contribute significantly to incident response capabilities. When a potential security incident is detected in real-time, these tools provide detailed information about the nature of the threat, its origin, and its potential impact. This level of granularity facilitates a more precise and targeted response, allowing security teams to contain, eradicate, and recover from security incidents swiftly. The integration of continuous monitoring with incident response workflows enhances the organization's overall resilience by ensuring a coordinated and well-informed response to emerging threats.

The implementation of continuous monitoring tools is not confined to traditional network boundaries but extends to encompass cloud environments and mobile devices. As organizations increasingly adopt cloud services and mobile technologies, the attack surface expands, necessitating a holistic approach to security. Continuous monitoring tools that extend their reach to the cloud and mobile environments provide a unified and comprehensive view of the organization's entire digital infrastructure. This integrated approach enables security teams to detect and respond to threats regardless of where they originate or manifest, ensuring a consistent security posture across diverse and dynamic digital landscapes.

The role of automation in continuous monitoring is paramount, driving not only efficiency but also accuracy in threat detection and response. Continuous monitoring tools automate the collection, analysis, and correlation of vast amounts of data, enabling security teams to focus on strategic decision-making rather than routine tasks. Automated response mechanisms, such as the isolation of compromised systems or the blocking of malicious IP addresses, can be integrated into continuous monitoring workflows. This automation not only accelerates incident response times but also minimizes the risk of human error in the face of rapidly evolving threats.

To maximize the efficacy of continuous monitoring tools, organizations must prioritize integration with existing security infrastructure and frameworks. Seamless integration with Security Information and Event Management (SIEM) systems, intrusion detection/prevention systems, and endpoint security solutions creates a unified security ecosystem. This integration enables continuous monitoring tools to leverage data from diverse sources, enriching their analytics and providing a more comprehensive understanding of the threat landscape. Furthermore, integration facilitates a synchronized response to security incidents, ensuring that actions taken by continuous monitoring tools align with broader security strategies.

The regulatory landscape and compliance requirements also underscore the significance of continuous monitoring in contemporary cybersecurity initiatives. Many industry regulations and compliance frameworks mandate not just periodic assessments but ongoing monitoring of security controls. Continuous monitoring tools provide organizations with a proactive means of demonstrating adherence to these regulatory requirements by showcasing a real-time commitment to maintaining a secure operating environment. This proactive stance can be instrumental in regulatory audits and assessments, contributing to the organization's ability to meet and exceed compliance expectations.

Challenges in implementing continuous monitoring tools include the need for adequate resources, including skilled personnel and robust infrastructure. The effectiveness of continuous monitoring relies on the ability to analyze and interpret large volumes of data in real-time. This necessitates skilled cybersecurity professionals who can configure, manage, and interpret the output of continuous monitoring tools effectively. Additionally, organizations must invest in scalable and resilient infrastructure to support the constant influx of data generated by these tools. A holistic approach that combines skilled personnel, appropriate technology, and strategic planning is essential to overcome these challenges and derive maximum value from continuous monitoring initiatives.

In conclusion,

implementing continuous monitoring tools for real-time threat detection is a cornerstone of modern cybersecurity strategies. These tools offer organizations a dynamic, proactive, and adaptive approach to security, providing continuous visibility into the evolving threat landscape. By leveraging advanced analytics, machine learning, and automation, continuous monitoring tools enhance threat detection capabilities, reduce dwell time, and improve incident response efficiency. The real-time nature of continuous monitoring is instrumental in addressing the rapid evolution of cyber threats, and its integration with incident response workflows ensures a coordinated and well-informed response. As organizations navigate the complexities of the digital landscape, continuous monitoring emerges as a crucial component in fortifying defenses, mitigating risks, and maintaining a resilient security posture.

Regular assessments to identify and address evolving security challenges.

Regular assessments to identify and address evolving security challenges are foundational elements of a proactive cybersecurity strategy essential for navigating the complex and dynamic landscape of digital threats. In an era where cyber adversaries continuously refine their tactics, organizations must adopt a comprehensive and ongoing approach to evaluating and fortifying their security posture. Regular assessments serve as a structured mechanism for systematically identifying vulnerabilities, assessing risks, and implementing targeted measures to address emerging security challenges.

The essence of regular assessments lies in their recurrent and systematic nature. Unlike one-time evaluations, regular assessments are iterative processes designed to adapt to the evolving threat landscape and the dynamic nature of organizational ecosystems. They encompass a diverse range of evaluations, including vulnerability assessments, penetration testing, risk assessments, and compliance audits. These assessments are not isolated events but rather components of a continuous cycle aimed at maintaining a vigilant and responsive security posture.

Vulnerability assessments represent a fundamental aspect of regular security evaluations, offering organizations insights into potential weaknesses in their digital infrastructure. These assessments involve the systematic scanning and analysis of systems, networks, and applications to identify known vulnerabilities. By leveraging automated tools and manual analysis, organizations gain a comprehensive view of their susceptibility to common exploits. Regularity in vulnerability assessments ensures that emerging vulnerabilities are promptly detected and mitigated, reducing the window of opportunity for potential attackers.

Penetration testing, a proactive and simulated form of hacking, is another crucial element of regular security assessments. Penetration tests involve ethical hackers attempting to exploit vulnerabilities in a controlled environment to assess the effectiveness of existing security controls. By simulating real-world attack scenarios, organizations can identify and address potential weaknesses before malicious actors can exploit them. Regular penetration testing provides a dynamic understanding of evolving threats and helps organizations fine-tune their defensive measures accordingly.

Risk assessments play a central role in regular security evaluations by providing a holistic view of the organization's risk landscape. These assessments involve the identification and analysis of potential risks to critical assets, considering factors such as threat actors, vulnerabilities, and the potential impact of security incidents. By conducting regular risk assessments, organizations can prioritize their security efforts, allocate resources effectively, and make informed decisions to address evolving security challenges. The dynamic nature of risk assessments ensures that organizations remain agile in responding to emerging threats and changing business environments.

Compliance audits, while often driven by regulatory require-ments, contribute to the regular assessment process by ensuring that organizations adhere to established security standards and legal frameworks. Compliance audits evaluate whether security controls align with industry standards and regulatory mandates. Regular au-dits provide organizations with a continuous mechanism for validat-ing their adherence to compliance requirements, thus reducing the risk of legal and financial repercussions. Additionally, the insights gained from compliance audits contribute to overall security im-provements by highlighting areas that may require additional atten-tion or enhancements.

Regular assessments are instrumental in fostering a proactive cy-bersecurity posture that goes beyond mere compliance. The evolving nature of cyber threats demands a forward-thinking approach that anticipates potential challenges and vulnerabilities. By conducting regular assessments, organizations gain a deeper understanding of their security strengths and weaknesses, enabling them to develop and implement strategic and tailored security measures. This proac-tive stance is crucial for mitigating risks associated with emerging threats, such as zero-day vulnerabilities, advanced persistent threats (APTs), and novel attack vectors.

The frequency of assessments is a critical consideration in main-taining the relevance and effectiveness of security measures. The rapid pace of technological change, coupled with the agility of cyber adversaries, necessitates assessments that align with the dynamic na-ture of the threat landscape. While the specific cadence of assess-ments may vary based on organizational needs and risk profiles, a consistent and adaptive schedule is essential. Regularity ensures that organizations remain resilient in the face of evolving security chal-lenges and positions them to respond swiftly to emerging threats.

The collaborative nature of regular security assessments involves multiple stakeholders within an organization. Security teams, IT personnel, compliance officers, and executive leadership all play crucial roles in the assessment process. Effective communication and collaboration among these stakeholders ensure that assessments are conducted comprehensively, findings are accurately interpreted, and remediation efforts are aligned with organizational objectives. Regular assessments, therefore, serve not only as a technical exercise but also as a strategic and collaborative initiative that aligns security efforts with broader business goals.

The insights derived from regular security assessments contribute to informed decision-making within organizations. Executives and decision-makers rely on the findings of assessments to allocate resources, prioritize security investments, and establish strategic directions for cybersecurity initiatives. By providing a data-driven understanding of the organization's security posture, regular assessments empower decision-makers to make informed choices that enhance overall resilience against evolving security challenges.

The integration of automation and advanced analytics enhances the efficiency and effectiveness of regular security assessments. Automated tools can continuously scan and analyze vast amounts of data, identifying potential vulnerabilities and anomalous activities in real-time. Machine learning algorithms contribute to the predictive analysis of emerging threats, enabling organizations to proactively address vulnerabilities before they can be exploited. The synergy between automation and human expertise ensures a comprehensive and timely assessment process, allowing organizations to stay ahead of evolving security challenges.

The role of regular security assessments extends beyond the technical realm to encompass a cultural shift within organizations. A security-aware culture, fostered through continuous assessments, instills a sense of responsibility and vigilance among employees at all levels. Regular security training, awareness programs, and simulations contribute to a workforce that is well-versed in identifying and responding to security threats. This cultural transformation ensures that security becomes an integral part of daily operations, reducing the likelihood of human error and enhancing the overall resilience of the organization.

Regular security assessments contribute to the ongoing refinement of incident response plans and strategies. By simulating real-world attack scenarios and identifying potential weaknesses, organizations can enhance their readiness to respond effectively to security incidents. Regular assessments enable security teams to test and validate incident response procedures, ensuring that the organization is well-prepared to mitigate the impact of security breaches. This proactive approach is essential in a landscape where the speed and effectiveness of incident response can significantly impact the outcome of security incidents.

The ever-evolving nature of security challenges necessitates a continuous cycle of assessment, adaptation, and improvement. Organizations must not view security assessments as isolated events but rather as integral components of an ongoing security lifecycle. The iterative nature of this lifecycle ensures that organizations remain responsive to emerging threats, proactive in addressing vulnerabilities, and resilient in the face of evolving security challenges. Regular assessments, driven by a commitment to continuous improvement, position organizations to navigate the complexities of the cybersecurity landscape with agility and confidence.

Developing comprehensive incident response plans for effective crisis management.

Developing comprehensive incident response plans (IRPs) for effective crisis management is an indispensable component of a robust cybersecurity strategy in the contemporary digital landscape. An incident response plan serves as the guiding framework that outlines a systematic and well-coordinated approach to identifying, managing, mitigating, and recovering from security incidents. In an era where cyber threats are pervasive and continually evolving, organizations must proactively prepare for the inevitability of security incidents, ranging from data breaches and ransomware attacks to advanced persistent threats (APTs). A comprehensive incident response plan not only helps organizations minimize the impact of security incidents but also enhances their ability to recover swiftly, thus maintaining business continuity and preserving the trust of stakeholders.

The first critical step in developing a comprehensive incident response plan is to conduct a thorough risk assessment. This involves identifying and evaluating potential threats, vulnerabilities, and the potential impact of security incidents on the organization's critical assets, operations, and reputation. A meticulous risk assessment lays the foundation for tailoring the incident response plan to the unique risk landscape of the organization. By understanding the specific threats and vulnerabilities that may pose a risk, organizations can prioritize resources, define response strategies, and establish clear roles and responsibilities for incident response team members.

The incident response plan should encompass a well-defined and hierarchical structure that delineates the roles and responsibilities of key personnel. This includes the appointment of a dedicated incident response team, composed of individuals with specialized skills in cybersecurity, digital forensics, legal, communications, and other relevant domains. The plan should clearly articulate the chain of command, decision-making processes, and communication protocols within the incident response team. By establishing a structured and coordinated approach to incident response, organizations can ensure swift and effective crisis management during security incidents.

Communication is a cornerstone of effective incident response, and the incident response plan should outline comprehensive communication strategies. This involves both internal and external communication, with clear guidance on how to communicate with employees, executives, customers, regulatory bodies, law enforcement, and the media. Transparent and timely communication is crucial in maintaining trust and credibility during a security incident. The incident response plan should include predefined templates for communication, ensuring that messages are consistent, accurate, and aligned with the organization's overall crisis management strategy.

Developing an incident response plan necessitates a detailed understanding of the organization's digital assets, critical systems, and network architecture. This includes mapping out the organization's information technology (IT) infrastructure, identifying key data repositories, and documenting the interdependencies between systems. By creating an inventory of assets and understanding the flow of information across the network, organizations can enhance their ability to detect and respond to security incidents effectively. This asset inventory is integral to the development of incident response playbooks, which provide step-by-step procedures for responding to specific types of incidents.

Incident response playbooks are a crucial component of a comprehensive incident response plan, offering predefined and structured response procedures for different types of security incidents. These playbooks are developed based on scenarios identified during the risk assessment, and they outline the specific actions to be taken at each stage of an incident. Playbooks cover a wide range of incidents, including malware infections, data breaches, denial-of-service attacks, and insider threats. By having predefined response playbooks, organizations can streamline decision-making, reduce response times, and ensure a consistent and effective approach to incident resolution.

A critical aspect of incident response planning is the establishment of an incident detection and monitoring system. This involves deploying technologies such as Security Information and Event

Management (SIEM) solutions, intrusion detection/prevention systems, and endpoint detection and response tools. These technologies provide real-time visibility into network activities, system behaviors, and potential indicators of compromise. By continuously monitoring for abnormal patterns or activities, organizations can detect security incidents in their early stages, enabling a swift and targeted response. The incident response plan should specify the parameters for monitoring and define the thresholds that trigger incident response actions.

The development of a comprehensive incident response plan requires organizations to establish a robust incident triage process. Triage involves the initial assessment of an incident's severity, impact, and scope to determine the appropriate response actions. This process helps incident responders prioritize their efforts, allocate resources efficiently, and escalate incidents based on their criticality. Triage criteria should be clearly defined in the incident response plan, ensuring a consistent and objective evaluation of incidents. Additionally, the incident response plan should include procedures for documenting and preserving evidence during the triage process, supporting forensic analysis and potential legal proceedings.

A critical component of effective incident response planning is integrating legal and regulatory considerations into the process. Organizations must be cognizant of legal obligations related to data breach notifications, privacy regulations, and industry-specific compliance requirements. The incident response plan should outline procedures for legal and regulatory compliance, including the timely notification of relevant authorities, affected individuals, and other stakeholders. Collaboration with legal counsel during incident response planning ensures that the organization's actions align with legal standards and mitigates potential legal liabilities.

The incident response plan should incorporate a comprehensive approach to digital forensics, recognizing its significance in understanding the root causes of incidents, preserving evidence, and supporting legal investigations. Procedures for collecting, analyzing, and preserving digital evidence should be clearly outlined, with an emphasis on maintaining the integrity of the forensic process. Collaboration with external forensic experts may be included in the incident response plan to augment internal capabilities and ensure a thorough and impartial forensic analysis.

Regular and realistic incident response training and simulations are crucial to validate the effectiveness of the incident response plan and enhance the preparedness of the incident response team. These exercises involve simulating real-world scenarios, allowing incident responders to practice their roles, refine response procedures, and identify areas for improvement. Regular training ensures that the incident response team remains proficient in their skills and can adapt to evolving threats. Furthermore, post-exercise evaluations provide valuable insights that can be used to update and enhance the incident response plan.

The incident response plan should include a comprehensive post-incident analysis process to evaluate the effectiveness of the response and identify opportunities for improvement. This involves conducting a thorough review of the incident, analyzing response actions, documenting lessons learned, and updating the incident response plan based on the insights gained. The post-incident analysis contributes to the organization's overall resilience by facilitating a continuous improvement cycle that incorporates feedback from each security incident into future incident response planning.

The incident response plan should be a living document that evolves alongside the organization's digital landscape, business processes, and threat landscape. Regular reviews and updates ensure that the plan remains current, reflecting changes in technology, organizational structure, and the regulatory environment. The incident response team should conduct periodic tabletop exercises, which involve scenario-based discussions to assess the plan's effectiveness and identify areas for refinement. This iterative approach ensures that the incident response plan remains a dynamic and adaptive tool for crisis management.

In conclusion, developing a comprehensive incident response plan for effective crisis management is an imperative for organizations seeking to navigate the complex and evolving cybersecurity landscape. Such a plan serves as a strategic blueprint, providing a structured and coordinated approach to identifying, managing, and recovering from security incidents. Through risk assessments, communication strategies, incident response playbooks, and a commitment to continuous improvement, organizations can enhance their resilience, minimize the impact of security incidents, and maintain the trust of stakeholders. In a world where cyber threats are pervasive, a well-developed incident response plan is a linchpin in the overall cybersecurity strategy, empowering organizations to respond effectively to the challenges of the digital age.

Conducting drills and simulations to ensure preparedness.

Conducting drills and simulations to ensure preparedness is a pivotal component of a comprehensive and proactive approach to managing crises and emergencies across various domains, including cybersecurity, disaster response, and organizational resilience. These exercises serve as strategic tools for evaluating, refining, and validating existing plans, procedures, and response mechanisms. In the context of cybersecurity, where the threat landscape is dynamic and constantly evolving, drills and simulations are instrumental in fortifying an organization's ability to detect, respond to, and recover from security incidents. These simulated scenarios, often referred to as tabletop exercises or cyberwar games, provide a controlled environment for participants to navigate through hypothetical but realistic situations, enabling them to hone their skills, enhance decision-making capabilities, and identify areas for improvement in a risk-free setting.

The primary goal of conducting drills and simulations in the realm of cybersecurity is to enhance organizational preparedness for handling security incidents effectively. These exercises simulate a range of potential scenarios, from common cyber threats like malware infections to sophisticated and targeted attacks such as advanced persistent threats (APTs). Participants, including members of the incident response team, IT personnel, and relevant stakeholders, are presented with a detailed narrative of a hypothetical incident, and they are required to make decisions and take actions as if they were responding to a real incident. This immersive and interactive approach allows participants to experience the complexities and challenges associated with cybersecurity incidents, fostering a proactive mindset and better equipping them to tackle real-world situations.

The planning and design of cybersecurity drills and simulations involve creating scenarios that closely mirror the organization's specific threat landscape, business processes, and digital infrastructure. These scenarios should be diverse, encompassing different types of attacks, potential vulnerabilities, and response challenges. Scenarios may range from simulated ransomware attacks to social engineering campaigns or even scenarios involving insider threats. Tailoring scenarios to the organization's unique environment ensures that participants engage with situations that are relevant to their roles, responsibilities, and the specific risks facing the organization. This customized approach maximizes the realism and effectiveness of the drills.

The execution of cybersecurity drills often involves a multidisciplinary approach, bringing together various stakeholders across the organization. The incident response team, IT security personnel, legal and compliance experts, communications professionals, and even external partners or third-party service providers may be involved, depending on the nature of the scenario. This collaborative approach ensures that the organization's response is holistic, considering not only the technical aspects but also legal, regulatory, and communication dimensions. The diversity of perspectives enriches the learning experience and fosters a culture of cross-functional collaboration, which is crucial in the complex landscape of cybersecurity.

Simulations provide a controlled environment for testing and validating the effectiveness of incident response plans and playbooks. Incident response plans outline the steps to be taken during a security incident, and playbooks provide detailed procedures for specific types of incidents. Cybersecurity drills offer an opportunity to assess how well these plans and playbooks hold up in practice. By observing how participants execute response procedures, organizations can identify gaps, bottlenecks, or ambiguities in their plans. This insight allows for iterative improvements to the incident response framework, ensuring that it remains current and aligned with emerging cyber threats and organizational changes.

The value of cybersecurity drills extends beyond technical proficiency to include the enhancement of decision-making capabilities among participants. In the high-pressure environment of a security incident, effective decision-making is crucial. Simulations allow participants to practice making critical decisions under realistic time constraints and resource limitations. It enables them to assess the impact of their decisions on the overall incident response and the organization's ability to mitigate the threat. This experiential learning fosters a culture of adaptability and resilience, empowering participants to make informed decisions when faced with the uncertainties and complexities of actual cybersecurity incidents.

One of the significant advantages of cybersecurity drills is the opportunity they provide for testing and optimizing communication strategies. Effective communication is a linchpin in incident response, involving both internal communication within the response team and external communication with stakeholders, management, customers, and, in some cases, the public or media. Simulations help organizations evaluate the clarity, timeliness, and accuracy of their communication protocols. Participants learn to coordinate communication efforts, disseminate critical information, and manage public relations aspects during a security incident. This holistic approach to communication ensures that the organization presents a unified and transparent front in the face of a security crisis.

In addition to technical skills and decision-making, cybersecurity drills contribute to the development of strong leadership within the incident response team. Leaders emerge and refine their ability to guide the team through the incident lifecycle, from initial detection to containment, eradication, and recovery. The drills allow leaders to practice prioritizing tasks, delegating responsibilities, and maintaining a cohesive and focused response in the midst of chaos. Leadership skills cultivated during simulations contribute to the effectiveness of incident response teams when dealing with real-world cybersecurity incidents, where strong and decisive leadership can be the key to a successful resolution.

Cybersecurity drills also play a pivotal role in cultivating a culture of continuous improvement within an organization. Post-exercise debriefings and analyses provide a forum for participants to reflect on their performance, share insights, and collaboratively identify areas for enhancement. These discussions generate a wealth of lessons learned that can be used to refine incident response plans, update playbooks, and address organizational weaknesses. The iterative nature of cybersecurity drills ensures that organizations adapt their strategies and procedures based on evolving threats, technological advancements, and changes in the organizational landscape.

To maximize the effectiveness of cybersecurity drills, organizations often engage in red teaming or penetration testing exercises. Red teaming involves the simulation of adversarial activities by ethical hackers to identify vulnerabilities and weaknesses in the organization's defenses. This advanced form of simulation challenges the incident response team to detect and respond to simulated attacks in real-time. The insights gained from red teaming exercises provide organizations with a realistic understanding of their security posture and allow them to bolster their defenses and incident response capabilities accordingly.

Beyond the technical aspects of incident response, cybersecurity drills contribute to the development of a cybersecurity-aware organizational culture. When employees across various departments participate in these exercises, they gain a better understanding of the importance of cybersecurity, their role in incident response, and the potential impact of their actions on the organization's security posture. This increased awareness fosters a proactive mindset, encouraging employees to be vigilant, report suspicious activities promptly, and adhere to cybersecurity best practices in their daily activities. The drills, therefore, serve as a holistic approach to cybersecurity education and awareness.

Challenges associated with cybersecurity drills include the need for careful planning and coordination to ensure that the simulations are realistic without causing disruption to normal operations. Balancing the realism of the scenario with the need to maintain a safe and controlled environment is essential. Additionally, organizations must invest in creating and maintaining an up-to-date testing infrastructure that mirrors their production environment, allowing for accurate and relevant simulations. Addressing these challenges requires a strategic and resource-intensive approach to ensure that the drills align with organizational objectives and contribute meaningfully to cybersecurity preparedness.

In conclusion, conducting drills and simulations to ensure preparedness is an indispensable aspect of contemporary cybersecurity strategies. These exercises provide organizations with the means to evaluate, refine, and validate their incident response capabilities in a controlled and realistic environment. From technical proficiency and decision-making to communication strategies and leadership development, cybersecurity drills contribute to the holistic preparedness of organizations facing the dynamic and evolving landscape of cyber threats. By investing in regular and well-designed simulations, organizations not only enhance their ability to withstand and recover from cybersecurity incidents but also cultivate a culture of continuous improvement and proactive cybersecurity awareness across the entire organization.

The importance of ongoing security training for users and IT staff.

The importance of ongoing security training for users and IT staff is a cornerstone of a resilient cybersecurity posture in today's complex and dynamic digital landscape. Recognizing that both end-users and IT professionals play integral roles in safeguarding organizational assets, ongoing security training serves as a proactive strategy to mitigate the evolving and sophisticated nature of cyber threats. Users, as the first line of defense, need to be equipped with the knowledge and skills to recognize and respond to potential security risks, while IT staff must stay abreast of the latest threats, technologies, and best practices to fortify the organization's defense mechanisms. This continuous learning approach is not merely a one-time event but rather an iterative process that adapts to emerging threats, technological advancements, and organizational changes.

For end-users, who constitute the largest attack surface within an organization, ongoing security training is pivotal in fostering a culture of cybersecurity awareness. Users are targeted by a myriad of tactics, ranging from phishing attacks and social engineering to malware infections and insider threats. Regular training sessions provide users with the knowledge to identify phishing emails, recognize social engineering attempts, and understand the importance of strong password practices. Beyond recognizing threats, ongoing training empowers users to adopt secure behaviors in their daily activities, such as avoiding the use of unsecured Wi-Fi networks, updating software promptly, and reporting suspicious activities. The goal is to transform users from potential vulnerabilities into active participants in the organization's cybersecurity defense.

An integral aspect of ongoing security training for end-users is the cultivation of a security-conscious mindset. Users need to understand the impact of their actions on the overall security posture of the organization. Training programs often include real-world examples, case studies, and simulations to illustrate the consequences of security lapses. By contextualizing security practices within the broader organizational context, users develop a sense of responsibility and ownership for maintaining a secure environment. Ongoing training reinforces the idea that cybersecurity is a shared responsibility, with each user contributing to the collective defense against cyber threats.

The dynamic nature of cyber threats necessitates ongoing training that addresses emerging risks and vulnerabilities. Cybercriminals continually refine their tactics, exploiting new vulnerabilities and devising innovative attack vectors. Ongoing security training ensures that end-users are informed about the latest threats, such as ransomware, zero-day exploits, and business email compromise, and are equipped with the skills to recognize and respond to these evolving challenges. Training content is regularly updated to reflect the current threat landscape, providing users with relevant and actionable information. This adaptability is crucial in preparing users to navigate the ever-changing terrain of cybersecurity threats.

For IT staff, who are responsible for designing, implementing, and managing the organization's cybersecurity infrastructure, ongoing training is indispensable in staying ahead of the rapidly evolving threat landscape. IT professionals need to possess in-depth knowledge of the latest cyber threats, attack methodologies, and vulnerabilities to design and implement effective defense strategies. Training programs for IT staff cover a spectrum of topics, including threat intelligence, penetration testing, incident response, and secure coding practices. This breadth of knowledge ensures that IT professionals are well-equipped to design robust security architectures, identify and patch vulnerabilities, and respond effectively to security incidents.

In the realm of IT, ongoing training plays a pivotal role in developing and maintaining technical skills. The rapid pace of technological innovation, coupled with the sophistication of cyber threats, requires IT professionals to continually update their skillsets. Training programs cover a range of technical domains, from network security and encryption to cloud security and mobile device management. Continuous learning ensures that IT staff are proficient in leveraging the latest technologies to secure the organization's digital infrastructure. This adaptability is critical in responding to the ever-evolving landscape of cybersecurity challenges and technological advancements.

Beyond technical proficiency, ongoing training for IT staff emphasizes strategic and risk management aspects of cybersecurity. IT professionals need to understand the business context, regulatory landscape, and organizational risk appetite to align security measures with broader business objectives. Training programs cover topics such as risk assessment, security governance, and compliance frameworks. This holistic approach ensures that IT staff not only possess technical expertise but also the strategic acumen to make informed decisions that balance security requirements with business priorities.

Ongoing security training for IT professionals extends to specialized areas such as threat hunting, malware analysis, and security architecture design. These specialized skills are essential in proactively identifying and mitigating emerging threats. Training programs often include hands-on exercises, labs, and simulations to provide IT professionals with practical experience in applying their knowledge. This experiential learning approach enhances their ability to respond to real-world scenarios, whether it involves analyzing a new strain of malware or conducting a forensic investigation following a security incident.

The interconnected nature of IT systems, coupled with the increasing prevalence of hybrid and cloud environments, necessitates ongoing training for IT staff to effectively manage and secure these complex infrastructures. Training programs cover topics such as cloud security, virtualization, and containerization to ensure that IT professionals can navigate the intricacies of modern IT architectures. This knowledge is crucial in designing secure and resilient systems that can withstand the diverse and evolving nature of cyber threats.

A critical aspect of ongoing security training is the cultivation of a security-aware organizational culture within the IT department. Security should be ingrained in the mindset and decision-making processes of IT professionals. Training programs often emphasize the importance of proactive security measures, adherence to best practices, and the need for continual improvement. By fostering a culture of security awareness, IT staff become more vigilant, responsive, and collaborative in addressing security challenges. This cultural shift is instrumental in creating a cohesive and unified approach to cybersecurity within the IT department.

Ongoing security training for both end-users and IT staff is integral in addressing the human factor in cybersecurity. The majority of security incidents involve some form of human error, whether it is clicking on a malicious link, falling victim to a phishing email, or misconfiguring security settings. Ongoing training programs for end-users focus on raising awareness about these common pitfalls and providing practical guidance on how to avoid them. For IT staff, training programs incorporate human-centric considerations in the design of security measures, recognizing that technology alone cannot eliminate the impact of human behavior on cybersecurity.

The dynamic nature of the cybersecurity landscape requires ongoing training programs to be adaptable and responsive to emerging trends and challenges. This adaptability is not limited to the content of the training but extends to the delivery methods. Online courses, webinars, workshops, and hands-on labs are among the diverse approaches used to deliver ongoing security training. The flexibility of these methods accommodates the diverse learning preferences and schedules of both end-users and IT professionals. Leveraging a combination of training formats ensures that individuals receive a well-rounded and engaging learning experience.

The effectiveness of ongoing security training is not solely measured by the acquisition of knowledge but also by the application of that knowledge in real-world scenarios. Training programs often include assessments, quizzes, and practical exercises to evaluate participants' understanding and retention of the material. Additionally, the impact of training on actual security outcomes is assessed through metrics such as incident response times, the frequency of security incidents, and the success of security awareness campaigns. This data-driven approach enables organizations to gauge the effectiveness of their training initiatives and make informed decisions about refining and expanding their training programs.

In conclusion, the importance of ongoing security training for users and IT staff cannot be overstated in the context of modern cybersecurity. This continuous learning approach recognizes the dynamic and evolving nature of cyber threats and the pivotal role that both end users and IT professionals play in safeguarding organizational assets. By fostering a culture of cybersecurity awareness, providing relevant and up-to-date knowledge, and cultivating technical and strategic proficiency, ongoing security training contributes to the resilience of organizations in the face of an ever-changing cybersecurity landscape. It is not merely a periodic obligation but an integral and ongoing commitment to equipping individuals with the skills and awareness needed to navigate the complexities of the digital age securely.

Fostering a culture of security awareness throughout the organization.

Fostering a culture of security awareness throughout the organization is a foundational and multifaceted strategy crucial for building resilience against the ever-evolving landscape of cybersecurity threats. This cultural shift involves instilling a collective understanding of the importance of cybersecurity, making security considerations an integral part of everyday activities, and empowering individuals at all levels to actively contribute to the organization's defense against cyber threats. Such a culture not only enhances the organization's ability to prevent and respond to security incidents but also creates a proactive and vigilant mindset among employees, making security a shared responsibility.

At the heart of a security-aware culture is the recognition that every individual within the organization plays a pivotal role in safeguarding sensitive information, digital assets, and overall organizational well-being. This inclusive approach acknowledges that security is not solely the responsibility of the IT department but a collective effort that involves every employee, from executives to front-line staff. By fostering this sense of shared responsibility, organizations create a robust foundation for building a culture where security is not seen as a hindrance but as an integral aspect of day-to-day operations.

Communication and education lie at the core of instilling security awareness. Organizations invest in regular communication campaigns that convey the importance of cybersecurity, the potential risks faced, and the role each individual plays in mitigating those risks. These campaigns utilize diverse communication channels, including emails, posters, intranet portals, and newsletters, to reach employees at various touchpoints. The messaging emphasizes the impact of individual actions on the organization's overall security posture and the potential consequences of security lapses, creating a sense of personal responsibility.

Ongoing security education and training programs are pivotal components of a security-aware culture. These programs cater to employees at all levels, ensuring that each individual receives relevant and targeted information based on their roles and responsibilities. Training modules cover a spectrum of topics, including password hygiene, safe browsing practices, social engineering awareness, and data protection principles. The goal is to equip employees with the knowledge and skills needed to identify and respond to potential security threats, transforming them from potential vulnerabilities into active contributors to the organization's defense.

Simulations and exercises are integral to security training, providing employees with hands-on experience in recognizing and responding to real-world security scenarios. Phishing simulations, for instance, allow employees to practice identifying and avoiding phishing emails, a common attack vector. By immersing employees in realistic scenarios, organizations enhance the practical applicability of security knowledge, fostering a deeper understanding of potential threats and effective mitigation strategies. These exercises also contribute to building a resilient workforce capable of adapting to emerging security challenges.

Leadership commitment is fundamental to the success of a security-aware culture. When organizational leaders visibly prioritize and champion cybersecurity initiatives, it sends a powerful message about the significance of security throughout the organization. Leaders set the tone by participating in security training, adhering to security policies, and consistently reinforcing the importance of security in their communications. This top-down approach ensures that security awareness becomes ingrained in the organizational DNA, influencing the behavior and attitudes of employees at all levels.

Beyond formal training programs, organizations promote informal channels for sharing security knowledge and best practices. Peer-to-peer learning, mentorship, and collaborative forums create opportunities for employees to discuss security concerns, share insights, and learn from each other's experiences. This grassroots approach fosters a sense of community and collective responsibility, where employees feel comfortable seeking advice, reporting security incidents, and actively participating in the organization's security initiatives.

Integrating security considerations into the organizational culture requires aligning security practices with business objectives. Security measures should be designed to complement, rather than hinder, day-to-day operations. For instance, implementing multi-factor authentication may be framed not only as a security necessity but also as a measure that enhances user convenience and protects individuals from unauthorized access. By presenting security measures in a positive light, organizations encourage compliance and cooperation, fostering a culture where security is viewed as an enabler rather than an obstacle.

Recognition and reward mechanisms play a pivotal role in reinforcing positive security behaviors. Organizations acknowledge and celebrate individuals or teams that demonstrate exemplary security practices, whether it's promptly reporting a phishing attempt, implementing a security improvement, or contributing innovative ideas to enhance cybersecurity. By highlighting and rewarding positive behaviors, organizations create a positive feedback loop that reinforces the desired security-aware culture. Recognition may take various forms, including public commendations, awards, or even small incentives, contributing to a culture where security diligence is valued and acknowledged.

Transparent and accessible communication channels for reporting security concerns are essential components of a security-aware culture. Employees should feel empowered to report suspicious activities, potential vulnerabilities, or security incidents without fear of reprisal. Establishing secure and anonymous reporting mechanisms, such as incident reporting hotlines or dedicated email addresses, ensures that individuals can contribute to the organization's security without hesitation. This open communication approach not only facilitates early detection of potential threats but also signals to employees that their vigilance is valued.

Regular security updates and communication about emerging threats are vital elements in sustaining a security-aware culture. Cyber threats are dynamic, and organizations must keep employees informed about the latest tactics, techniques, and procedures employed by cybercriminals. Regular communication about current threats, recent incidents, and evolving attack vectors ensures that employees remain vigilant and are well-informed about potential risks. This information empowers employees to recognize and respond to new and emerging security challenges, contributing to the organization's overall security resilience.

Cultivating a security-aware culture extends to remote and mobile work environments, recognizing the increasing prevalence of flexible work arrangements. Security awareness initiatives should address the unique challenges posed by remote work, such as the use of personal devices, reliance on home networks, and potential exposure to public Wi-Fi. Training programs and communication campaigns should emphasize secure remote work practices, the importance of using virtual private networks (VPNs), and the need for heightened vigilance in recognizing phishing attempts in virtual environments.

Organizations integrate security considerations into the development of new projects, systems, and processes from the outset, adopting a security-by-design approach. This involves collaborating with security professionals during the planning and design phases to identify and address potential security risks. By embedding security into the fabric of organizational projects, organizations ensure that security is not an afterthought but an integral part of the development lifecycle. This proactive approach contributes to the creation of a security-aware culture where security is ingrained in organizational practices and workflows.

Regular security assessments and audits are essential components of maintaining a security-aware culture. These assessments evaluate the effectiveness of security measures, identify potential weaknesses, and validate the organization's overall security posture. Conducting regular audits ensures that security practices align with industry standards, regulatory requirements, and best practices. The findings from these assessments inform continuous improvement initiatives, enabling organizations to address emerging threats, update security policies, and refine training programs to reflect the evolving security landscape.

A security-aware culture is not static; it requires continuous evaluation and adaptation to address evolving threats and organizational changes. Regular feedback loops, surveys, and assessments gauge the effectiveness of security awareness initiatives and identify areas for improvement. This feedback-driven approach allows organizations to refine their strategies, tailor training programs to address specific needs, and adapt communication campaigns to resonate with employees effectively. The iterative nature of this process ensures that the organization's security-aware culture remains dynamic, responsive, and aligned with current cybersecurity challenges.

In conclusion, fostering a culture of security awareness throughout the organization is a holistic and adaptive strategy that goes beyond traditional security measures. It involves embedding security into the organization's values, practices, and communication channels. By creating a culture where security is a shared responsibility, valued by leadership, reinforced through positive reinforcement, and integrated into everyday operations, organizations empower employees to be active participants in the collective defense against cyber threats. A security-aware culture is not merely a set of rules but a mindset that permeates every aspect of the organization, creating a resilient and proactive response to the challenges of the ever-evolving cybersecurity landscape.

Exploring emerging trends such as zero-trust architecture and AI-driven security.

Exploring emerging trends in cybersecurity, such as zero-trust architecture and AI-driven security, unveils transformative approaches that reflect the evolving nature of cyber threats and the increasing complexity of digital environments. Zero-trust architecture represents a paradigm shift from traditional perimeter-based security models to a more dynamic and granular approach that challenges the inherent trust assumptions within networks. In a zero-trust model, every user, device, and application is treated as untrusted, regardless of their location or previous access privileges. This approach is especially relevant in today's landscape, where the traditional network perimeter is increasingly porous due to factors like remote work, cloud adoption, and mobile devices.

Zero-trust architecture emphasizes continuous verification and strict access controls based on least privilege principles. Authentication and authorization occur on a per-session basis, requiring users and devices to prove their identity and adhere to the principle of least privilege before accessing resources. This model minimizes the attack surface, reduces the risk of lateral movement by cyber adversaries, and enhances overall security posture. As organizations navigate the complexities of modern IT infrastructures, zero-trust architecture becomes a crucial strategy for mitigating the risks associated with insider threats, compromised credentials, and advanced persistent threats.

On the other hand, AI-driven security is revolutionizing the cybersecurity landscape by leveraging artificial intelligence and machine learning to proactively detect and respond to threats in real-time. Traditional security approaches often rely on predefined rules and signatures to identify malicious activities, but these methods can struggle to keep pace with the speed and sophistication of contemporary cyber threats. AI-driven security solutions address this limitation by continuously learning and adapting to the evolving threat landscape, enabling organizations to detect and respond to previously unseen or rapidly changing attack vectors.

One of the key advantages of AI-driven security is its ability to analyze massive datasets and identify patterns indicative of malicious behavior. Machine learning algorithms can detect anomalies, recognize deviations from normal user behavior, and correlate seemingly unrelated events to uncover sophisticated attacks. This proactive threat detection capability enhances an organization's ability to identify and mitigate potential threats before they escalate. Moreover, AI-driven security solutions often incorporate automation and orchestration, enabling rapid response to incidents and reducing the burden on cybersecurity teams.

Machine learning models in AI-driven security are trained on diverse datasets, allowing them to develop a nuanced understanding of normal and abnormal behavior across an organization's digital ecosystem. This contextual awareness is invaluable in distinguishing between benign anomalies and actual security incidents, minimizing false positives and negatives. As organizations grapple with the increasing volume and complexity of cyber threats, AI-driven security emerges as a force multiplier, augmenting human capabilities and providing a more adaptive and scalable defense against a broad spectrum of attacks.

The application of AI in cybersecurity extends beyond threat detection to include predictive analysis, behavioral analytics, and even autonomous decision-making. Predictive analysis leverages historical data and machine learning algorithms to forecast potential future threats and vulnerabilities. By identifying emerging patterns and trends, organizations can proactively implement preventive measures, staying ahead of cyber adversaries. Behavioral analytics, powered by AI, enables the identification of subtle deviations in user behavior that may indicate a compromised account or insider threat, allowing for timely intervention.

Autonomous decision-making, an advanced aspect of AI-driven security, involves automated responses to security incidents based on predefined policies and machine learning insights. This capability streamlines incident response times, reduces the impact of attacks, and ensures a more consistent and rapid reaction to evolving threats. However, the adoption of autonomous decision-making also raises important considerations regarding the ethical implications, accountability, and transparency of such systems, requiring careful evaluation and governance.

While zero-trust architecture and AI-driven security represent distinct trends, their convergence holds the potential to create a robust and adaptive cybersecurity framework. The zero-trust model, with its emphasis on continuous verification and strict access controls, aligns seamlessly with the proactive threat detection and response capabilities of AI-driven security. By combining the principles of zero trust with the intelligence and automation offered by AI, organizations can fortify their defenses against an ever-expanding threat landscape.

Integrating AI into zero-trust architectures allows organizations to enhance their ability to detect and respond to threats in real-time, leveraging machine learning algorithms to analyze vast amounts of data and identify subtle indicators of compromise. The continuous monitoring and verification aspects of zero-trust architectures complement the dynamic threat detection capabilities of AI-driven security, creating a synergistic approach to cybersecurity. This integration enables organizations to move beyond reactive strategies and adopt a more anticipatory and adaptive stance against cyber threats.

Moreover, the integration of AI into zero-trust architectures contributes to the evolution of security analytics. Traditional security information and event management (SIEM) systems often struggle to cope with the scale and complexity of modern digital environments. AI-driven security analytics platforms can ingest, correlate, and analyze massive datasets in real-time, providing a more comprehensive and context-aware understanding of the security landscape. This evolution is crucial as organizations transition from legacy, on-premises infrastructures to cloud-based environments and face the challenges associated with distributed workforces.

As organizations explore the convergence of zero-trust architecture and AI-driven security, they must also address challenges related to implementation, interoperability, and human-machine collaboration. Implementing zero-trust architecture requires a comprehensive understanding of an organization's digital assets, user behaviors, and access requirements. Integration with AI-driven security solutions necessitates careful planning to ensure seamless interoperability and effective collaboration between human cybersecurity professionals and automated systems.

Human-machine collaboration emerges as a critical aspect of the evolving cybersecurity landscape. While AI-driven security can provide unprecedented speed and scale in threat detection, human expertise remains essential for contextual interpretation, decision-making, and adapting security measures to the organization's specific risk profile. The convergence of zero-trust architecture and AI-driven security emphasizes the need for a balanced approach that leverages the strengths of both human and machine intelligence.

In conclusion, exploring emerging trends such as zero-trust architecture and AI-driven security underscores the dynamic nature of cybersecurity strategies in response to evolving threats. Zero-trust architecture challenges traditional notions of network trust and emphasizes continuous verification, aligning with the proactive and adaptive capabilities of AI-driven security. As organizations grapple with the complexities of modern IT landscapes, the convergence of these trends holds the promise of creating a resilient, anticipatory, and adaptive cybersecurity framework that can effectively counter the diverse and sophisticated threats of the digital age.

The potential impact of quantum computing on encryption and security practices.

The potential impact of quantum computing on encryption and security practices looms as a paradigm-shifting challenge, stirring discussions and prompting organizations to reconsider the foundations of their cryptographic infrastructure. Classical encryption, which relies on mathematical problems that are computationally hard to solve, faces a substantial threat from the computational prowess promised by quantum computers. Quantum computing leverages the principles of quantum mechanics, such as superposition and entanglement, to perform certain calculations exponentially faster than classical computers. This advancement poses a formidable risk to widely used encryption algorithms, particularly those based on factoring large numbers, such as RSA, and solving discrete logarithm problems, as quantum computers excel in solving these problems efficiently.

The most eminent threat quantum computing poses to encryption lies in its ability to execute Shor's algorithm. Shor's algorithm, designed specifically for quantum computers, has the potential to efficiently factor large numbers and compute discrete logarithms, rendering widely deployed public-key cryptography vulnerable. RSA, a widely used asymmetric encryption algorithm, relies on the difficulty of factoring large composite numbers into their prime factors for its security. Shor's algorithm, when executed on a sufficiently powerful quantum computer, could significantly reduce the time required to factor large numbers, thus breaking RSA encryption. This prospect has sparked concerns about the long-term security of data encrypted using RSA and similar algorithms.

Similarly, elliptic curve cryptography (ECC), another popular choice for public-key cryptography, is susceptible to quantum attacks through algorithms like the Quantum Elliptic Curve Discrete Logarithm Problem (QEDLP). ECC offers strong security with shorter key lengths compared to RSA, making it a favored choice for resource-constrained environments. However, the vulnerability of ECC to quantum algorithms puts it in the line of fire, necessitating a reevaluation of cryptographic strategies for securing communications, transactions, and sensitive information.

Post-quantum cryptography has emerged as a response to the looming threat of quantum attacks on existing encryption algorithms. This field aims to develop cryptographic schemes that remain secure even in the face of quantum computing capabilities. Various approaches are being explored within post-quantum cryptography, including lattice-based cryptography, hash-based cryptography, code-based cryptography, and multivariate polynomial cryptography. These alternatives are designed to withstand the potential threats posed by quantum algorithms, providing a transition path for organizations seeking to maintain the confidentiality and integrity of their data in a quantum-powered future.

Lattice-based cryptography stands out as a particularly promising post-quantum alternative. Lattice problems are considered hard even for quantum computers, making them resistant to Shor's algorithm. By building cryptographic primitives on the difficulty of lattice problems, researchers aim to create encryption schemes that remain secure in the era of quantum computing. These efforts are not merely theoretical; several lattice-based cryptographic algorithms are being actively considered for standardization by organizations such as the National Institute of Standards and Technology (NIST).

Hash-based cryptography, relying on the security of hash functions, presents another avenue for post-quantum resilience. Hash functions are considered quantum-resistant due to their one-way nature. Schemes like the Merkle signature scheme leverage hash functions to provide digital signatures that remain secure even when confronted with the computational capabilities of quantum computers. As the cryptographic community works towards standardizing post-quantum algorithms, hash-based cryptography stands as a candidate for securing digital signatures in a quantum-threatened landscape.

Code-based cryptography introduces a different approach by leveraging error-correcting codes. The hardness of decoding specific linear codes is believed to withstand quantum attacks, making this approach a potential candidate for secure communications in a quantum era. The McEliece cryptosystem, an early example of code-based cryptography, has drawn attention for its resistance to quantum attacks and is under consideration for standardization.

Multivariate polynomial cryptography explores cryptographic primitives based on the difficulty of solving systems of multivariate polynomial equations. The complexity of solving such equations is expected to provide security against quantum algorithms. Algorithms like the Unbalanced Oil and Vinegar (UOV) signature scheme, a multivariate polynomial signature scheme, are being studied for their resistance to quantum attacks and suitability for post-quantum cryptographic applications.

Transitioning to post-quantum cryptography, however, poses its own set of challenges. Compatibility with existing systems, the need for standardized algorithms, and the performance impact on resource-constrained devices are critical factors that demand careful consideration. Organizations face the task of developing migration strategies that ensure a smooth transition from current cryptographic standards to post-quantum alternatives.

Quantum-resistant cryptographic algorithms must not only be secure but also efficient enough for practical deployment in various computing environments. Striking a balance between security and performance is essential, especially in scenarios where computational resources are limited, such as in the Internet of Things (IoT) devices. The cryptographic community, industry stakeholders, and standards organizations are actively engaged in the evaluation and standardization of post-quantum cryptographic algorithms to facilitate a seamless transition while ensuring the security of digital communications.

In addition to advancements in post-quantum cryptography, quantum key distribution (QKD) emerges as a complementary approach to fortify security in a quantum era. QKD leverages the principles of quantum mechanics to enable secure communication through the distribution of quantum-entangled keys. The fundamental tenet of quantum mechanics, namely the observation effect, ensures the security of key distribution. Attempts to eavesdrop on the quantum-entangled keys inherently disrupt the quantum state, providing a mechanism to detect unauthorized access attempts.

While QKD holds promise for securing communication channels, its practical deployment faces challenges, including the limitations on communication distances, the impact of noise on quantum states, and the need for specialized infrastructure. Despite these challenges, ongoing research and technological advancements aim to address the practical constraints of QKD, positioning it as a potential tool for enhancing the security of communications in a quantum-powered world.

The impact of quantum computing on encryption and security practices extends beyond the realm of data confidentiality to encompass the integrity and authenticity of digital signatures. Traditional digital signatures, reliant on algorithms vulnerable to quantum attacks, may become insecure in a post-quantum era. The adoption of quantum-resistant digital signature schemes, such as those based on hash-based cryptography or other post-quantum approaches, becomes imperative to ensure the ongoing trustworthiness of digital communications.

In the context of organizational cybersecurity strategies, the potential advent of large-scale quantum computers underscores the importance of adopting a quantum-ready mindset. Organizations need to conduct thorough risk assessments, evaluate the longevity of their cryptographic infrastructure, and develop migration plans that account for the evolving landscape of quantum computing. The timeline for the realization of practical quantum computers remains uncertain, but the need for proactive measures is clear.

As the field of quantum computing progresses, the quantum-resistant cryptographic landscape will continue to evolve. The collaboration between researchers, industry experts, and standards organizations plays a crucial role in shaping the future of post-quantum cryptography. The journey towards quantum-safe cryptographic practices involves not only the development and standardization of new algorithms but also the establishment of best practices for implementing, managing, and transitioning cryptographic systems in the face of quantum threats.

In conclusion, the potential impact of quantum computing on encryption and security practices necessitates a proactive and strategic approach to safeguarding digital assets in a quantum-powered future. From the vulnerabilities of classical encryption algorithms to the promise of post-quantum cryptography and quantum key distribution, the journey towards quantum-safe cybersecurity requires a collective and concerted effort. Organizations must navigate the complexities of migration, consider the interplay of quantum-resistant technologies, and remain adaptable to the dynamic landscape of quantum advancements. As quantum computing progresses, the resilience of cryptographic systems will be defined by the collaborative efforts of the global cybersecurity community in anticipating and mitigating the transformative impact of quantum technologies.

9 798887 587508 3